Cognitive Approaches in Special Education

Cognitive Approaches in Special Education

Edited by

David Sugden
University of Leeds

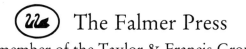 The Falmer Press

(A member of the Taylor & Francis Group)
London . New York . Philadelphia

UK   The Falmer Press, Falmer House, Barcombe, Lewes,
East Sussex, BN8 5DL

USA   The Falmer Press, Taylor & Francis Inc., 242 Cherry Street,
Philadelphia, PA 19106-1906

©Selection and editorial material copyright David Sugden
1989

First published 1989

British Library Cataloguing in Publication Data

Cognitive approaches in special education.
   1.   Educational institutions. Students with special educational
needs. Cognitive development. Teaching methods
   I. Sugden David
   371.9

   ISBN 1-85000-419-6
   ISBN 1-85000-418-8 Pbk

Jacket design by Caroline Archer

*Typeset 10½ on 13 Garamond by Chapterhouse, The Cloisters,
Formby L37 3PX*
*Printed and bound in Great Britain by Redwood Burn Limited,
Trowbridge, Wiltshire.*

Contents

Introduction

The view is now widespread that special education is a fundamental part of every school, and is not restricted to special schools using highly technical, complex and different teaching methods. Special education involves a broad spectrum of children, placements, and teaching methods. During the 1980s, following the Warnock Report (1978) and the Education Act (1981), there has been an emphasis on a continuum of need that is served by a corresponding continuum of provision in the form of types of school, curriculum and instruction.

My aim in this text is to present a number of approaches in special education which are based upon some common assumptions. These assumptions are introduced in Chapter 1 and expanded in Chapter 2 and include the notion that the child is a problem-solver and constructs his or her own meaning to material that is available. Learning is seen as an active process with the successful learner being able to retain a skill over a period of time and use it flexibly in a variety of situations. The learning process can be described and involves cognitive processing skills. These skills include the selection of detail to attend to, the holding of information in some working memory, the comparing of incoming information with that held in a permanent store, the generating of a plan of action, the implementation of this plan and the use of feedback. These assumptions are the same whether or not the child is deemed to have special educational needs.

The authors who have contributed to this text use these assumptions to a greater or lesser degree. Some are very much concerned with the actual teaching process and how to modify this; others are more involved in presenting a framework from which difficulties can be analysed and programmes initiated. Despite these differences the authors would tend to agree on how children learn skills and would emphasize the cognitive nature of this activity.

A variety of topics are presented involving these assumptions and Chapter 1, written by myself, attempts to set the scene for the rest of the book. Current in special education are described with a particular emphasis on events post-Warnock, 1978. I then examine the role that psychology has played in providing guidelines for teaching in special education. Methods and approaches are briefly described and evaluated. Finally, I present a broad overview of the assumptions underlying cognitive psychology.

Chapter 2 is written by Peter Tomlinson, a well-known author in educational psychology, whose text *Understanding Teaching* (1981; 2nd edn now in press) has influenced large numbers of practising teachers and teachers in training. This is an ideal chapter to bridge the gap between the assumptions of cognitive psychology in Chapter 1 and teaching in special education that many of the other chapters present. Peter takes cognitive psychology and translates it into the teaching process, noting that this involves a number of interactive parts and is not the simplistic activity that some would have us believe. He emphasizes the skilled nature of teaching and breaks this down into its constituent parts. He rejects a 'cookbook' approach and instead stresses that teachers examine the interactive nature of the learner, the material to be learned, the context in which it is learned and the teachers themselves.

In Chapter 3, Ronald Gallimore, Roland Tharp and Robert Rueda describe how children learn with assistance from a more capable other person. They use what Vygotsky called 'the zone of proximal development' to reflect the difference between unassisted performance showing the child's current level of achievement and development, and assisted performance reflecting the nearest or next steps of development still to come. They describe some of the work from KEEP (the Kamehameha Early Education Project) which had a goal of developing an effective reading programme. Their main emphasis is on understanding and giving meaning to texts, and they use questioning techniques to assist pupils to relate experience to text. The teacher is providing the child with opportunities to learn and flexibly use a variety of processing strategies in the reading situation.

In Chapter 4 the idea of a more capable other person assisting is used in trying to promote generalization in children with moderate learning difficulties. Poor generalization is a fundamental characteristic of many of these children, and any success in teaching it has been hard earned. The generalization process is described with an emphasis on the cognitive activity that is involved. A programme teaching the skill of verbal elaboration is described in detail followed by some suggestions as to how generalization can be encouraged.

Jacqueline Rutherford brings together much of Chapters 3 and 4 with her chapter on Instrumental Enrichment. This programme of instruction originally devised by Reuven Feuerstein for immigrants into Israel has received world-wide publicity. It is a programme very much based on a cognitive approach and aims to teach thinking skills to children. It is not subject-specific although some derivatives of it are moving in that direction. One could suspect that with such a global aim the programme is quite non-specific in its nature. Nothing could be further from the truth with the 'instruments' being highly structured and sequential. Jacqueline has both researched and taught the programme, giving her unique insights into its philosophy and practice. Her section on the evaluation of the programme is particularly interesting, showing that we are not trying to present 'cure-alls' and also that we recognize support for total success is a rarity.

In Chapter 6 Diane Shorrocks deals with the development of language and communication. The previous three chapters have all stressed the importance of language in the programmes they have described, and interaction with a more competent other has been another common theme. Diane's chapter does not examine language problems, but provides a framework for the analysis of children's language based on so-called normal progression. This framework enables detailed and accurate diagnosis of the language difficulties experienced by some children, which hopefully leads to more creative and individually based developmental programmes. Diane's thesis is that a thorough understanding of the processes of language learning is necessary for effective and efficient programmes.

In Chapter 7 Sally Beveridge develops the increasingly important idea of parents as teachers. The chapter links nicely with the one by Diane Shorrocks, sharing the common ideas of 'transactional' development. This term is used to describe the nature of the process whereby mutual influences operate between child and environment. Sally describes the implications of this for parents of children with special educational needs. A major thrust in the chapter is to encourage a move away from what can be called a 'training model' and move towards more flexible ways of working which involve a more educationally oriented approach. This has broader goals than a training model and aims to further the parents' own existing skills in a way that facilitates problem-solving such that over time there is a decreased reliance on so-called professional expertise.

Three chapters complete the book and are all firmly entrenched in classroom practice. In Chapter 8 Peter Galvin examines programmes designed to redirect children's inappropriate behaviour. Peter's view appears to be that programmes based on behaviouristic psychology have taken us a long way forward in teaching appropriate behaviours, and that the introduction of the cognitive aspect within this framework takes us even further. He uses 'cognitive behaviour modification' a term coined by Meichenbaum (1977) and stresses the structure and tightness emphasized by behavioural programmes, together with the active involvement of the child's cognitive processes which is the central assumption of a cognitive approach. As he says, with this combination, anyone working with children showing behaviour problems should be able to 'have his/her cake and eat it'. Programmes involving self-talk and problem-solving are described and overlap with those of rational emotive therapy and cognitive behavioural therapy.

In Chapter 9 Alan Dobbins skilfully takes us through the myriad of approaches using computers. He argues against computer based learning (CBL) for children with special educational needs, and instead promotes computer assisted learning (CAL). He describes how software programs can promote cognitive gain when used as part of a computer assisted learning approach. He explains how the developments have taken place over time, with the use of CBL with both normal and children with special educational needs. Popular programmes such as LOGO are described. He then details computer assisted learning, moving from drill and practice, simulation through to word processing and information handling. A final section describes some of the work he is doing in mainstream classes with children showing special educational needs.

The final chapter by Rosie Connell is on motor problems, a topic that is near and dear to me. At first glance motor problems would appear to be the last place to look in order to examine the effects of cognitive processes. But a closer look will reveal that in a skill such as ball-catching, a child obviously has to 'know' something as well as 'do' something. Perceptual/cognitive skills such as selective attention, tracking, prediction, anticipation, judgement of speed and distance are all involved. Rosie takes current theories in motor control and learning to illustrate the cognitive involvement in motor tasks. In addition her own research work not only shows this involvement, but also describes how this involvement changes with development. She skilfully brings these together into a framework for analysing motor skill performance and for remediation purposes. If some are still unconvinced about the cognitive involvement in motor skills, consider the following from Turvey (1974) who using the work of Polanyi (1964) said of bicycling:

> As the cyclist starts to fall to the right he turns the handlebars to the right, deflecting the bicycle along a curve to the right. The result of this manoeuvre is a centrifugal force pushing the cyclist to the left and off-setting the gravitational force pulling him to the ground to the right. Consequently, the cyclist is thrown out of balance to the left and responds by turning the handlebars to the left deflecting the bicycle along a curve to the left, which results in a centrifugal force pushing him to the right etc., etc. In the course of these manoeuvres the cyclist is obeying the following injunction: adjust the curvature of the bicycle's path in proportion to the ratio of the unbalance of the square of the speed.' Keeping one's balance on a bicycle is a very cognitive act. (p. 312).

The essence of teaching children with special educational needs is not that it is necessarily special, although some specialist techniques are available. These children need carefully structured teaching that encompasses the needs of the children, the resources the children bring to the learning situation, the material to be learned and the context in which learning takes place.

David Sugden
University of Leeds

References

Department of Education and Science (1978), *Special Educational Needs* (The Warnock Report, London: HMSO).

Meichenbaum, D. (1977), *Cognitive Behavior Modification* (New York: Plenum Press).

Polanyi, M. (1964), *Personal Knowledge: Towards a Post Critical Philosophy* (New York: Harper).

Tomlinson, P. D. (1981) *Understanding Teaching: Interactive Educational Psychology*, 2nd edn. in press (London: McGraw Hill).

Turvey, M. (1974), A note on the relation between action and perception, in M. Wade and R. Martens (eds.) *Psychology and Motor Behavior in Sport* (Champaign, Illinois: Human Kinetics).

Chapter 1

Special Education and the Learning Process
David Sugden

It is not surprising that the field of special education has provoked the interest of those investigating the learning process. Children receiving special education are having difficulty in learning. This may be because of some 'within child' problem such as sensory, physical or cognitive impairment; it may be because of poverty of experience before entering school; or it could be because of some earlier inappropriate schooling, or a combination of these variables. Whatever the reason, the failure to learn in these children provides a unique opportunity to explore the learning process and find the most efficient way of teaching previously unlearned skills.

During the last fifteen years special education has had a particularly high profile. In Europe and in the USA the move towards educating as many children as possible in mainstream schools has brought special education to the fore, whereas previously it had been the domain of a skilful and enthusiastic minority. As soon as ideology and the law changed, special education became a concern for all educators, with the fundamental assumption that mainstream schools would have to cater effectively for a wider range of pupils

The history of special education is littered with methods of teaching. Some are based on sound theoretical foundations, with a natural progression from these foundations to the classroom or clinical situation. There is consistent support for such methods across time, place and persons. Others appear to revolve around the outstanding clinical and teaching skills of the proponent of a particular method, and support for these is more fragmented. The success of these methods is more dependent upon the personal qualities of the teacher or therapist rather than upon a strict interpretation of methodology. Finally, there are a group of techniques which at first glance appear to be only tangentially related to the desired educational outcome.

This text comprises a number of articles all coming from a particular frame of reference, which emphasizes the active cognitive involvement of the child. There is not one method to present but a group of methods representing a common background, and therefore a similarity of approach. A strong theoretical background is present for the total approach, and each individual article has its own body of literature further strengthening its case.

In this chapter I am proposing to describe and discuss some of the recent developments in special education and link them through teaching to the developments in the field of cognitive psychology. Thus the chapter starts by a description of special education in the United Kingdom with particular reference to developments since the Warnock Report in 1978. A second section examines approaches to teaching in special education, and chronicles the changes in time and how they have mirrored the emphasis in other more fundamental disciplines, especially psychology. Finally, I will describe the broad area of cognitive psychology, as it is this area that the contributors are using as their theoretical base.

Recent Developments in Special Education

Pre-1978

The various contributors to this text have taken children as the focus of study, and have not concerned themselves with where the children are placed, only with educational methods aimed at overcoming their various difficulties. However, in order to put some of these methodologies in perspective, it is relevant to examine the overall special educational context in which they have arisen.

The 1944 Education Act placed a duty upon all local education authorities to bring special education under the same control as mainstream. They now had to provide special education, and children could be deemed by a school medical officer to be suffering from 'a disability of mind or body'. Galloway (1985) notes two reasons for the influence of the medical profession at this time. First, handicap was seen primarily as a 'within child' problem and therefore the concern of the medical profession. Second, doctors were the only professionals in sufficient numbers to respond to the demand for assessment. Educational psychology was in its infancy as a profession, and the psychologists who were available, helped the doctors by training them to use assessment instruments such as the Stanford Binet Intelligence Test. This eventually led to the widely criticized use of intelligence tests for the placement of children in educational settings.

The 1944 Act firmly established the concept of special education by laying down ten categories of handicap: educationally subnormal, maladjusted, blind, partially sighted, deaf, hard of hearing, physical handicap, delicate, speech defect, and epileptic. This, coupled with an extensive postwar building scheme, resulted in a rapid increase in the special school population with the concomitant belief that special education only took place in special schools. We are still left with this legacy and it is a major attitudinal stumbling block to our current provision.

Thus from the early 1950s, children with problems were assessed by the school medical officer and placed in special schools. However, this procedure slowly started to break down. First, educational psychology as a profession started to wield some influence. The literature on the process of learning became more widespread and was being used by the professionals. The total influence of the medical profession was being questioned and by the late 1950s there was strong opinion that placement of children should be the concern of educationalists and psychologists and not just the medical profession.

Second, even with psychological and educational assessment, the assessment procedures were still problematic. For example, the largest category of educationally subnormal (moderate) was very ill-defined, and a child in one authority who was in a special school could be matched by one in another who was in the mainstream. This was also true of the equally ill-defined category of maladjustment.

A third reason was that the ten categories forced administrators to fit a child into a particular category; very often a child had more than one difficulty and thus 'qualified' for more than one category, and choice of placement became almost arbitrary.

Fourth, there was growing concern that the transfer from special educational placement was very limited. Once a child was placed in a special school, there was rarely movement back into the mainstream. This made the implicit assumption that ability was a fixed and permanent condition, something which researchers in child development had argued against for years.

Finally, research had shown us the damaging effects of labelling and segregation, with the result that there was a world-wide move towards the concept of integration. In the USA, Public Law 94–142, 1975, granted free education to all children, no matter what their disability. School Boards were to ensure that this education took place in 'the least restrictive environment' which in the majority of cases was in the mainstream school. Various European countries also passed laws facilitating the integration process, and in the United Kingdom, ideological and legal issues were addressed by the Warnock Report, 1978, and the 1981 Education Act respectively.

Warnock Report, 1978

This inquiry started in 1974 and investigated the state of special education in England and Wales and was published as a collection of over 200 recommendations covering ideology, assessment, pre-fives, teacher training, ordinary schools, and special schools. It is not relevant here to detail the extent of these recommendations, merely to point out the major ideological changes that influenced our thinking about special educational needs. There were several important areas:

1   It was recommended that the ten categories of handicap be abolished and replaced by the concept of need. Thus children were not described in terms of their handicap or what they could not do, but in terms of their educational need. A deficit orientation was replaced by an educational-need orientation.

2   It was estimated that one child in six at one time or one in five at some time during schooling would require special educational provision. This estimate had important implications for the concept of integration. Special schools have catered for children with particular difficulties, but only around 2–2½ per cent of the school population are educated in these schools. Thus if 20 per cent of children require some form of special education, 18 per cent of these are, and always have been in mainstream schools.

3   Special educational provision should, in the first instance, be provided in the mainstream school. Special schools were recommended for children with severe cognitive, sensory or physical problems, for those with emotional and behavioural problems, or for those with diverse and complex difficulties.

4   It was recognized that the term integration could refer both to the process by which children in special schools were moved back into mainstream, and the different forms that the state of integration could take. The Report addressed the latter point by describing three forms of integration. There was locational integration with children showing special needs on the same mainstream site; social integration where the children mixed at lunch, breaktime and in clubs etc., and finally there was functional integration which was the fullest form with children showing special educational needs being educated in the same classroom as those evidencing few or no problems.

5   A range of special educational provision was recommended. It was not a simple choice between special and mainstream schools, but a range from full integration in the mainstream classroom with support, through temporary help in a resource centre in the mainstream school, short-term placement in some offsite unit, to short- or long-term stay in a special school. In all of these placements, contacts with a mainstream school were recommended.

6   Assessment was recommended to be a continuous process with structure and detail of the procedures increasing with the severity and complexity of need. Thus five levels of assessment were proposed which started with the class teacher and finished with formal proceedings carried out by outside professionals.

Other categories of recommedations were made, including those on education of children under five years of age, the transition between school and work, and the training of teachers. Many of the recommendations were not startling or innovative, but merely recorded current practice from various parts of the country. However, together they provided guidelines for the direction of special education and brought it from the back seat of education to a position of high visibility.

1981 Education Act

The government response to the Warnock Report was the 1981 Education Act which came into operation in April 1983, and provided a new legislative framework for special educational needs. The Act only addressed a small number of the Warnock recommendations, and has been widely criticized, but it contains many implications for all teachers in special and mainstream schools, and affects parents, governors, LEAs and ultimately children with special educational needs.

First the Act dealt with definitional issues, and replaced the former categories of handicap with the generic concept of learning difficulty, which includes physical, sensory, intellectual and behavioural problems. A child with a learning difficulty requiring educational provision which is additional or different from that of similar age children in a mainstream school is said to have a special educational need. Thus the idea of two types of children is removed and replaced by the concept of need, embracing the Warnock figure of 20 per cent of children at some time having such a need that special educational provision is necessary.

Section Two of the Act noted that with certain conditions met, the child with special educational needs should be educated in the mainstream school. These conditions however, did lend themselves to differing interpretations by the various local education authorities. The first condition was that integration should be compatible with the child receiving the appropriate education for his/her need. Second, it should be compatible with the educational needs of the other children. Third, it should be done with respect to the efficient use of resources. As all education is carried out with resources in mind, it is invidious to select one aspect of it as a financial target. Finally, the wishes of the parents must be addressed.

We are starting to see the implications of this part of the Act. In various authorities there is some movement of children with special educational needs back from special to mainstream schools. Certainly special schools will become fewer in number, but it is not yet clear which ones will stay and which will close. Many children with physical and sensory difficulties will be educated in mainstream, and children with moderate learning difficulties may be kept in mainstream rather than being referred out. However, children with emotional and behavioural difficulties in the majority of cases will still be in separate placements, as in all probability will children with severe and profound learning difficulties.

Under the exclusionary clauses, any authority could easily make a case for keeping these children in special schools, as indeed they could for many of the other children showing special educational needs. Much of the success of the integration measures contained in the Act depend upon the intent and good will of the local education authorities.

The Act requires LEAs to identify children with special educational needs, and in Circular 8/83 there is an explanation of the LEA's duty to show schools how to assess and identify children with special educational needs. The principle of assessment is based upon the Warnock recommendations that it should not be performed in a single session but should be the culmination of on-going monitoring throughout the year. Assessment should be seen as a continuous process with various levels involved. Only when classroom assessment and intervention methods have been tried and found wanting should the formal proceedings as specified by the Act come into play.

These formal proceedings require LEAs to seek advice on the child from the child's teacher, the school medical officer, an educational psychologist and any other relevant professional such as a social worker, speech or physical therapist. The parents' wishes and reports must also be considered, and parents must also be informed of the times and dates of any formal assessments, and in general have the right to be present. The reports are considered by the LEA and a decision is made as to whether a 'Statement' will be provided. If the decision is made to go ahead, a draft must be sent to the parents who will have the right of representation if they feel that it ought to be amended. If the LEA and parents still disagree there are other procedures for appeal.

The Statement spells out the special educational provision that should be made for the child. Thus the place of schooling, the type of curriculum, the social grouping in which the education is to take place and any other necessary support should all be specified in the Statement. In reality the content of Statements varies considerably across and within LEAs. Some give great detail about the child's needs and how these needs should be accommodated. These are very much akin to the American Individual Educational Programme as specified under the 1974 95-142 Act. Others however are pale imitations of a document which is meant to spell out an educational response to a child's needs.

Despite variations in the way LEAs have interpreted the assessment part of the Act, there are strong implications for teachers to keep on-going, up-to-date accurate records of a child's progress, noting both strengths and weaknesses. Many LEAs have responded well to this by giving detailed guidelines to teachers in mainstream schools as to how they should assess, monitor and record children's progress. Others have responded in a less admirable fashion.

The involvement of parents in the decision-making process of their children's education was also a important feature of the Act. It was noted above that parents have various rights with respect to the assessment and placement of their children. They can request that their child be assessed; they can comment upon and add to the assessment procedure; they can discuss the findings of the assessment; they can discuss the draft Statement, and appeal against it through various channels. All of these rights are made specific, and this emphasis on parents being partners in their child's education is consistent with the recommendations of the Warnock Report.

The 1981 Education Act has had many critics; indeed many have proposed that it has done little for real integration and provision because of the 'softness' of the legislation. Certainly it is open to interpretation in a number of important areas, and eventually its effectiveness will depend upon the importance a given LEA will attach to it. At best it has encouraged some teachers to become actively involved in producing programmes for a wider range of children on an individual basis; it has encouraged some to keep more accurate records of children; it forces LEAs to face the issues and make decisions, even if these decisions are not what one might hope for. At worst, the concept of special education can still be ignored, but this is becoming more difficult as the field takes a higher profile.

As this text is being produced, the Education Reform Bill of 1987 is appearing. The Act from this Bill will totally change education from what we have known since 1944. The implications for special education whether in mainstream or special schools will be immense. The regulations governing curriculum may restrict the kind of programme offered to children with special educational needs. For those children without a Statement in mainstream, they will have to follow the National Curriculum whether or not it is suited to their needs. At the time of writing it is not clear what are the curricular implications for those children with a Statement.

Education is in a state of change, special education has become a major issue and is now firmly entrenched in the mainstream of educational thought. Recent commentators are not only saying that the starting point for special education is the mainstream school, but also within that school there has to be positive discrimination towards children with special needs (Dessent,1987). There is not a distinct separate placement for children with special educational needs, because there is no distinct line between those who have special needs and those who have not. A continuum of need is present which ought to be matched by a continuum of provision.

With these principles in mind we have some quite fundamental questions to ask about children with special educational needs. First, where do we place children to receive the education they need? We have tried to move towards the concept of a continuum of provision such that transfer between them can occur more easily and as often as is required. Secondly, what is the curriculum that should be offered to children with special educational needs? Obviously, this will depend upon the needs of the child, and of course the provision laid down by the National Curriculum. Thirdly, what is the best way in which to present the curriculum; that is what methods of teaching should we use? Although by necessity this text draws upon the second and to some extent the first point, the focus is on the third question and examines methods of teaching and interacting from a particular viewpoint.

Psychological Influences on Teaching Approaches in Special Education

The complex relationship between pupil learning outcomes and theories of learning, teaching and instruction has generated a vast research literature. A number of models have been proposed to try and explain these relationships, and educators have often turned to psychology for guidance. Psychology as part of its domain involves the study of human learning and the simple logic would appear to follow that if we know how individuals learn, we have prescriptions for how to teach. Entwistle (1985) concurs with this by saying:

> educational psychology aims at guiding teachers' and students' under-standing of behaviour within the specific contexts where learning and teaching take place. (p. 4).

He continues by saying that there is a long history of the relevance of psychology to the practice of teaching, which does not require cookbook type prescriptions, but involves a range of guidelines to take into account a variety of pedagogical aims.

However, this view is certainly not universal, and not only is it questioned, but there are those who claim:

> psychology is not used in teaching because it is not useable under the circumstances in which teachers operate. (Desforges,1985. p.121).

This quote does not represent an isolated opinion with the relevance of psychology being questioned by other educators (Alexander, 1984). Even psychologists such as Claxton (1985) admit that:

> psychology too often leaves only a faint smear on memory, a slightly bitter taste in the mouth, and as much effect on spontaneous com-petence as a passing face leaves on a mirror. (p.83).

Claxton does continue by saying that it is possibly because psychology promises so much that we are doubly disappointed when it fails to deliver.

If the above statements were true, classroom teaching would be an exception in not benefiting from psychology because we have effectively used principles from psychology in teaching individuals to operate industrial machinery, track on a radar screen, fly planes, drive tanks, play the piano, ski, speak foreign languages, read a book, overcome stressful incidents and many others.

So why do some people see a problem with psychology and teaching? First, I ought to stress that I believe there are several courses involving teachers or trainee teachers where principles from psychology have been effectively used. They are derived from recent psychological thought, they are pedagogically oriented and they are interactive in nature involving the pupil, the teacher, the material to be learned and the setting in which learning takes place. Thus I obviously believe that courses which are not of this nature are the ones that promise much and often offer little. I also believe that some critics of the psychological influence or lack of it are often using dated psychological models. Texts such as this and others in the pedagogical field are what Entwistle (1985) would regard as guidelines within a range of pedagogical aims. There is still the link to be made between the text and the classroom, and this can only be made by practice with guidance.

Earlier I stated that children with special educational needs are having some difficulties in the school situation. These difficulties may be those of learning subject skills such as numeracy and literacy; they may involve problems with personal and social skills; they may be more general involving problems with comprehension, analysis of material and transfer. These difficulties may be the result of a number of factors, probably ultimately being a transaction of within-child attributes and environmental events as espoused by Sameroff and Chandler (1975). For these children questions surrounding assessment, curriculum and teaching methods are of paramount importance, and there is strong debate surrounding the potential answers. Accurate assessment of the child's difficulties would appear to be a prerequisite for any form of intervention, but the manner of assessment will vary. Similarly with curriculum and methodology. Mainstream education has constantly addressed these, and indeed the 1987 Education Reform Bill is our latest answer. In special education a myriad possible solutions to the questions have been proposed, and before detailing the basis for the approaches advocated in the present text, it is relevant to briefly examine some of the more important methods that have been influential.

Ability Training

Ability training is a crude title given to a group of approaches that were popular in the 1960s and early 1970s. Their basis lies in a psychometric factor analytic view of human behaviour together with a fairly static explanation of abilities. The Illinois Test of Psycholinguistic Abilities will serve as an example of the thinking behind this type of approach. The subtests of the ITPA were based upon psycho-linguistic constructs derived from Osgood's (1957) model of communication, and involved items such as auditory and visual reception; auditory, visual, verbal and manual expression; grammatic, visual and auditory closure; auditory and visual sequential memory. These are the abilities that were thought to be involved in communication. Factor analytic studies had been used to identify the independence of the abilities from each other. These were the abilities a child had to bring to a situation which involved communication. Thus if a child was found to be deficient in any of the areas, instruction was aimed at that particular sub-component, with the hope that it would be remediated and thus improve overall communication.

The concept of ability is not an easy one to define or describe. As used in the ITPA it is a fairly rigid predisposition that the child brings to any learning situation. It is a set of discrete components which underpins the task; it is not the task itself, but a collection of resources that are relevant to a particular task. Thus when I learn to play squash, I bring to that squash situation speed, strength, agility, balance, co-ordination, and other abilities. The analogy with squash is that if I can improve my ability of speed, I will become a better squash player. Similarly if I can improve my visual or auditory receptions skills, I will become better at communication. Ainscow and Tweddle (1979) coined the term 'ability training' from Ysseldyke (1973) and are rather dismissive of the approach when measured against success in learning basic academic subjects. They contrast it with a more direct teaching approach which they propose and which is detailed later in the chapter.

A summary of the arguments surrounding the efficacy of teaching abilities was presented by Hammill and Larsen (1974). Their conclusions cast doubts upon this method concluding that the idea that psycholinguistic abilities could be trained was not proven. Controversy then arose concerning the efficacy of the training methods, plus the validity of the evaluation methods of Hammill and Larsen until confusion and chaos seemed to be the result (Hammill and Larsen, 1978; Lund *et al.* 1978; Minskoff, 1975; Newcomer *et al.* 1975).

In a series of articles and in a recent book Kavale and colleagues have made the most complete evaluation of this minefield of information. (Kavale, 1980; 1981a; 1981b; 1982; Kavale and Forness, 1985). They use a technique called meta-analysis which is an inductive method of research synthesis, and summarizes data from a number of research projects thus clarifying the phenomena under consideration. Meta-analysis is based upon a statistic that represents the size of experimental effect or relationship. For experimental programmes or treatments this 'effects size' statistic is:

$$ES = (Xe - Xc)/SDc$$

where Xe is the mean score for the experimental group on the outcome measure, Xc is the mean score for the control group on the outcome measure, and SDc is the standard deviation of the control group. This ES statistic can be translated into a standard score and thus any score of $+1.0$ indicates that a pupil at the 50th percentile has risen to the 84th percentile following the educational intervention.

ES can be used with respect to the duration of intervention, such as the effect after one year's programme; and it can be used to compare teaching methods. ES cannot be made in isolation; it has to be placed in the context of decision-making or policy, e.g. is an ES of *x* worth the deployment of resources *a* and *b* over time span *c*? Meta-analysis does not confirm or reject hypotheses in the classical sense but seeks general conclusions which have been empirically confirmed. It summarizes a multitude of different investigations and brings them together under one common statistic such that overall meaning can be viewed. A final point is that meta-analysis is appropriate only for examining group as opposed to individual data.

Using the ITPA as an example of psycholinguistic training, Kavale (1981a) performed meta-analysis on 34 studies to evaluate its effectiveness. There were 1850 children with an average age of 7.5 years and IQ of 82, and who received 50 hours of psycholinguistic training. An overall ES of .39 was produced indicating that the children who received the training moved to the 65th percentile compared to those not receiving the training who remained at the 50th percentile. In some subcomponents such as verbal expression, the results are particularly encouraging, with roughly 50 hours of psycholinguistic training producing results in excess of what would be expected from half a year's schooling.

The ITPA is an often quoted example of the so-called ability training approach. Another one comes from the area loosely called 'perceptual-motor training'. The logic of this training is that motor skills are really perceptual-motor in nature because they involve taking in and making meaning of information; reading also involves perception as it may be possible to improve reading by using perceptual-motor methods. When the ES statistic is applied to these studies we find that their effect is negligible, with the probability of a positive result after a teaching programme being only slightly better than that which is expected by chance. Even when the outcome variables are broken down into the various subject areas rather than global fields, there is still no evidence of positive results.

The ability training or diagnostic prescriptive model has shown some positive results, certainly more than would be admitted by Ainscow and Tweddle (1979). However there has been a drift away from this type of approach with the relevance to a school curriculum and everyday functioning being questioned. The methodologies have become more direct, and behavioural models have taken over as the foundation for the approaches.

Behavioural Approach

During the last fifteen years, approaches coming from the behavioural model have had the greatest impact in special education. What started as influence on individual programmes for children with severe difficulties has expanded not only into a wider group of children showing both behaviour and learning difficulties, but also into a greater range of methods.

One of the difficulties in describing and analysing behavioural approaches lies in the shifting ground of its proponents. Tomlinson (1981; 2nd edn. in press) provides a novel antidote to this by evaluating behaviourism from theoretical, methodological and technological perspectives. He argues that theoretically it has been widely criticized for being overly simple and reductionist, while its methodology has strong support, with the emphasis on direct measures. Tomlinson does stress, however, that a method with a heavy emphasis on observation and experiment is not necessarily a behaviourist one. It is in the area of practice that behaviourism has made most gains with techniques such as shaping being particularly powerful. The confusion and in some cases direct contradiction between theory, method and practice opens it to fierce criticism. When a solution to a child's difficulties is being sought, a sequence of questions is asked. What is the difficulty? What is the immediate cause? What programme of remediation is most appropriate, and why? It is the linking of the last two questions which causes the confusion. Many of today's behavioural advocates are using methods which are very effective and efficient in terms of pedagogy, but are quite a way from the original assumptions of behaviourist psychology. Indeed in the influential publication by the *British Journal of Educational Psychology* (Fontana, 1984), Blackman notes,

> It is simply not true, however, to say that contemporary behaviourists have no place for private experience in their explanatory system (p.7).

a clear example of how the ground has shifted, although not changed entirely as later Blackman points out,

> although it should be recalled that those private events are conceptualised as themselves being the result of behavioural interactions between members of a social community rather than the autonomous causes of behaviour (p.11).

It is most appropriate to examine first the fundamental general assumptions upon which the behavioural approach is based, and then outline the pedagogical approaches that have arisen from them. Wheldall and Merrett (1984) have summarized these assumptions as follows:

1   The concern is with the observable; thus in education the interest is in what the child actually does as opposed to what the child thinks or feels.
2   For most practical purposes, behaviour is learned. While recognizing that genetic influences do have effects, and may set the limit for what individuals can learn, the observable behaviour is still the result of learning.
3   Learning is a change in behaviour. Whereas cognitive psychologists will argue that learning is a change in an internal construct which may result

in a change in behaviour, for behaviourists learning is a change in behaviour relying on the logic; it is the only way we know that learning has taken place.

4   Learning is governed by the law of effect, that is, individuals learn on the basis of repeating behaviours that are followed by desirable consequences, and will eliminate behaviours with punishing or undesirable consequences.

5   Linked closely with 4, behaviours are governed by the contexts in which they occur. Learning is concerned with the when and where of performance. Thus the antecedents of the behaviour are as important as the consequences.

From these assumptions or ones very similar, the behavioural approach has given us the tools and structure with which to teach children with special educational needs. There is such a vast body of literature that all I can do is summarize a number of approaches and recommend Fontana (1984).

The first area in which this approach has had effect is in the area of classroom management. Originally this was called behaviour modification, but now its proponents prefer to use the term applied behavioural analysis. The approach is very simple, consisting of several carefully structured and sequenced steps. First identify the problem behaviour; what is the behaviour that you wish to change? Second, how often, for how long, under what conditions, does this behaviour occur? In other words carefully analyse the occurrence of the behaviour, particularly with respect to the immediate antecedents. Third, with what do you wish to replace the problem behaviour? Fourth, what reinforcer will be used to achieve the desired goal? Fifth, continually monitor the behaviour, and finally evaluate the results. This method has its origins in the USA, but research work has now been replicated in this country (Wheldall and Merrett, 1984).

A second area gaining recent popularity has been the use of behavioural objectives. Tweddle and Francis (1984) argue that this rise in popularity has been the result of the demise of child centred assessment, and replaced by one which is firmly linked in the curriculum. Behavioural objectives are descriptions of learning outcomes, describing what the child will do after a period of instruction. They are not vague descriptions of teaching intentions, but rather precise statements of what the pupil will or should be able to do. They contain three important components:

1   A verb stating what the child will do.
2   Some standard or criterion of performance required of the child.
3   A description of the conditions under which the behaviour will occur.

An example would be: 'child writes the answer to twenty double digit addition sums when requested by the teacher, making no more than two errors'. Thus any teaching programme would contain a number of these objectives in different areas. This has led to the curriculum being made up of these objectives, particularly in some special schools. There are now on the market a number of commercial packages and LEA-produced materials (DATA-PAC, Ackerman *et al.*, 1983; LISSEN, Leeds LEA (1984); SNAP, Ainscow and Muncey, 1981).

In order to use an objectives-based approach, subject, skill or experience areas have to be broken down into their component parts, and placed in sequence. Task analysis has always been a cornerstone of the behavioural approach, although sole rights to task analysis do not reside within the behavioural field. Again the essence of this approach appears to be simple: instead of presenting a whole skill that the pupil cannot perform, break it down into its component parts that can be managed by the learner, an approach which is central to behavioural methods but which also would be embraced by almost all other approaches. The process of task analysis involves a variety of techniques leading to teaching methods using forward and backward chaining, slicing, error discriminate learning, fading and shaping (Ainscow and Tweddle, 1984; Gold, 1981).

Precision teaching is linked to the use of objectives and attempts to provide the answer to five key teaching questions (Raybould, 1984):

1   Is the pupil on the right task?
2   Is the pupil learning?
3   Is the pupil learning fast enough?
4   What is to be done if the pupil is not learning?
5   What level of performance is to be expected?

Certainly these questions are entirely reasonable for any teacher to ask, and precision teaching uses similar procedures to those detailed from applied behavioural analysis in order to answer them. Thus there is the description of the child's difficulties followed by the specification of the desired outcome in observable measurable terms. There is the recording and charting of the child's performance on a daily basis, the recording of teaching methods used in relation to the pupil's performance, and finally the analysis of the progress to evaluate the effectiveness. The essence therefore is very simple, although its impact has often been lessened in a plethora of jargon.

There are other influential offshoots of behavioural methods such as direct instruction, using many or all of the techniques mentioned above and put into some large pedagogical package. Again it is based on the same fundamental principles.

We have a substantial amount of evidence evaluating the efficacy of a behavioural approach, with several benefits being evident. First, the approach demands that teachers be organized; it is impossible to be effective without a good sense of structure and organization, these being the cornerstones of the approach. If teachers are organized they are automatically in a better position to help children with special educational needs. Second, it is an optimistic approach. It relegates home background and constitutional defects, and concentrates on what can be done in the educational setting. This is what teachers have control over, and thus it is where we should place our resources. An obvious extension of this has been to involve parents using similar techniques. If a child is not learning, then the instruction is at fault not the child. Third, the approach is based on giving the child success and encouragement. The programmes of learning are structured for the child to experience success and be moved on in sequential small steps so that this success is cumulative. Similarly with behaviour problems, the emphasis is on positively rewarding desirable behaviour, and teaching socially acceptable skills to take the place of less desirable ones.

The behavioural approach has given us some effective tools to use, but as one might imagine it is rare indeed for any educational philosophy to go unchallenged, and the behavioural approach is no exception. The following is a global summary of criticisms of the approach.

1 The approach itself is reductionist in nature. It is difficult to capture the essence of the educational process in some stark behavioural objectives. Even Ainscow and Tweddle (1979) argue that behavioural objectives are very difficult to write in some subject or skill areas. For example, mathematics would appear to be an easier area in which to specify objectives than in say the humanities. Tomlinson (1981; 2nd edition in press) has pointed out that an extreme and rigid use of objectives can limit the curriculum by encouraging convergence.

2 The approach does not take into account the cognitive processes thus the learning processes of the child. Two simple areas where this is evident. First, when task analysis is being performed, it is assumed that each child will learn the task in the same order, because it is the task that is analysed not the learning context, which involves the child. Second, in the area of motivation, from a behavioural point of view, a child will be motivated to repeat an action because of the result of previous experience on that action: that is how they did, good or bad. Again this appears simplistic with a great deal of evidence showing it is not the previous result that is effective, but why the child thinks the result happened. To what did they attribute the result (Weiner, 1981)? Thus if I am successful, I want to know whether it was because of my ability, effort, the difficulty of the task or some other general factor like luck. These are what will affect the way I approach this task a second time, rather than solely the result of my previous experience.

3 There is still the assumption that a child's learning is externally driven and directed. When feedback is given to the child, from the behavioural point of view it is seen as reinforcing rather than informing. The child is still viewed as a passive recipient of information rather than an active seeker who reconstructs what the environment offers.

The cognitive perspective takes up the second and third points by stressing that the learning processes and styles of the child are a crucial factor and cannot be ignored in the teaching situation. In a limited form these are even being used in some behavoural programmes, involving the child in decision-making, self-monitoring, goal setting and reinforcement. This is effective pedagogy, but a long way from the original assumptions of the behavioural tradition.

Psychodynamic Approach

One chapter in the book is solely concerned with children evidencing emotional or behavioural difficulties, and it would be a notable omission if some account was not given of the psycho-educational approach to helping these children. This term is a general one referring to a group of approaches loosely based upon the psychodynamic theory of Freud, and the humanistic principles of workers such as Rogers and Maslow.

In the Freudian tradition, it is the unconscious motives within the individual that drive behaviour. Defences and symptoms develop to deal with conflict and anxiety, and these conflicts occur as the child goes through early psychosexual stages. The mastery of each of these stages is necessary for a child to achieve appropriate mental stability (Erickson, 1963; Freud, 1949). If the child does not resolve these developmental conflicts, then emotional instability of various types can be the result. In the humanistic tradition as proposed by Maslow, there is a striving for self-actualization, with a hierarchy of needs that have to be met. When a lower level need has been met, the individual moves to the next, and anything that impedes the progress towards self-actualization can lead to emotional instability (Maslow, 1970).

As Hewett and Taylor (1980) have pointed out, contemporary psycho-dynamic and humanistic explanations for the development of emotional disturbance are long and complex. It is somewhat unfair to summarize them in such a brief section. However, the detail is well described elsewhere and the fundamental explanation for the development of emotional disturbance rests on conflict in childhood and faulty relationships during the early critical years.

When we examine the influence of such theories on our approaches, we first see that the child is viewed as emotionally disturbed. This is the result of inadequate resolution of various critical conflicts during childhood (Erickson, 1963) or when there is a discrepancy between the child's experiences and his self-concept (Rogers, 1969). A child has certain life goals and expectancies and if life experiences are not in accord with these, then conflict is the result. Hewett and Taylor (1980) describe a six-year-old who evidenced behaviour that was aggressive, destructive, verbally abusive, violent and overly active and propose that from a psychodynamic and humanistic viewpoint, this behaviour is the result of one or more of the following:

1   Previous unsatisfactory interpersonal and affective relationship with others.
2   Anger and hate toward others.
3   Mistrust and suspicion toward others.
4   Self-doubt and guilt.
5   Withdrawal, fearfulness and anxiety.
6   Lack of feelings of self-worth.
7   Conflict between previous experience and innate actualising tendencies.
8   Poor sense of identity. (p. 58).

It is not surprising that when a teacher begins to work from this viewpoint, a role of therapist is assumed. A fundamental principle is the establishment of positive relationships between the child and teacher. This often involves initial unconditional acceptance of behaviour with a gradual introduction of limits; allowing aggressive behaviour to run its course; developing trust first before making demands on the child; and creating a warm friendly environment for learning, concentrating on this rather than on academics (Hewett and Taylor,1980).

Modern programmes incorporating psycho-educational techniques rarely advocate total permissiveness in the manner of Aichorn (1975), but they are still concerned with developing relationships, enhancing self-concept, changing attitudes, developing trust and encouraging emotional growth. Certainly most educators would agree that these are laudable if somewhat ill-defined goals. However, a major concern is that they are rather elusive terms and it is very difficult indeed to be specific about the instruction and methodology for achieving them. Samuels (1980) notes the imprecision of the theory, pointing out that class size often preludes the method, and it is a skilled activity requiring extra training for the teachers. Finally, she argues that it does not take into account the cognitive development of the child.

There have been a number of offshoots which have their origins in psychodynamic and humanistic theories. Crisis intervention strategies such as life space interviews (Redl, 1959), and communication skills to facilitate interpersonal relationships (Jones, 1980) are such examples, although they also draw upon other theoretical bases.

Cognitive Processes and Learning

The diversity of topics in this text illustrates the range to which the general label of cognition applies. There is a great width to the field, and it is certainly not restricted to specific topics as cognitive psychologists are interested in perception, learning, development, memory, problem-solving plus school subject areas such as reading, maths and sciences, together with everyday experiences outside of the educational arena (Smyth *et al.*, 1987). Such is the width that Eysenck (1984) notes that an American survey reported three-quarters of all academic psychologists claimed to be in the cognitive tradition.

Despite the varying interests of cognitive psychologists, they are linked by a fundamental aim involving the need to provide a detailed and specific account of cognitive processes. Cognition involves knowledge and how it can be applied to everyday situations. The roots of cognitive psychology are to be found in investigations involving communication systems, verbal skills, motor skills, and in child development. Now cognitive approaches have taken a firm hold of explanations of everyday behaviour, and the influence of this mode of study is felt in a number of academic disciplines. It influences what to teach beginners; it can help determine the nature of knowledge differences between expert and novices; and aids in how best to accomplish the goals of instruction.

The essence of a cognitive approach is that cognitive processes such as attention, memory and problem-solving are analysed and explained. They are seen as crucial to the performance and learning of everyday tasks, and much of the research in experimental psychology is aimed at better methods of identifying and measuring these processes. The approach in this text is to take these psychological concepts and direct them towards pedagogical concerns.

An examination of cognitive processes is the starting point for the cognitive approach and to do this, experimenters have often broken down the process into subcomponents. The early attempts to do this were fairly simplistic with a computer analogy being quite common. Flow charts were produced representing the internal functioning of human beings in much the same way as had been done with computers. However, as Eysenck (1984) points out, this was questioned because of the enormous differences between humans and computers. Now the focus has turned around with some researchers trying to program a computer to perform human functions.

The concept of subcomponents remained an integral part of the cognitive approach, and in the 1960s and 1970s models showed information progressing through these components or stages in some sequential manner. These models usually involved the following: information is taken in through the sensory system; some filtering mechanism is used to direct attention to that information which is relevant; information is held in working or short-term memory as it progresses through the system; it is compared to previously learned information held in long-term store; it is co-ordinated to bring about a plan; the plan is put into action. Models of memory were common using this approach (Atkinson and Shiffrin, 1968), and reaction time studies were used to indicate speed of processing. The models provided a simple framework from which textbooks and lecturers could present cognitive processes.

Unfortunately, this approach was too simple, and modern models of cognition differ in two important aspects to the one described above. First the system above runs sequentially, with one operation being completed before the next one begins. But an everyday task may need five operations for its completion. It is possible that one follows the other in a special manner, but most tasks are not structured in this way. Some simultaneous or parallel processing has to take place. Thus more modern models of cognition involve both serial and parallel processing, and each will be used at the appropriate time according to the demands of the task.

A second difference is that the early models tended to be stimulus-driven in that the individual was dominated by the characteristics of the stimulus. They took little account of past experience, attitudes, expectations and motives of the individual, characteristics which we know have great impact upon cognitive processing. These stimulus-driven models are often referred to as 'bottom-up' processing, whereas 'top-down' processing refers to that processing which takes into account the characteristics noted above. Cognitive characteristics the individual brings to a situation have great effect on the type and quality of sub-sequent cognitive processing. As with serial and parallel processing, top-down and bottom-up approaches are both used in everyday cognitive functioning.

For example, when children read, they are guided by the stimulus, that is the text. However, the meaning they extract from the text is equally determined by the nature of the knowledge, attitudes, and expectations they bring to the reading situation. With these two processes working in tandem, they then construct their meaning of the text. Other everyday examples of this are very common; two people witnessing an accident or crime or any noteworthy incident will differ in the report they give. The stimulus is the same, but the resources of the observers will differ, thus affecting the reports. Listening to music, watching a play, viewing some art exhibit, all involve cognitive and in some cases emotional experiences that will use bottom-up and top-down processes.

A textbook on cognitive psychology will usually include chapters on percep-tion, memory, learning, development and language. In these chapters are reports of experiments investigating some component of the area in question. Smyth *et al.* (1987) note that sometimes the components of the system have been emphasized at the expense of the overall function of the activity. They take an action and make it the focal point of a particular chapter, bringing to bear on this action, those studies that they believe to be relevant. So instead of starting with the components of a memory system and working towards some meaningful task, they start with the task and ask the question 'how do we do this?' Using this format, they describe the actions of investigating a murder; problem solving; witnessing an accident; reading a book; finding your way around a new city; doing mental arithmetic; and even reaching for a glass of beer!

Models of cognitive processing have destroyed the myth of the 'black box' by identifying, describing, predicting and measuring cognitive actions. Like Smyth *et al.* (1987), our concern is not with the subcomponents of cognition; they are merely aids to our understanding of how individuals use their knowledge to interact with the environment. In our case these interactions are pedagogically oriented.

We have narrowed the focus of our study to children who are experiencing difficulty in school. Some of the chapters are concerned with *describing* the problem, which may involve language and reading performance, motor behaviour, social and personal competence or a more general difficulty in learning any skill. A second concern is with an *explanation* of the problem. Cognition is concerned with knowledge and how it is applied to everyday situations. Thus explanations will examine where this has broken down; how inappropriate or inefficient cognition activity will lead to faulty or poor skills. The third concern is with *prescription*, and examines the most effective ways these skills can be taught. Most of the chapters deal with all three of these issues while a few concentrate on just one or two.

References

Ackerman, T., Gunelt, D., Kenward, P., Leadbetter, P., Mason, L., Matthews, C. and Winteringham, D. (1983) *DATAPAC* (Department of Educational Psychology, University of Birmingham).

Aichorn, A. (1965). *Wayward Youth*. (New York: Viking Press), originally published 1925.

Ainscow, M. and Muncey, J. (1981), *Tutors' guide: SNAP Learning Difficulties Course* (Coventry LEA Publications).

Ainscow, M. and Tweddle, D. A. (1979), *Preventing classroom failure: an objectives approach* (Chichester: Wiley).

Ainscow, M. and Tweddle, D. A. (1984), *Early Learning Skills Analysis* (Chichester: Wiley).

Alexander, R. J. (1984), *Primary Teaching* (Holt, Rinehart & Winston).

Atkinson, R. C. and Shiffrin, R. M. (1986), Human memory: a proposed system and its control processes, in K. W. Spence and J. T. Spence (eds.), *The Psychology of Learning and Motivation*, Vol.2. (London: Academic Press).

Blackman, D. (1984), The current status of behaviourism in learning theory in psychology, in D. Fontana (ed.), *Behaviourism and Learning Theory in Education* (British Journal of Educational Psychology, Monograph 1. Edinburgh: Scottish Academic Press).

Claxton, G. L. (1985), The Psychology of Teaching Educational Psychology, in H. Francis (ed.), *Learning to Teach: Psychology in Teacher Training* (Lewes: Falmer Press).

Department of Education and Science (1983), *Assessments and Statements of Special educational needs*, Circular 1/83 (London: DES).

Department of Education and Science (1978), *Special Educational Needs* (The Warnock Report, London: HMSO).

Desforges, C. (1985), Training for the management of learning in the primary school, in H. Francis (ed.), *Learning to Teach: Psychology in Teacher Training* (Lewes: Falmer Press).

Dessent, T. E. (1987), *Making the Ordinary School Special* (Lewes: Falmer Press).

Dillon, R. F. (1986), Issues in cognitive psychology and instruction, in R. F. Dillon and R. J. Sternberg (eds), *Cognition and Instruction* (Orlando: Academic Press).

Education Act (1944) (London: HMSO).

Education Act (1980) (London: HMSO).

Education Act (1981) (London: HMSO).

Education Act (1986) (London: HMSO).

Education Reform Bill (1987) (London: HMSO).

Education of All Handicapped Children's Act (1975), *Public Law 94-142*.

Entwistle, N.J. (1985), Contributions of psychology to learning and teaching, in N.J. Entwistle (ed.), *New Directions in Educational Psychology 1 Learning and Teaching* (Lewes: Falmer Press).

Erickson, E. (1963), *Childhood and Society*, 2nd edn. (New York: Norton).

Eysenck, M.W. (1984), *A Handbook of Cognitive Psychology* (London: Lawrence Erlbaum Associates).

Fontana, D. (ed.) (1984), *Behaviourism and Learning Theory* (*British Journal of Educational Psychology*, Monograph 1, Edinburgh: Scottish Academic Press).

Freud, S. (1949), *An Outline of Psychoanalysis* (New York: Norton).

Galloway, D. (1985), *Schools, Pupils and Special Educational Needs* (London: Croom Helm).

Gold, M.W. (1981), *Try Another Way: Training Manual* (Champaign, Illinois: Research Press).

Hamill, D.D. and Larson, S.C. (1974), The effectiveness of psycholinguistic training, *Exceptional Children*, **41**, 5–14.

Hamill, D.D. and Larson, S.C. (1978), The effectiveness of psycholinguistic training: a re-affirmation of position, *Exceptional Children*, 44, 402–414.

Hewett, F.M. and Taylor, F.D. (1980), *The Emotionally Disturbed Child in the Classroom*, 2nd edn. (Boston: Allyn & Bacon).

Jones, V.F. (1980), *Adolescents with Behaviour Problems: Strategies for Teaching Counseling and Parent Involvement* (Boston: Allyn & Bacon).

Kavale, K.A. (1980), Auditory-visual integration and its relationship to reading achievement: a meta-analysis, *Perceptual and Motor Skills*, **51**, 947–955.

Kavale, K.A. (1981a), Functions of the Illinois Test of Psycholinguistic Abilities (ITPA): are they trainable? *Exceptional Children*, **47**, 496–510.

Kavale, K.A. (1981b), The relationship between auditory perceptual skills and reading ability: a meta-analysis, *Journal of Learning Disabilities*, **14**, 539–546.

Kavale, K.A. (1982) 'Meta-analysis of the relationship between visual perceptual skills and reading achievement', *Journal of Learning Disabilities*, **15**, 42–51.

Kavale, K.A. and Forness, S.R. (1985), *The Science of Learning Disabilities* (Windsor: NFER-Nelson).

Leeds Local Education Authority (1984), *Leeds In-Service for Special Education Needs (LISSEN)*.

Lund, K.A., Foster, G.E. & McGall-Perez, F.C. (1978), The effectiveness of psycholinguistic training: a re-evaluation, *Exceptional Children*, **44**, 310–319.

Maslow, A.H. (1970), *Motivation and Personality*, 2nd edn., (New York: Harper & Row).

Minskoff, E. (1975), Research on psycholinguistic training: critique and guidelines, *Exceptional Children*, **42**, 136–144.

Newcomer, P., Larsen, S. and Hamill, D. (1975), A response, *Exceptional Children*, **42**, 144–48.

Osgood, C.E. (1957), Motivational dynamics of language behaviour, in M. Jones (ed.), *Nebraska Symposium on Motivation* (Lincoln: University of Nebraska Press).

Raybould, T. (1984), Precision teaching with pupils with learning difficulties, in D. Fontana (ed.), *Behaviourism and Learning Theory in Education* (*British Journal of Educational Psychology*, Monograph 1, Edinburgh: Scottish Academic Press).

Redl, F. (1959), Strategy and techniques of the life space interview, *American Journal of Orthopsychiatry*, 19, 130–9.

Rogers, C. (1969), *Freedom to Learn* (Columbus, Ohio: Merrill).

Sameroff, A.J. and Chandler, M.J. (1975), Reproductive risk and the continuum of caretaking casualty, in F.D. Horowitz (ed.), *Review of Child Development Research*, Vol. 4 (Chicago: University of Chicago Press).

Samuels, S.C. (1980), *Disturbed Exceptional Children: an Integrated Approach* (New York: Human Sciences Press).

Smyth, M. M., Morris, P. E., Levy, P. and Ellis, A. W. (1987), *Cognition in Action* (London: Lawrence Erlbaum Associates).

Tomlinson, P. D. (1981, 2nd edn. in press), *Understanding Teaching: Interactive Educational Psychology* (London: McGraw Hill).

Tweddle, D. and Francis, L. (1984), The formulation and use of educational objectives, in D. Fontana (ed.), *Behaviourism and Learning Theory in Education. British Journal of Educational Psychology*, Monograph 1, Edinburgh: Scottish Academic Press.

Weiner, B. (1981), *Theories of Motivation: From Mechanism to Cognition*, 2nd edn. (Chicago: Markham).

Wheldall, K. and Merrett, F. (1984), The behavioural approach to classroom management, in D. Fontana (ed.), *Behaviourism and Learning Theory in Education. British Journal of Educational Psychology*, Monograph 1, (Edinburgh: Scottish Academic Press).

Ysseldyke, J. E. (1973), Diagnostic-prescriptive teaching: the search for aptitude treatment interactions, in L. Mann and D. A. Sabatino (eds), *The First Review of Special Education* (Philadelphia: JSE Press).

Chapter 2

The Teaching of Skills:
Modern Cognitive Perspectives
Peter Tomlinson

This chapter may be seen as an extension of David Sugden's introduction, in that it offers a general overview of the nature and relevance of cognitive skills psychology to the teaching of useful competences in special education. It may therefore function as a background introduction to various other chapters. Like the book of which it forms part, such a chapter seems necessary for a variety of reasons, including the following: (1) In everyday 'common sense' talk, skilled competence sometimes seems to be viewed in a rather simplistic way; (2) in special education circles, this way of thinking has been reinforced by ideas from Skinnerian psychology, with which it has much in common; (3) all this in spite of the existence of a large body of relevant theory and research concerning human action and learning. These ideas have long been dominant in experimental psychology, yet have only recently begun to penetrate educational thinking. Why this should be so is another issue, beyond my present scope; but it is also part of the reason why this chapter will start with some reflections on what we need to bear in mind when seeking useful insights and ideas for teaching. Having considered this, I will then offer an account of what modern cognitive psychology has to say about skill and its acquisition, so as to look at the nature of teaching functions in relation to skill development, with particular reference to special educational needs.

Introduction

Before Jumping on any Bandwagon...

Whether in special education or elsewhere, any teacher who thinks about the matter knows that there are considerable problems in understanding and promoting effective teaching. Part of the reason for this must surely lie in the complexity and uniqueness of the tasks teachers are faced with, not to mention issues like resources, class size and so forth. But to some extent it may also be due to our expectations, often implicit, concerning what new ideas can achieve and how they may relate to our existing practices. We sometimes succumb rather too readily to the assumption (often encouraged by those who would offer their ideas and commercial packages) that to be useful, a new idea must magically transform the whole picture for the better, while still not being so new and different that we can't understand it immediately! It must give a sure-fire way of dealing with what we perceive as problems, offer a bandwagon we can join with confidence. If such an assumption does exist, however, it's surely a very unfortunate one. Among other things, for example, it promotes premature, defensive rejection ('You can't tell me this is going to work!'). And should such a reaction be overcome, we may then get the zealous convert who seeks to frame everything in terms of their new 'gospel', seeing nothing else.

Yet most of us surely suspect, if only intuitively, that matters are never so clear-cut in real life: no idea or approach is going to tell us everything, though some may offer us something. The more intelligent stance is surely to weigh up the strengths and weaknesses, to be open-minded yet critically aware at the same time, as we first encounter new ideas and then try out any of their implications that seem plausible (see Tomlinson, 1989, ch.1 for a development of this viewpoint). Some writers (e.g. Claxton, 1985) feel that such reflection is a luxury teachers neither want nor need: intuition and immersion in practice are enough. Others, such as Schön (1983), stress that for professional effectiveness, practitioners such as teachers need not just to think before acting, but also to 'reflect-in-action'.

My own view is that intuition and involvement are vital in various respects, as we shall shortly see confirmed by skill psychology. But so are reflection and strategy. This is true of skilled performance itself, but all the more important when it comes to appraising the potential of new concepts, ideas, concepts, strategies to inform our teaching, whether generally or in special education. In making such appraisal there are at least two central matters about which we ought to be as clear and explicit as possible.

The first is the nature of teaching: what is involved, how do we currently conceive of the practice we're seeking to illuminate? The second is the nature of the ideas being offered for that purpose: what exactly is being proposed, how coherent is it and how does it relate to our existing ideas, how well-grounded is it and to what aspects of teaching does it seem relevant? To a closed-minded practitioner, this explicit reflection on current practice seems irrelevant and possibly even threatening. To the more thoughtful, it may seem so obvious when spelled out that they wonder why it even needed to be mentioned!

One answer is that if in fact we had always insisted on such explicit analysis, not a few sterile controversies and educational bandwagons might have been avoided and teachers' adoption of particular ideas and strategies would probably be more measured and intelligent. Since I shall shortly be presenting cognitive skill psychology as a suitable source of illumination for special education, I ought at this point to practise what I've just been preaching by offering a brief analysis of what in essence teaching seems to involve, with some reference to the meaning of 'special' education.

What is this Teaching We're Trying to Illuminate/Improve?

Even when stripped down to its essential features, teaching is still something rather complex. It always involves a number of elements, these elements interact, and their interaction is of a particular, purposeful kind. That is, teaching always involves at least: *(1) a learner:* a person who, whatever else they may have or be, lacks some *(2) intended competence or learning outcome,* the intention (hopefully share by the learner) being to gain it by means of *(3) a learning process,* a set of activities thought likely to promote acquisition of the competence in question; *(4) a teacher:* a person whose understanding of the competence in question and the nature of learning enables them to influence the learning process (i.e. teach) in whatever ways enhance learning, other things equal.

The bare essentials of this interactive view of teaching can be portrayed diagrammatically, as in Figure 2.1. Even such a minimal view as this has many implications. Thus, amongst other things, to summarize the above as saying that teaching is a *purposeful interaction* means that traditional polarizations into 'teacher centred', 'learner/child centred', 'subject/objectives' approaches seriously reduce the notion of teaching and thereby limit our understanding, at the very least. Thus, in fact, all teaching must be learner centred, in that it's the learner's acquisition of competence that is the basic reason for the activity in the first place. Yet the teacher is also an essential figure, otherwise he or she wouldn't be teaching: why involve a teacher if the learner could acquire the competence equally effectively? Second, successful teaching will depend on the combination of elements interacting at the time. Learners, teachers, intended learning outcomes and types of learning/teaching process can all vary. So an interactive conception of teaching immediately highlights the need to seek suitable

Figure 2.1 Teaching as a purposeful interaction

combinations that will *match* requirements: different types of learning/teaching process may be needed for different types of competence outcome, for learners with differing characteristics by way of ability, specific experience, cognitive style, motivation.

Thus an interactive analysis gives an explicit rationale for the truth of the old saying that 'all education is special education': every pupil is different from every other in at least some respect, and since this may make a difference to 'what they get out of' any particular teaching approach, the intelligent teacher needs in principle to attend to pupil differences. In practice, one might argue, the very notion of special education has only come about because of an implicitly non-interactive view of teaching: traditionally, teaching is done in a particular way (or restricted set of ways), and pupils who don't seem to be catered for by this general approach are seen as 'special'. Doubtless, such a 'simple orthodoxy' view of teaching approach is fostered by a whole range of factors in addition to the above, including resource limitations of the teacher–student ratio kind.

Although the curriculum implications of an interactive conception of teaching include all sorts of issues regarding the nature and definition of 'special' educational needs and provision, and though these clearly require careful discussion, that is beyond my scope here. In order to clear the ground for the remainder of the chapter, therefore, I will proceed on the following basis. An interactive analysis of teaching implies that intelligent teaching requires an understanding of the nature of possible learning processes and of the nature and variation among learners, so that in principle, the teaching approach can be matched to the requirements of learners and intended outcomes (topics). This alerts us generally to relevant learner characteristics in all educational settings and it may well be the case (the sources cited later confirm this, in fact) that individual pupils' making sense and learning from new experiences depends very specifically on the competences and experience they bring to learning/teaching situations. In these terms, a 'special educational' focus means a focus on the types of variation we may find in pupils' psychological resources for learning *in relation to* types of learning/teaching process adaptation to take account of these resources. It also tends to mean something of a focus on the extremes of such variations in what pupils bring to the learning/teaching situation.

Any psychological viewpoint recruited to help illuminate teaching will therefore have implications for all of these constituent aspects, whether it does so explicitly or implicitly. One problem here is that there is something of a trade-off dilemma: the more simple, direct and comprehensible the viewpoint, the more relevant and promising it may seem to the educator – but the more likely it is to be one-sided. On the other hand, the more a psychological viewpoint does justice to the complexities of teaching, the less easy it is to grasp and apply. Perhaps the eventual acid test of applicability is whether we can derive a relatively precise set of strategies and procedures, which the teacher can attempt to follow in practice.

The Psychology of Skill and the Processes of Teaching

It seems important to recognize explicitly that the cognitive skill perspectives I shall review are not being offered in a vacuum, to an audience with no previous thoughts on the matter. So let's start by considering 'common sense' views of skill that are taken for granted more or less generally and the existing 'theoretical' views that have been prevalent in special education. Both sets share much in common, as we shall see.

Some Current Views of Skill

Common sense

Everyday talk about human competence typically contains a variety of strands, some involving very subtle ideas. However, one major tendency seems to be to see capacities as coming purely from within the person, inborn, you've 'either got them or you haven't'. We might call this the 'talent' model, because of its tendency to use artistic examples: thus, parents may ask 'Does my child have ''musical ability''?' Whatever else, such a viewpoint is clearly rather pessimistic from the educational point of view and where, for instance, parents do imply it, there may be a need to alter their stance if any backup co-operation is to be forthcoming from them. They may, for instance, have a more optimistic view of other capacities and one might help them see things in terms of that model. As a music teacher once pointed out to me, even if in former times the common folk weren't thought to have the gift of literacy, nowadays few parents would ask the equivalent 'Does my child have reading ability?' They're more likely to ask when she/he is going to be reading, why she/he isn't doing so, and what is being done about it. This alternative everyday conception may see capacities as forms of skill. In so far as it does, however, we also need to be on the lookout for a quite widespread implicit notion of skill that is seriously lacking because of its one-sidedness.

As I suggested above, any viewpoint on skill actually contains two strands: a view of what skilled action consists in and an idea of the nature of the performer of skill, the person. A prevalent common-sense view of action sees skill as 'simple motor habit' and tends to think in terms of physical actions such as biting one's nails, raising one's hand, and the like. Skills are thus 'brute action', bits of behaviour that have become habitual through repetition: 'practice makes perfect'. There isn't any thought or reflection associated with such actions, that's what makes them skills. Observation and imitation may have been involved in their acquisition, but this doesn't matter now, and the way such awareness may influence action is left out of consideration.

Corresponding to this view of skilled action is a conception of the person, an 'implicit psychology': much everyday talk implies a view of persons as made up of two separate and very different parts, the mind and the body. In this *dualist* view the mind is associated with conscious experience, thought and feelings, decisions, and tends to be seen as non-physical, the 'ghost in the machine', as the philosopher Gilbert Ryle put it. The 'machine' is the other part, the body, within which the mind resides somehow and somewhere (my own research on people's concepts of persons suggests that some people in our culture identify mind with brain, while others think that 'the mind' is separate from the brain).

Such a dualist view tends to have problems in trying to conceive how something totally non-physical (the mind) can influence the action of the physical part (the body), and much common sense adopts the neat (but one-sided) solution of seeing action in totally physical terms, cutting thought and awareness out of the picture. So skilled actions are seen as movements executed by the body without the involvement of the mind: kicking is basically knee-jerking.

Behavioural approaches

The formal psychology known as behaviourism leads to a very similar stance. Starting (in the early part of this century) in a culture which also shared the mind–body view of the person described above, behaviourism strove to be objective and scientific. This it did largely by leaving the notions of mind, spirit and other inner aspects of persons to the speculations of philosophy and religion and, using a rather narrow view of science (see Harré, 1972), it concentrated on what can be observed publicly. Human *action* was reduced to its externally visible features, to observable *behaviour*. Action was treated as observable response (physical movement) to observable stimulus (physical event). The person became the impenetrable 'black box' within which stimulus somehow elicits response. The central aim of this behaviourism was to see what causes tendencies to behave in certain ways, to predict and control what behaviour will be emitted in response to particular circumstances.

Under this conception skill becomes an appropriate *response* that is executed readily and rapidly. Because the emphasis was on observable events, behaviourism tended to focus on relatively specific 'bits' of behaviour, it had a tendency to be 'atomistic' and to see complex behaviour as the addition of many simpler behaviours. The view, as Carl Bereiter (1972) once put it, was that 'the soul builds its mansion by nailing boards together'. Later developments, in particular the work of Robert Gagné (1965), paid more attention to the ways such build-ups might occur. In essence, however, practice and reward were seen as the only factors necessary to convert a response to the status of habitual reaction and therefore, *by definition*, skills tended to be seen as trainable and teachable. In fact, we could describe this sort of behaviourism as a *technology* (an attempt at practical *control* using a minimum of theory) rather than as a *psychology* (an attempt to *understand* the processes involved) which might subsequently inform practical techniques.

In spite of the fact that behaviourism repeatedly (see Tomlinson, 1989, ch.2) strove to go beyond its externalist focus to understand the inner processes governing human action, this simple externalism has been central to the influential work of B. F. Skinner (see Modgil and Modgil, 1987), which in turn has had a major effect on educational applications such as direct instruction, precision teaching and teaching by objectives (see for instance Fontana, 1984).

I will return later to an appraisal of these movements in the light of the cognitive psychology of skill. For the moment, however, I should point out what I regard as some of the positive, healthy features of these behaviourist-inspired approaches. (1) Emphasis on the learning and trainability of behaviour has provided a healthy counter to the sometimes fatalistic assumptions of common sense, particularly in the area of interest, special education. Thus, for instance, 'backwardness' becomes 'learning difficulty'. (2) Focus on particular behaviours highlights the vagueness of traditional norm-referenced assessment (e.g. IQ tests) in the diagnosis of such learning difficulties. Attention switches instead to precise analysis of performance on specific, relevant tasks. (3) The stress on concrete, observable behaviour has yielded specific procedures that are relatively easy for teachers to grasp and apply. One would not wish to lose these sorts of advantage and in so far as they're based on a somewhat inadequate conception of skill, then we might be able to build further on them by getting a better understanding of it – though we may also need to modify these behavioural emphases in more or less important respects. This brings us, then, to the modern psychology of skill.

Cognitive Psychology of Skill

Whereas behaviourist ideas were rooted historically in motivational studies of animal behaviour, the ideas I'm about to present originated in the detailed study of human performance, particularly involving military tasks such as flying, using radar, and so on (see Tomlinson, 1989; Gellatly 1986). These ideas are now seen to apply to a very broad range of activities including social interaction and thinking, as well as the more obviously physical and sports activities often associated with the word 'skill'. In fact, it's hard to think of human competences that *don't* exhibit the characteristics of skill.

So what are these characteristics? When we look closely at skill, as experimental psychologists have done, we find that it has a range of typical features: the concept of skill is relatively complex. In what follows I want first to consider the general characteristics of skill and then to look at the way skills studies have led us to think about human persons and their capacities. I'll then go on to look at what seems to be involved in the acquisition of skill, so as to examine the specific functions teaching may fulfil, with consideration of 'special' needs. On the way, there will be some comparison with the behavioural approaches to skill and teaching mentioned above.

The nature of skill

The range of characteristics skills exhibit may be presented under three headings. Skills are: (1) puposeful and systematic; (2) complex in an organized, co-ordinated way; (3) acquired by learning. As you read the following points, think of one or more examples of what you count as a typical skill and see how the range of features are embodied in your particular examples.

(1) Skills are purposeful and systematic Skill may be thought of as an actual performance or as a capacity to perform, but the activity in question will have a *purpose* or 'point'. It's systematically geared towards achieving a desired state of affairs. This is sometimes expressed by saying that skilled action is 'goal-oriented', but we must remember that skills vary in the type of goal involved. Sometimes it's relatively *discrete* (e.g. hitting the target in archery), sometimes it's *continuous* (e.g. keeping the car on the correct side of the road, while avoiding obstacles, going at a suitable speed, and much else, in driving). Skilled action is interactive with the context, the action is adapted so as to bring about the goal, and this adaptiveness involves both *anticipation* and *reaction*. Thus, skilled action must somehow be guided by some sort of *internal plan* or programme, since the skilled performer has to know how to anticipate and react in ways appropriate to achieving the purpose: he or she must know 'what to do next'. Note, however, that knowing how to interact in the context is *not necessarily or even typically conscious* and explicit knowledge. As Ryle (1949) put it, we may 'know how' without 'knowing that', that is, without consciously knowing or being able to say what the constituents of our action are (see Griffiths, 1987).

Therefore modern skills psychology is a cognitive psychology, in the following sense. There must be some sort of internal plan of means and ends within the skilled performer, which gives rise to his or her reliable capacity to achieve the relevant goals in the relevant contexts. This plan must include information about, representations of, the outside context, of 'what to look out for' so as to do useful actions at appropriate points (like putting my arm in the second sleeve of the jumper). In order to understand skilled action we need to develop and test ideas about this internal information processing that regulates our skilled interaction with the outside context. Since 'cognition' is the term generally used in psychology to refer to internal representations and processes involving such information, then an understanding of skill will include insights into these processes: it will be a cognitive psychology of skilled interaction.

When, as psychologists did, we start on this path by investigating in detail the activities at which people have reliable competence (skill) we find that these activities vary greatly. They vary in the complexity of their goals and of what needs to be taken into account and reacted to in order to achieve these goals (compare hoopla with, say, tennis). They vary in the predictability of the factors involved (compare the behaviour of snooker balls with that of tennis balls). They vary in the subtlety and clarity of these factors (compare fast bowling with spin bowling as regards how to cope with it). Skills dealing with relatively complex, unpredictable contexts are sometimes referred to as *open skills* in comparison to more *closed skills* dealing with simpler, better defined, regular demands.

Skills also vary as regards the concreteness or abstractness of their constituent goals and activity. Thus people have competences in physical activities such as sports, but also in intellectual ones like arithmetic, chess and reasoning, in social one like persuasion and teaching. So all skills have cognitive processes involved in their regulation, but some skills are more cognitive than others. They nevertheless share the quality of purposefulness, including adaptive anticipation and reaction, as well as the following two sets of features.

(2) Skills are complex co-ordinations of awareness and action Really skilful performances look and feel simple, the person has 'got it all together' in a seamless sort of way. But when the novice tries to do it, it becomes apparent that a lot is going on. At the very least, there's a co-ordination of intention, awareness and action, as we've just seen. To return to an earlier example: kicking isn't just any movement of the leg, it's a leg movement designed to impact on, say, a football with a certain force; therefore the leg movement must be co-ordinated with awareness of the position of the ball. More than this, skills typically turn out on close inspection to involve the co-ordination of a number of subskills going on at the same time. This involves at least two things.

First, there is a co-ordination of awareness and action at these more specific levels (e.g. I have to find the gear lever and move it). Second, these subskills have to be co-ordinated and meshed with each other in an organized way (I have to move the gear lever between depressing and releasing the clutch pedal). The organization of subskills tends to be hierarchical. That is, any skill involves various co-ordinated subskills, subskills tend in turn to involve further co-ordination of subskills (driving involves gear changing, which involves clutch control, which involves locating the clutch). The more regular processes and subskills tend to become intuitive, done without consious attention.

(3) Skills are acquired through learning The 'ready-made' look of the really skilled performance perhaps tempts us to think that such actions are just 'inborn' and waiting to emerge. People do seem to vary in their aptitudes for some constituents of skills and in their capacity to acquire particular skills. However, there are very few co-ordinated actions that are 'hard-wired' into the nervous system so that they occur fully programmed (sneezing would be one example). In human life we have to deal with great ranges of particular contexts and purposes – all of which could hardly be built in to each individual in advance of knowing which contexts they will encounter! What we do seem to come equipped with is a set of basic powers involving senses and behaviour, and the capacity to co-ordinate

these into actions. These co-ordinations can become skilful. That is, from having to do things 'one at a time', in a conscious and often painstaking way, we become able to do a number of things at once, to do so intuitively, without the conscious thought or effort that characterized our initial attempts. Such improvement is gradual in some respects, but can be sudden in others, as when subskills each become efficient enough to be put together. What produces such aquisition is another issue, to which we will return shortly. In order to consider that and the nature of skill teaching more effectively, it's worth looking first at what experimental research tells us about the nature of persons as learners and performers of skill.

Cognitive psychology's view of the learner

Research on human cognitive processes is very much an on-going enterprise; however, enough major features of our information processing have received broad experimental confirmation (see for instance Eysenck, 1984; Sanford, 1985) for them to function as major assumptions in any educational application. The following is a rather drastic summary of these features, organized under five headings: complexity, limitation, active selectivity, learning capacity and idiosyncracy. These abstract labels indicate some familiar but important human features.

(1) Complexity In contrast to the traditional view of the mind as a transparently simple container of ideas and feelings, it is clear from experimental cognitive research that human 'intellectual equipment' has many parts and aspects, though they are highly interconnected. Thus, for instance, one sort of brain damage may lead to *aphasia* (loss of ability to name objects) yet not to *agnosia* (loss of ability to recognize a named object) with respect to the same everyday thing, such as a cup (see for instance, Blakemore, 1976), while other forms of damage may do the opposite. This sort of finding indicates that our everyday cognitive processes are skilful integrations of very many constituent subprocesses. A further example is that cognitive research indicates humans have at least three different types of *memory* function: sensory after-image storage, short-term storage over a period of seconds, and long-term memory over minutes, hours and years. It also confirms that we have three *levels of awareness*: the familiar sharp form of focal or conscious attention, the more vague type of pre-attentive or peripheral awareness 'out of the corner of the eye', and fully subconscious or unconscious awareness, that is, where we're not aware *that* we are aware of something (see Dixon, 1984). These examples only begin to scratch the surface, but at the very least they caution against any assumption that we as teachers can easily see what is going on at any point in a teaching interaction, especially within the learner.

(2) Capacity limitations Some of our capacities to deal with information are very limited indeed. When attending in a conscious, focal way, for instance, we're

limited to dealing with one new item at a time, and then only at a certain speed (it takes about a third of a second before we can in any way react to a next item). Likewise, our short-term memory or capacity to 'hold in mind' is limited in adults to about seven or so independent items, and some of these are probably held as the most recent entries to our apparently limitless long-term memory store. There is longstanding evidence (cf. Tomlinson, 1971; Welford, 1968) that short-term retention is enhanced by familiarity of items and use of mnemonic strategies such as grouping and rehearsal. So we have a further illustration of the centrality of the skill notion for human understanding: short-term memory may have seemed like a core piece of the 'hardware' utilized in skilful action, but it turns out itself to depend on learning. In children (see Kail, 1984) this short-term grasp is still more limited, and the evidence is that this has very much to do with their lack of familiarity and mnemonic skill development. By the same token, however, the length of time it takes children to get to typically adult performance levels (i.e. childhood and adolescence) also gives some idea of the speed of skill acquisition, and the magnitude of the task facing those who would remedy the deficits typically found in the educationally subnormal (see, for instance, David Sugden's chapter on generalization).

The special needs of those with cognitive learning difficulties are very likely to include heavy limitations in cognitive grasp, which will obviously have implications for their ability to understand explanation and demonstration, as well as affecting the complexity of their thinking. At the crudest level, the implication for the teacher is a need to switch into whatever skills the learner does bring, which includes dealing with material with which the learner is relatively familiar.

(3) Selective (inter)Action I must apologize for the jargon-like nature of this expression, but it refers economically to a feature that is central to the cognitive picture of human processing, in strong contrast to equally central assumptions of common sense and behaviourism. Namely, human cognition, including its more basic aspects such as perception and understanding, is not just a matter of passively receiving and reacting to impressions of data from the outside world. Because human awareness is limited, it must also be selective. We can't take it all in at once, certainly not consciously, we can only deal with some of it. And even what we make of that is partly due to what we bring to the situation. Such extreme possibilities as visual illusions exemplify what cognitive experimentation has shown to occur less noticeably all the time, namely that our past experience, expectations and values play a deeply implicit role even in our awareness of 'objective' reality. We go round 'making sense' of what we encounter by trying our existing ideas and resources on it; we try, as one writer recently put it, to 'headfit' reality, to interpret it in our terms. Piaget (cf Piaget, 1970) made this sort of 'assimilation' a basic axiom of his appoach; experimental cognitive

research (e.g. Eysenck, 1984; Sanford, 1985) provides evidence for it. Thus our awareness is not only 'data driven' by external reality, but also 'concept driven' by our existing knowledge and experience. Likewise, in attempting new tasks, we may have existing skill or subskills that can help in the new situation. We 'latch on' to the familiar bits, both implicitly and consciously.

This can be summarized by saying that our encounters with and actions on reality are interactions in which we are actively selective and interpretive, though it occurs largely unconsciously. This has the important implication for teaching that imposition of meaning or approach from outside the learner tends to be a rather difficult thing to achieve: one may place a person before something, but what they make of it depends at least and in the first instance on them and their resources. The emphasis therefore needs to shift from the passive reception assumptions of common sense and behaviourism at least to a more interactive conception, in which the learner's existing resources are diagnosed so that one can enlist their competences and tendencies. More of this later.

(4) Learning capacity In spite of these limitations and selectivity, most humans are nevertheless able to deal efficiently, smoothly and easily with large numbers of things at a time – when they've become skilful. In skill acquisition constituent processes become more economical, integrated and automatized. This process appears to continue, even in the case of relatively simple skills and subskills, over a very large amount of practice. Once accuracy of co-ordination has been achieved, then further practice tunes, economizes and speeds up the action. Because behaviourist approaches only considered accuracy of response, they tended to refer to this further consolidation under the rather ambivalent label of 'overlearning'. Yet this consolidation is of great importance in that further economization of subskills through practice tends to be required for them to be capable of amalgamation by our still limited capacities.

However, in skill acquisition we make these gains at certain costs. The gains include overcoming the capacity limitations of conscious attention and short-term memory, and exceeding the slow speed of one-at-time ('serial') focal attending. The costs (apart from the price of practice) are loss of conscious awareness as the subprocesses become intuitive, entering the less accessible levels of pre-attentive and subconscious awareness. Hence one of the ancient dilemmas of teaching: the expert has almost by definition become unaware of their own processes, so it's difficult to convey them to the learner. Of course, one of the other features of skill is that it is to some extent 'cognitively penetrable': we can raise subprocesses to conscious awareness (e.g. I can focus on exactly how I hold the handle as I open the door this time). But (a) such awareness requires this extra effort and (b) it's typically a matter of reconstructing what we normally do: we 'watch ourselves' do it. If we try to do each bit consciously, the danger is that we then 'de-skill' ourselves and do it inefficiently, if at all, like the novice who can only attempt it in such a deliberate manner.

(5) Idiosyncracy and individual variation All of this implies that learners will show considerable variation and idiosyncracy in what they bring to the learning situation. They may vary in 'basic abilities', and there may be very many of these relevant to the learning in question. Learners may vary considerably in the experience and existing skills they bring. Not only may they understand or be able to do different things, they may do the same things in different ways, for the purposeful nature of skill means that different strategies, different forms of action may achieve the same goal. This is easily masked by the automatized and intuitive status skilful activity achieves, and this insight itself implies that teachers require to diagnose what learners bring by way of knowledge, understanding, subskill and strategy that is of any potential relevance to the competences about to be taught. It further argues that teacher-based prescriptions concerning the path of skill acquisition must always, at the very least, be tried out for their effectiveness with particular learners, with whose existing resources they may match to varying degrees. Thus this and other aspects of cognitive skill psychology support the implication of the interactive analysis of teaching presented at the outset of this chapter, that effective teaching requires attention to be paid to the matching of teaching/learning strategy to learner and task characteristics.

Before leaving this brief treatment of modern cognitive psychology, it's perhaps worth pointing out that although dealing with action and skill (and not just with inner, conscious thinking), this approach is concerned primarily with understanding the 'how' of action. Behaviourist approaches tend to have concentrated on the 'why', the motivation and payoff aspects. To some extent the two approaches may therefore be 'talking past each other about different aspects' when it comes to teaching applications. Unfortunately, however, it doesn't appear to be a matter of simply combining the two, since the understanding of skilful action processes eschewed by the behavioural approach tends to alter the ways the motivation and regulation of such action might be seen – even though we might allow that the less complex the cognitive processing (which does tend to be one characteristic of some members of the special educational clientèle), the more relevant the simple assumptions of a behavioural approach may be. However, saying this is really bending over backwards to be open-minded towards that approach, since the more effective stance appears to me to require taking on the more sophisticated conception of persons and their action offered by cognitive psychology, so as then to raise issues of motivation in its terms (see Tomlinson, 1989, chs. 5 and 8 for developments of this line).

Learning and Teaching Skills

What does it take to acquire a skill? As mentioned earlier, common sense and behaviourism share a simple answer: practice – 'Practice makes perfect', as the proverb has it. The teaching implication is that we set up the activity and get the learner to practise it, rewarding efforts in so far as they approximate to the desired action, because this is held to 'reinforce' the connections and make that behaviour more likely in the same circumstances. This is all quite consistent with a view of skill as 'brute', habitual behaviour. But a closer look at skill has shown that it's more complicated than this, and experimental study of skill acquisition reveals that it, too, involves more than simply practice. In this section, therefore, I want to look first at what has shown to be required for the acquisition of skill and then at the specific roles and influences attempts to facilitate skill acquisition (i.e. teach) can have.

Learning skills

What skill acquisition does involve can be summarized in the flow-diagram form of Figure 2.2, which connects with the characteristics of skill performance outlined earlier. The diagram requires some explanatory comment:

(1) Plan The first requirement is for the learner to have some idea of what they're trying to do, i.e. of the end and the means, of what and how. This is perhaps the most basic expression of the anticipatory nature of skilled action. Even in the everyday notion of 'trial and error', the trial isn't just any random action, so there has to be some plan or programme within the learner which guides it. To be successful, the plan has both to be adequate to direct all the anticipations and reactions involved in the activity, and to be deployable by the learner. It mustn't, for example, be beyond their capacity to hold in mind. On the other hand, if there are already relevant subskills within their existing repertoire, then these familiar 'chunks' may be stored more economically. A learner may acquire a plan by a variety of means: from direct observation, particularly when repeated, as a product of their own imaginative thinking about

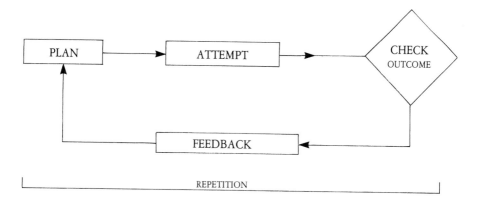

Figure 2.2 Skill acquisition essentials

strategy, as the recipient of instruction in verbal or whatever other form. It would appear that some modalities of awareness, such as vision, enable us to process more at once than others, because we can process many aspects in parallel ('a picture is worth a thousand words'), whereas verbal descriptions, in addition to being 'second-hand', present information in a much more serial way, and can therefore load memory storage heavily. On the other hand, visual presentation alone requires the learner to pick out the relevant action, as well as inferring the goal. In this way imitation can lead to some strange 'acquisitions', particularly by child novices, who bring that much less experience to help them interpret matters!

(2) Attempt The next requirement is that the learner make an active attempt to execute their plan of action and realize the goal.

(3) Check outcome The result of the attempt next needs to be checked against the intended outcome state of affairs. To the extent that they don't correspond and the attempt falls short of success, specific information about the difference between actual and intended outcomes needs to be picked up.

(4) Feedback This specific information needs to be fed back as a basis for modifying the plan for the next attempt where necessary. Simply knowing that one has failed to achieve the goal is not in itself useful information. What is required is information specific enough to enable some sort of translation from awareness to action, as for instance, when the archer misses to the left and therefore needs to aim further to the right. 'Further to the right' means 'further than last time', of course, and this signals the general need for feedback information not only to be specific, but also to be relatable to the original plan. This typically means that the information must come soon after the previous attempt, and that the next attempt be soon enough to retain the memory of the now adjusted plan.

(5) Repetition All of this needs to be repeated. It's not as if one could simply practise actions and nothing else; in doing so one would in any case be practising the processes that guide and regulate the action. Also, as has often been pointed out in the skills literature (e.g. Bartlett, 1958), even with simple physical skills, we never repeat completely the same action twice. Nevertheless, skill acquisition does require repeated plan-governed attempts and the use of feedback information to progressively modify the plans and action. It requires what we might therefore call 'meaningful' or 'reflective' practice. As mentioned above, while the effects of practice may be great, it can also be that massive amounts are required for the gradual acquisition of proficiency. The kind of expertise one associates with, for instance, international sports stars, concert pianists, chess grandmasters, all share

a dependence on massive amounts of feedback-influenced practice. The same is true of the sorts of skills we take for granted most of the time, but which may be lacking in varying degrees in some learners, such as the capacity to understand and produce communication in a natural language such as English. So while wishing to get rid of the externalist focus of traditional teacher-centred teaching, we do not want to overlook the need for learners to economize and consolidate their competences through suitably meaningful practice.

With the repeated operation of the cycle shown in Figure 2.2 learners can pass from a stage where they had hardly any idea of how to go about achieving a given outcome, to a point where they're so skilled at doing so they forget that they ever learned it, let alone how they did or how it felt! It does seem possible that at least some of us unconsciously pick up plans and strategies of considerable complexity from those around us, when we are exposed to such skills (e.g. language and other forms of social communication). However, when we look at the actual acquisition processes in these cases, we find a certain degree of gradualness, with some aspects of these skills being picked up before others, and not necessarily the most detailed first, as the behaviourist 'bottom-up' approach tends to assume. Young babies, for instance, typically learn 'turn-taking' at a very early stage in their interaction with their caregivers. We also find the more specifically human capacities of representational thought and reflection being used in the building of plans and strategies for action. Creativity is perhaps an inherent aspect of skill development, because negative feedback may be so heavy as to require radical alteration or reinvention of plans for headway to be made.

This bring us to an important point which needs to be made explicit, namely that the above represents an outline of what seems to be involved in the acquisition of skill, when skill acquisition does occur. There is no guarantee that it will: the range of factors seen to be involved in the learning of skill is such that we cannot simply *assume* that skill can necessarily be taught. There is a notable contrast between this view and the simple response-repetition view of behaviourism and some common sense, in which skill is taken by definition to include trainability. Nevertheless, as teachers, skill acquisition is what we're in business to achieve. Although a broad understanding of skill learning may not guarantee infallible means of teaching it in any particular case, it ought to suggest ways to go about trying.

Before taking a look at these possibilities, a couple of further comparisons of the cognitive with the common-sense behaviourist views of skill and its acquisition are worthy of mention at this point. The cognitive approach reveals the need for *feedback*: awareness of useful, specific information as a basis for self-correction. The behaviourist approach stresses the role of *reinforcement*: a positive event or payoff that functions to increase the likelihood of the same response occurring in the context in the future. Feedback is primarily a matter of information, reinforcement a matter of motivation. The two are distinct, but overlap, particularly in the teaching context. In the first place, it is necessary to get the learner to make active attempts at the activity in question. So positive pay-offs may be useful, particularly the rewarding of successive approximations known as shaping, when the learner has difficulty understanding or keeping in mind the longer term payoff of skill acquisition. A second function is that nervous system arousal appears to consolidate memory traces, and significant events such as rewards tend to have an arousal effect. Nevertheless, if the actual action is to become skilled, internal action plans must be built and developed through the use, one way or another, of specific information which can inform the next efforts.

Teaching skill

Behaviourist approaches to skill development have been disseminated mainly through special educational teaching applications such as the types known as direct instruction, precision teaching, and teaching by objectives (see chapters in Fontana, 1984). Here the emphasis is very much the Skinnerian one of viewing the intended learning outcome as a behaviour to be performed under certain conditions – as opposed to a competence whose possession is to be assessed by way of such precise actions. The emphasis is on analysing the goal behaviour into constituent sub-behaviours (carrying out a *task analysis*) so as then to design a hierarchical sequence of teaching/learning objectives. That is, a sequence starting within the learner's competence and getting progressively more difficult by a series of steps until the step embodying the desired final learning outcome is achieved. This appears very logical, but it must be pointed out that the central issues in skill teaching are *psychological*. That is: how to optimize the learner's acquisition of skilled processing.

In so far as the teacher wishes or needs to plan the sequence of topics and tasks in the curriculum, then what is at stake is the difficulty order (a) as experienced by particular learners who may vary in this respect and (b) as influenced by the adoption of particular teaching strategies. There appears to be an interesting inconsistency in some versions of the behavioural approach (e.g. Ainscow and Tweddle, 1979) between the emphasis on following a hierarchical sequence of objectives on the one hand, and the recognition of a variety of possible sequences on the other. Admittedly these authors do acknowledge the need for more studies of actual learning sequences and levels of difficulty, and they are consistent with this view when they recommend flexibility in seeing how learners actually respond to what may have seemed a plausible sequence (in theory, or rather, on the basis of examining the purely external aspects of the 'goal behaviour', since this approach doesn't go for internal process theory). Though this stance appears to imply some recognition of the importance of cognitive process, an explicitly cognitive approach would perhaps come to a similar position, but from a different direction. Namely, plan your learning/teaching sequence on the basis of empirical evidence and theoretical understanding of the complexity and difficulty of tasks within a domain. In the absence of this, estimate likely sequences on the basis both of observable aspects and anything you know about cognitive processes likely to be involved. In any case, see what the learner brings to the task and makes of it, and attempt to build on that.

But, of course, teaching is more than selecting sequences of tasks, it's also, and if anything more centrally, the attempt to facilitate acquisition of competence at these tasks. Given what has been seen so far about the nature of skill and its acquisition, as well as the nature of human cognitive processes, certain teaching functions suggest themselves. Figure 2.3 summarizes things by adding these functions to the skill acquistion summary of Figure 2.2.

Before commenting on the various functions relating to the different phases of the skill acquisition cycle, a few general remarks must be made. First, these functions can generally be achieved in a variety of styles *varying in the extent to which they are structured by the teacher or elicited from the learner.* The earlier point about the active nature of human cognition cautions against too much imposition and control by the teacher, but argues for the encouragement of involvement of the learner. It is strengthened by recent confirmation of the relative effectiveness of parental tutors adopting a stance 'contingent' on their child's activity rather than a more regulatory approach (cf. Wood, 1988).

Second, as mentioned earlier, motivational as well as purely informational and competence issues are at stake, at least to the extent that one wishes to gain

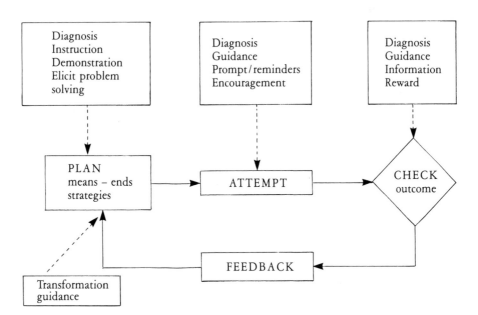

Figure 2.3 Teaching inputs in skill development

the active involvement which seems crucial to skill development. Therefore both informational and motivational functions are mentioned in relation to various phases of the skill learning outline in Figure 2.3. Let us turn to these.

(1) *Plan formation* At this stage the teacher needs to diagnose where the pupil stands in competence terms. This can be attempted directly, by seeing how the learner fares when presented with the overall skill task, but the teacher will usefully draw on general awareness of the learner's repertoire as noted in a variety of contexts. When attempts at the activity in question are used, then it's a matter of getting access by whatever way possible to the exisiting competence. This clearly involves observation, but ought also to include the learner's own reports about what he or she finds easy or difficult, how they are trying to go about the problem (e.g. via their attempts to teach someone else as well as their own ac- counts of their stategy). A decision may then be required as to whether to break things down and proceed to a subskill or to focus on getting some broader aspect across, perhaps by focusing on a different but more familiar activity, which share this aspect. This does raise the issue of transfer and its facilitation (see David Sugden's chapter on generalization).

Whatever the task or subskill, it's worth commenting that making sure the goal of the activity in question is clear to the learner enables him or her to bring to bear whatever resources they judge relevant. Beyond this, there is the question of didactic instruction or demonstration, as opposed to stimulating the learner to develop their own means, with the concomitant trade-off between short-term gains and longer-term demotivation. Relevant here is the Vygotsky notion of the *zone of proximal development*, within which the learner can achieve something assisted but not unassisted (see the chapter by Gallimore). Children with special needs perhaps present an especial temptation for the teacher to dominate and structure heavily.

Nevertheless, recent work (cf Wood, 1988) suggests that the best results are gained when the teacher makes his or her activity contingent, as far as possible, on the learner's attempts, rather than directing them through very specific sub- aspects. This does seem at base to involve a question of motivation, but it also serves to indicate that taking account of the active nature of human psychological functioning may be of importance in both motivational and cognitive aspects of skill teaching – not that they can ever be entirely separated anyway! Thus instruction under the guise of copying games, and the provision of surprise once a subroutine has become established, and the learner gives evidence of knowing what to expect next, may be suitable compromises which preserve aspects of the learner's felt independence.

(2) *Active attempt* At this following stage there is, as always, again the require- ment to keep tabs on how things are going. The more positive teaching function

here is to guide in various ways, from explicit verbal prompting and reminding, to covert removal of distractions, implicit orienting of attention towards appropriate features of the situation. At this point there is the possibility of promoting self-regulation by the learner, of getting him or her to engage in reflection on the course of the on-going process and in 'thinking in action'. This 'metacognitive' aspect may have considerable importance both as an automatized internal guidance means necessary in the case of certain types of learning difficulties (cf. Brown and Campione, 1981) and in order to promote the likelihood of transfer of the skill to new applications (again, see the later chapter by David Sugden). The aspect of encouragement is perhaps of particular importance during the attempt phase, which may involve apprehension at first and boredom in later stages, where consolidating practice is called for.

(3) *Knowledge of results* This and *feedback* gathering can, again, involve direct provision of relevant and specific feedback by the teacher or indirect prompting for the learner to gather such feedback for himself. Basic points here are that one does not simply assume that the learner can or will check results efficiently and that the feedback must be specific and relatable to the next attempt. This is also the point where reinforcement or reward is applied in a behaviourist approach. Given the tendency of the cognitive approach to ignore the payoff aspects of action, this certainly seems the juncture at which it can do with supplementing by an approach which doesn't. However, in addition to the earlier remarks on independence, something should be said about the intermingling of feedback and reinforcement functions.

For example, a reward following an attempt is, other things equal, likely to function as positive or confirmatory feedback. That is, it confirms the particular scheme or plan that generated the action. The teacher therefore needs to have some idea regarding that plan. Minimally, for instance, he doesn't want to reinforce a mistaken plan which happened to produce a positive outcome merely 'by fluke'. That is, the cognitive stance orients the teacher to a *diagnosis* of the learner's action plan, while the behaviourist approach looks at the similarity of the externally observable behaviour to that desired.

That observable behaviour is obviously of central importance in such a diagnosis, but it may not be the only basis. Put another way, we're interested in learners who can produce certain products; that is precisely why we attend to the correctness of the processes that generate such products, and not just at the products themselves. Thus the teacher is going to provide positive feedback (probably functioning also as reward) for guided attempts which were going in the right direction, even if they fell somewhat short of producing the desired outcome. The behavioural approach of *shaping*, that is the selective reinforcement of successive approximations to the desired performance, may instance the usual behaviourist confusion between reward and informational feedback, but in practice it tends to involve both. The cognitive approach may be clearer in distinguishing the nature of useful informational feedback, but needs to pay more attention to the payoff features on which behaviourism has concentrated.

(4) Feedback transformation This may need to be assisted, that is, help given to convert the information on what happened last time into what to try differently this time: knowing one has missed to the left doesn't always lead a learner, especially one with cognitive deficits, spontaneously to aim further to the right next time. Just as the teacher can provide feedback directly or attempt to get the learner to gain their own feedback, so also the teacher can vary the directness with which he influences the translation of feedback into action adjustment. The more indirect, the more the learner is being called upon to do and hopefully the more is being picked by way of learning how to learn. But to the extent that the learner's cognitive resources are limited, this kind of ambitiousness may be out of place. One may feel the need to narrow the scope to the particular competence in question, and within this, to the provision of as much support as compatible with the learner still having a plan to apply.

At this end of the possible range of approaches, then, we might have the feedback and translation being provided by the teacher (e.g. 'You missed to the right, so aim a bit to the left this time'), or where even that might confuse the cognitive resources of the learner, or where one wished to promote early success for motivational reasons, the teacher might go straight to the translation ('Try aiming more to the left'). Not only does this sort of approach narrow down what the learner is picking up, it will only work to the extent that the skill in question involves a simple, discrete type of action, rather than on-going feedback and adjustment.

Looking back over this chapter, then, it's unlikely that its ideas will be perceived as the sort of brand-new, simple, magical solution I accused closed-minded educators of seeking. Its view of skill and the human processes involved in them does, I think, nevertheless make contact with everyday insights and experience we all have of our own and others' action. Modern cognitive ideas give a framework within which to see a variety of such aspects, and further research is pinning things down in detail in particular areas, from language to social skills. The behavioural school's approach is not totally different in all respects, though I hope to have brought out the major differences of emphasis. Namely, the behavioural approach (or at least it Skinnerian version) attempts to maintain an external stance towards human action and learning, and tends to focus on motivation and external control of behaviour.

Modern cognitive psychology has by contrast attempted to understand the nature of action. This must include attempts to model and test theories about the inner processes that govern action and learning processes; thus modern cognitive psychology has very much favoured the experimental style of research (in fact, it has recently been accused of being too experimental and laboratory-based). This point bears some emphasizing, since there are some Skinnerian converts in education who seem to think that their approach is the only systematic and experimentally grounded one available.

While cognitive analyses and research have hitherto been somewhat short on the motivational side of human activity, their findings suggest that behaviorist conceptions of action systematically underestimate the nature of action and lead to a degenerate notion of skill as habitual response. Such a conception can only illuminate relatively closed skills. Nevertheless, the focus of its educational adherents on what can be done, whether by learners or by teachers to assist that learning systematically, is a positive and healthy development that is to be welcomed and built upon in the application of cognitive insights. This chapter has aimed to introduce these insights in a relatively general way, as a background to the further detail in other chapters of the book.

References

Ainscow, M. and Tweddle, D. (1979), *Preventing Classroom Failure* (Chichester: Wiley).

Bartlett, F.C. (1958), *Thinking: An Experimental and Social Study* (London: Allen & Unwin).

Bereiter, C. (1972), The soul builds it mansion by nailing boards together, *Interchange*, 2.

Blakemore, C. (1976), *Mechanics of the Mind* (Cambridge: Cambridge University Press).

Brown, A. and Campione, J. (1981), Inducing flexible thinking: The problem of access, in Friedman, M.P., Das, J.P. and O'Connor, N. (eds), *Intelligence and Learning* (New York: Plenum Press).

Claxton, G. (1985), The psychology of teaching educational psychology, in Francis, H. (ed.), *Learning to Teach: Psychology in Teacher Training* (Lewes: Falmer Press).

Dixon, N.F. (1984), *Subconcious Processing* (Chichester: Wiley).

Eysenck, M.W. (1984), *A Handbook of Cognitive Psychology* (London: Lawrence Erlbaum Associates).

Fontana, D. (ed.) (1984), *Behaviourism and Learning Theory in Education*, Edinburgh, Scottish Academic Press.

Gagne, R.M. (1965), *The Conditions of Learning* (New York: Holt, Rinehart & Winston).

Gellatly, A. (ed.) (1986), *The Skilful Mind: An Introduction to Cognitive Psychology* (Milton Keynes: Open University Press).

Griffiths, M. (1987), The teaching of skills and the skills of teaching, *Journal of Philosophy of Education*, 21, 203–14.

Harre, R. (1972), *The Philosophies of Science: An Introductory Survey* (London: Oxford University Press).

Kail, R.V. (1984), *The Development of Memory in Children*, 2nd edn (San Francisco: Freeman).

Modgil, S. and Modgil, C. (eds) (1987), *B.F. Skinner: Consensus and Controversy* (Lewes: Falmer Press).

Piaget, J. (1970), Piaget's Theory, in Mussen, P. (ed.), *Carmichael's Manual of Child Psychology*, 3rd edn, Vol.1 (New York: Wiley).

Ryle, G. (1949), *The Concept of Mind*, (London: Hutchinson).

Sanford, A. (1985), *Cognition and Cognitive Psychology* (London: Weidenfeld & Nicholson).

Schon, D. A. (1983), *The Reflective Practitioner* (New York: Basic Books).

Tomlinson, P. D. (1971), *An Investigation into the Development of Short-term Retention Capacity in Children as a Function of Age and Item Familiarity*, unpublished doctoral dissertation, OISE (University of Toronto).

Tomlinson, P. D. (1989, in preparation), *Understanding Teaching: Interactive Educational Psychology*, 2nd edn (London: Falmer Press; 1st edn, London: McGraw-Hill, 1981).

Welford, A. T. (1968), *Fundamentals of Skill* (London: Methuen).

Wood, D. (1988), *How Children Develop and Learn* (Oxford: Blackwell).

Chapter 3

The Social Context of Cognitive Functioning in the Lives of Mildly Handicapped Persons[1]

Ronald Gallimore, Roland Tharp and Robert Rueda

Introduction

Puzzling inconsistencies are revealed by studies of mildly handicapped individuals.[2] While apparently unable to perform a given task on one occasion, on another they perform it with reasonable competence. For example, learning disabled and mentally retarded adolescents, who cannot solve problems in an experimental setting, regularly use complex cognitive strategies in everyday life (Edgerton, 1967; Friedman *et al.* 1977; Rueda and Mehan, 1986).

Variations in performance as a function of context

What is there about settings that can produce differential levels of performance? Ethnographic and experimental studies of the past two decades have converged on a conclusion of significance to educators: *The performance of mildly handicapped individuals often improves when they can perform in collaboration with more competent and assisting others.*

Edgerton's (1967) classic studies of adults released from a government hospital for the retarded suggested that a crucial factor in adaptive success was collaboration with 'benefactors'. Benefactors were individuals who assisted the retarded person to solve problems required of an individual living independently, such as securing medical assistance, housing, dealing with government agencies, and resolving social conflicts. Through such collaboration, retarded individuals could perform at a much higher level and were able to survive outside the hospital.

Langness (1987) has recently completed a follow-up of one of Edgerton's original cohort members. This individual, now in his sixties, has lived in the 'skid row' area of a major US city since he left a state institution over 25 years ago. Langness's work reveals a man who has survived, and even prospered – when judged in his own terms of reference. At least one reason for this success is the network of reciprocity arrangements he has worked out, in which his limitations are compensated by collaborating with others when the occasion requires.

In a sheltered workshop for the retarded, Turner (1983) observed what can be called the 'social construction of competent performance'. Examples include: a wheelchair-bound, mildly retarded individual who was assisted by a severely retarded individual who in turn enjoyed the more interesting life that surrounded the former; small groups spontaneously formed and acted as 'sounding boards' for emotional distress and fears of individuals; individuals who were able, through collaboration, to interpret frightening dreams about dead relatives in ways that reduce anxiety and promote adaptive responses; more able workers in the workshop who assisted less able to perform tasks at a level much higher than the latter can normally manage.

Turner (1980) described a man who had lived a retarded identity for more than 20 years. Suspecting the man to be of normal intelligence, Turner arranged for testing and subsequently shared with the man the results, which placed him in the normal range. Using ethnographic and participant observer methods, Turner demonstrated that the individual gradually 'rewrote' his life history to conform to the discovery that he was not retarded. Life history events which were used to illustrate that retarded people have 'human' qualities were reinterpreted as proof that he was never retarded. But before and after his startling discovery, the man's competence level was a function of those with whom he interacted and collaborated. Before the discovery he 'constructed' a level of competence, in interaction with others, that was viewed by himself and the authorities as 'retarded'. After his discovery, he constructed 'normal' competencies with the aid of coworkers and room-mates. With assistance he succeeded in leaving the group home for developmentally disabled, over-turning the court order that made him a ward of the State of California, obtained regular employment, and eventually 'disappeared' into the community.

Assistance by experts, reciprocity, and complementarity can combine to normalize a marriage between mildly handicapped individuals. Kaufman (1988) described how such strategies enhanced the marital partnership of her retarded daughter and 'mildly handicapped' son-in-law. As experts, Kaufman and her husband provided instrumental assistance when the couple requested it; they solved problems and offered advice. Reciprocity was evident in the couple's borrowing of young nephews on weekends; the children's parents gained respite from childcare, while the borrowing couple enjoyed the pleasures of parenting without the continuing responsibilities. Complementarity was found throughout the marriage: the wife's energy and social skills compensated for her husband's lethargy and timidity, and his ability to read made up for her illiteracy.

For adult retarded individuals, such basic activity as interpersonal communication can depend on the assistance of nonretarded interlocutors. Sabsay and Kernan (1983) reported that the narratives of retarded adults contained all the essential elements for clear communication. However, there was often a lack of strategic management so that essential elements were presented in an order or manner which confused interlocutors. But when some interlocutors asked leading questions, or requested additional details, it often assisted a retarded person to construct a coherent narrative. Such sharing of the task components is analogous to experimental studies of memory strategies, in which experimenters assist research subjects to use mnemonic devices in timely fashion.

Finally, Rueda and Mehan (1986) reported that classroom observations of a learning disabled adolescent suggested a serious problem in reading. However, this student managed to 'pass' (i.e. conceal his inability to succeed in literacy-related tasks) in many everyday settings at least in part by using the assistance of more capable others to successfully complete tasks.

The previous examples are taken from studies of behaviour in natural contexts. Experimental studies suggest a similar conclusion: on artificial laboratory tasks, assistance by others can often substantially increase performance. For example, one line of research has demonstrated that mentally retarded and learning disabled students can be taught to use cognitive strategies on memory tasks which can improve their performance to the level of untrained college students (Brown, 1974; Torgeson, 1977; Brown and Campione, 1986). Teaching such strategies includes prompts or hints to use the strategy at given points in a task, and explanations of how the strategies work, why they work, and under what conditions they work best. In effect, the experimenter acts as a collaborator assisting the experimental participant to use strategies to improve recall.

Unfortunately, retarded individuals often cease using trained strategies once assistance ends. They require more assistance to transfer strategies to other tasks even when they are only slightly different from the original task on which they were trained. But this difficulty only serves to underscore the importance of collaboration to the performance level they can achieve.

The Concept of Assisted Performance

We can unite these ethnographic and experimental diverse findings in this way: the competence and performance of mildly handicapped individuals can sometimes be enhanced through collaboration with more capable others in the context of meaningful activity. The source of assistance in advancing performance is unimportant: parent, older children, expert, or teacher. The crucial factor appears to be that performance is assisted.

The idea of *assisted performance* was derived by Tharp and Gallimore (in press) from the ideas by Vygotsky (1978). Vygotsky, who died in 1934, grasped the role of assisted performance in cognitive development well before current interest arose (Fischer and Bullock, 1984). Vygotsky argued that psychology has too long ignored a major stage in the process of development and learning, the stage before full individual competence is achieved. This stage is characterized by the need for assistance for performance. As the child or learner advances through that stage, the amount of assistance needed steadily declines. Vygotsky called this stage 'the zone of proximal development'.

The Zone of Proximal Development

This zone of proximal development describes the difference between what a child can do alone, and what he or she can do with the assistance of a more capable other. *Unassisted performance* reflects the child's current level of achievement and development. *Assisted performance*, by contrast, reflects the nearest or next steps of development still to come. The zone defines those functions and skills that have not yet fully emerged, but are in the process of maturation.

A homely example of teaching illustrates this crucial point: a child cannot find her shoes, and notifies the father:

Daughter: I can't find my shoes.
Father: Where did you see them last?
Daughter: I don't know.
Father: Try to remember.
Daughter: I can't.
Father: Did you wear them to school?
Daughter: Yes.
Father: Did you change clothes when you came home?
Daughter: Yes.
Father: Well, where did you leave your clothes?
Daughter: In the bathroom. (Runs and fetches the shoes).

Who is doing the 'remembering' in this example? Both are. The child is not yet able to manage the entire sequence by herself. As her father's questions reveal, she is mature enough to have stored the bits of information needed to solve the problem. She can even recall them from memory when prompted. But she has not yet developed what researchers call the strategic or executive functions needed to organize a successful retrieval of information from memory (Brown, 1974; Brown and Campione, 1986). The father has a recall strategy for organizing retrieval of isolated bits of information in order to narrow the possibilities; the child has the memories. It is only through their joint collaboration that a satisfactory solution is produced.

More important than the successful resolution of the immediate memory problem, however, are the important developmental consequences illuminated by this example. Specifically, this commonplace interaction foreshadows the child's future cognitive activity. It reveals the roots of a powerful cognitive process which is associated with efficient memory recall. When the child is older, the father might have only to say, 'Well, think of where you last saw the shoes', leaving more of the strategic aspects of the task to the child.

Eventually the child will be able to self-regulate all aspects of the retrieval process, and perform it successfully without assistance. At some point, she will 'ask herself' the same questions that the father asked, and she will use, 'in her own head', a strategy for organizing the 'memory task' that is very similar to that observed in collaboration with her father. Assisted performance not only solves the immediate problem but draws the child into the use of more sophisticated cognitive strategies, thus preparing the ground for further cognitive development. What begins as a social process in the zone of proximal development will later be internalised into a psychological process as the competence is fully developed.

Since human activity is so complex, there is no single zone for each individual; for any domain of activity, a zone of proximal development can be created. Furthermore, development within this framework is best conceptualized as continuous, flexible, and most importantly, social in nature, moving initially from 'other-regulation' to eventual 'self-regulation'. Consider a mentally retarded boy who can piece together a detailed rendering of a folk tale, provided an interlocutor asks 'organizing' questions which assist him to recall relevant details and thereby order the recounting in a more coherent fashion. Through collaborative assistance,

> learning awakens a variety of internal developmental processes that are able to operate only when the child is interacting with people in his environment and in cooperation with his peers. Once these processes are internalized, they become part of the child's independent developmental achievement, (Vygotsky, 1978, p.90).

Much of the recent research on assisted performance has occurred in the field of language development, and mostly with pre-school non-handicapped children (see Shorrocks, this volume). Extensions of such work are now being seen in cognitive functioning. In his survey of the small body of available research, Wood (1980) concluded that instructional techniques which do not provide assisted performance markedly slow a child's cognitive development. Such results have caused researchers and theoreticians to reconsider the meaning of assisted performance. Rather than treating it as a bothersome problem in the conduct of research, there is now a trend toward integrating it into theories of cognitive development (Rogoff, 1982; Fischer and Bullock, 1984; Wertsch, 1985).

The distinction emphasized here between the proximal zone and the achieved zone (i.e. between assisted and unassisted performance), as well as the view of development and learning in which it is embedded, have important implications for educational practice (Tharp and Gallimore, in press). In the remainder of this chapter, we will explore the application of these ideas for special education practice. Our focus is first on assessment and then on instructional practices. We will end with broader issues that are raised by the educational application of the concepts discussed.

The Assessment of Student Achievement and Potential

Assessment has been problematic in the field of special education, especially in cases where cultural and linguistic differences exist between tester and testee (Figueroa, in press; Rueda and Mercer, in preparation). In the United States, controversies regarding the validity of existing tests, test bias, overrepresentation of ethnic and linguistic minority students in special education, usefulness of test data for instructional decisions, and other factors have led many to question current testing practices.

Curently, there are two widely used but differing approaches to assessment in special education (Rueda and Mercer, in preparation). On the one hand, standardized *norm-referenced tests* (of intelligence, achievement, and other related abilities such as perceptual-motor functioning) are used to assist in the classification of students in a given special education category. Such psychometric instruments evaluate a child's individual performance by means of comparison to an established norm group.

In a second approach to testing, *curriculum-based assessment*, a child is tested on one or more pre-specified behavioural learning objectives derived from actual classroom work (Tucker, 1985). The primary aim of this type of assessment is to decide what to teach an individual child. In place of normative comparisons, an attempt is made to determine which sequences of objectives a child can do and which have not yet been mastered.

These two views of the assessment process share an important characteristic: both focus on the performance of the child at the individual-developmental or unassisted level. Most often, strict limits are placed on the kinds of assistance the tester may give, and how it 'counts' in arriving at a score. The aim is an objective measure of how much the child can do alone; the examiner–examinee interaction is standardized, controlled, and minimized. Given this goal, to allow unrestricted aid to testees would introduce errors of measurement, make assessment unreliable and norms meaningless.

Providing assistance during a test would undoubtedly contaminate the assessment of the child's individual level of development. But what if the level of independent performance is far below what the child can do with some assistance? What if the child has a very wide zone of proximal development? This would have very clear implications for planning instruction. It would mean a child is ready for more advanced work than would be suggested by a conventional assessment. It makes risky the instructional placement of special education students based entirely on conventional testing.

A clear implication of these studies is that many special education clients – at risk for severe underachievement – will have skills that remain dormant and hidden, unless a zone of proximal development is created by the teacher/examiner. These skills will remain hidden when children are tested, if assessment is solely by the method of unassisted performance. And if hidden in the testing room, then they will also remain dormant in the classroom.

Assessing Competence: The case of Native Hawaiians

To illustrate the points under discussion, we will draw on studies of the academic difficulties of Native Hawaiian students. Like many ethnic and linguistic minority students in United States, Native Hawaiians are at extreme risk for educational underachievement. Many of US minority groups are overrepresented in special education classes, because of poor school performance. Extensive work with Native Hawaiian students suggests the same inconsistency of performance across settings described earlier for other clients of special education. Although as a group, Native Hawaiians are endowed with normal human intelligence and abilities, they display substantial gains in performance when collaboration and assistance are available. As we shall try to show in this chapter, generalization from studies of Native Hawaiians to other populations is warranted on theoretical grounds.

Beginning in 1972, the Kamehameha Early Education Project or KEEP (Tharp and Gallimore, 1979; 1982; in press; Tharp, *et al.*, 1984) operated a kindergarten to third-grade research and development school in urban Honolulu. The goal of KEEP was the development of a reading programme that was effective, required the least number of changes in standard public school practices, and would be accommodated to the culture and language of Native Hawaiian children. After some years, a successful programme evolved (Gallimore, *et al.* 1982; Tharp, 1982; Calfee, *et al.*, 1981).

Five years of naturalistic research in a Native Hawaiian community preceded the design of the KEEP project. This earlier work had focused on family, socialization, child development, and educational problems (Gallimore, Boggs and Jordan, 1974; Gallimore and Howard, 1968; Howard, 1974; MacDonald and Gallimore, 1971). When cohorts of such children entered KEEP, they were assessed in conventional ways: individual and group tests of cognition and language were administered by individuals familiar with local customs and dialect. The children scored well below national norms at entry to the KEEP kindergarten. Their test scores indicated extreme risk of poor educational achievement, and a high probability of referral to special education. Of particular interest is the fact that these tests suggested the children had a very low level of proficiency in standard English as well as school readiness.

Based on these measures of unassisted performance, there was no reason to expect such students were ready for instruction in the reading, writing, or ciphering of the primary grades. Indeed, these test results suggested the children would require instruction at a level far below that normally provided to 5-year-olds in North America. In blunt terms, on the tests, many were functioning at borderline or mildly handicapped levels.

These results were in marked contrast to observations during the earlier naturalistic investigations. Most notable was the contrast between the competence of Native Hawaiian children in the home and their incompetence at school. At school, teacher often reported the students to be nonverbal, and barely able to function as communicators (Boggs, 1985; Gallimore *et al.*, 1974; MacDonald and Gallimore, 1971). Few achieved at normative levels.

Yet in their homes and families, Hawaiian children assumed major responsibilities for childcare and cooking; they learned to play musical instruments and to dance. Their interactions with fieldworkers were marked by initial shyness, giving way to warmth and spontaneity; their verbal behaviour indicated no signs of linguistic deficit. In fact, many Native Hawaiian youngsters displayed highly refined verbal skills and routines. These home observations suggested that the children were competent and making normal progress in cognitive and linguistic development by the standards of the natal culture, and indeed appeared superior to the majority culture youngsters in coping, responsibility, and initiative.

What accounts for these inconsistencies? What does the paradox imply? As a result of the variability of performance in different contexts, KEEP investigators focused on naturalistic teaching and learning situations of these students in everyday settings. For example, it was found that Native Hawaiian children come to school with much experience in collaborative work and learning activities. This pattern derives from the structure of family life, and from specific socialization practices. Hawaiian families tend to be large, and related households often live in close proximity, sharing activities and resources. Even when physically separated, several households may function as one, so that children are reared in an atmosphere of interdependence and shared work.

Siblings and slightly older relatives are given major childcare responsibilities. By age 3, children operate as part of the sibling group and turn to siblings for help with many things, including teaching (Gallimore, *et al.*, 1974; Jordan, 1978*a*; 1978*b*; Weisner, Gallimore and Tharp, 1982; Weisner, Gallimore and Jordan, 1986). Children thus learn and develop in the context of a 'shared function' system which involves role flexibility and joint responsibility. Teaching takes place in the context of goal-directed activities, in which teacher and learner share responsibilty for the work and the product. Collaboration, co-operation and assisted performance are therefore commonplace in the everyday experience of Hawaiian children.

Consistent with our earlier formulation, this research of the past 20 years supports the conclusion that measures of unassisted performance can greatly underestimate the range of performance which minority culture children will display, and such measures will lead to instruction pegged at inappropriately low levels.

This conclusion was also supported by related lines of experimental research, including a series of studies which suggested Native Hawaiian children did not spontaneously or independently use certain cognitive strategies in testing situations (for example, mnemonics and other strategies which experimental research shows enhance learning and performance (e.g. Brown, 1978)). Observations of these learners suggested they were unlikely to apply such strategies in appropriate situations (Gallimore *et al.,* 1974; Gallimore and Au, 1979). Moreover, in primary grades, they tended to rely on inefficient and lower-level strategies, especially when faced with tasks that were separated from meaningful contexts. This finding is very similar to the extensive body of research which suggests that often mildly handicapped students fail to spontaneously use strategic information in problem-solving tasks even when it is supplied for them (Brown and Campione, 1986).[3]

When even limited assistance was provided, however, Hawaiian children were able to generate and use effective strategies. In one study, kindergarten children achieved significantly better long-term recall of shape names when they were prompted by an experimenter to associate the shape name with a commonplace, e.g. circle-plate Gallimore, Lam, Speidel and Tharp, 1977). In a second experiment, students were taught a simple labelling strategy which they did not generalize to a similar task, until contextual cues were provided by an assisting adult (Speidel, Gallimore, Kobayashi and Hao, 1984). Similar effects of assistance by an adult were demonstrated on a standard memory task. Without prompts, Hawaiian children showed no evidence of clustering as a recall strategy; in a cueing condition, a high degree of clustering was obtained (Ciborowski and Price-Williams, 1974).

The ethnographic and experimental research with Native Hawaiian children led to the design of an overall instructional programme that was compatible with significant features of contemporary Hawaiian culture. Research and programme design, addressed from a Vygotskian perspective, has been summarized in some detail by Tharp, Jordan, Speidel, Au, Klein, Calkins, Sloat and Gallimore (1984).

For example, the previously mentioned Hawaiian pattern of assisting performance through sharing work and learning responsibilities has been adapted into the day-to-day KEEP instructional activities. KEEP concentrated on finding ways to assist the performance of Native Hawaiian students in order to make available for instruction their full range of competence. One approach has been to draw from the natal culture the ways performance is assisted, and then to develop classroom analogues. In the KEEP classes, an important programme element is peer-learning centres. In these centres, children work together. A study of the centres indicated that an act of peer assistance occurs every 3 minutes in kindergarten and every 2.5 minutes in first grade (Jordan, 1977; 1978*a*; 1978*b*).

A wide range of assistance is provided by the children to one another, including modelling and direct intervention, such as assisting a peer to perform part of a task, or physically help the other child perform. Skills are practised in which children are not equally competent. But with reciprocal aid, they can perform beyond the level at which each child could perform alone. Thus peers assist each other to perfom in that zone which Vygotsky defined as critical to development and learning.

How do we interpret these results? Many capacities that might affect performance – in the classroom or on a test – lie in the zone of proximal development for Native Hawaiian children. Sometimes only minimal assistance is required to activate such capacities and substantially raise performance levels. Without assistance, however, it is easy to underestimate the level at which the children are ready to benefit from instruction. In case after case unassisted test results grossly underestimated the level at which Native Hawaiian students could achieve with assistance.

Approaches which only account for the unassisted or independent level of functioning may seriously underestimate the abilities of many mildly handicapped and at risk students. In general, these approaches take the *individual* as the unit of analysis, while failing to account for the improvement in performance as a function of mediation and/or collaboration with a more competent other, i.e., the examiner or teacher. Furthermore, these approaches focus on the 'end products' of learning, and ignore both the *process* of learning (acquisition) as well as *potential* for learning as revealed in the gap between assisted and unassisted performance.

The proper unit of analysis (focus of assessment) is the examiner and examinee (or teacher and learner) in joint activity. Assisted *vs* unassisted level of performance (zone of proximal development) is a more sensitive indicator of developmental level than more commonly used 'static' tests that focus only on what a student has already accomplished. This information can be used to make instruction responsive to individual development. Until such an approach is considered, many underachieving children will be taught at inappropriately low levels. Only when teachers and testers can detect and be responsive to the discrepancies can we be assured that they are teaching in the zone of proximal development, which is also the zone of maximum benefit (Gallimore, Dalton and Tharp, 1986; Tharp *et al.*, 1984; Tharp and Gallimore, 1987).

Instructional Implications of Assisted Performance

Many mildly handicapped and language/ethnic minority students perform poorly in school while displaying competence in other settings. Much of this puzzle can be accounted for by the amount of assistance/collaboration in the immediate environment. Stated in another way, cognitive competence can be seen as universal across various cultural and linguistic groups, with differences in performance residing in the context in which it is displayed (Cole and Bruner, 1971; LCHC, 1982); a crucial characteristic of this context is its pattern of social assistance.

To activate these underlying competencies, the level of instruction must not be too low. Rather, it must be aimed at a level just above what a student can independently accomplish, i.e. what has been previously mastered. Within the present framework 'good' instruction is that which is 'responsive' to the zone of proximal development. It is instruction which provides the appropriate level of individually sensitive collaboration and assistance.

One implication of these ideas is a powerful definition of teaching that may be derived: in Vygotskian terms, teaching is good only when it *'awakens and rouses to life those functions which are in a stage of maturing, which lie in the zone of proximal development* (Vygotsky, 1956, p.278, quoted in Wertsch and Stone, 1985, italics original)'. Based on these ideas, Tharp and Gallimore (in press) proposed a general definition of teaching: teaching consists of assisting performance through the Zone of Proximal Development. Teaching can be said to occur when assistance is offered at points in the ZPD at which performance requires assistance.

Taking this perspective of teaching into account, the following sections will illustrate the use of 'assisted performance' teaching with classroom examples. More specifically, we will examine assisted performance in two areas which are often problematic for mildly handicapped and minority students: situations where there are differences in the child/adult understanding of the task (and therefore lack of meaning for the child); and situations where students lack the specific academic skills needed to succeed.

The Role of Motivation: The Problem of Making Text Meaningful

It is commonly assumed that low achievement of disadvantaged children is due to a lack of specific academic skills or of academic motivation. Therefore many progammes attempt to provide intensive instruction in these basic academic 'building blocks' or basic skills, and despair when children are not 'motivated' to engage the academic tasks. However, there is mounting evidence that some special education and some low-achieving minority students may not only lack specific academic skills but may lack an appropriate 'larger context' in which to fit these small 'building blocks'. Stated another way, their understanding of a complex task is so incomplete that reading, for example, is meaningless (Erickson and Mohatt, 1982; Phillips, 1972; 1983; Scollon and Scollon, 1981). This commonly occurs in schooling when there is little correspondence between the background and life experiences of the child and the school texts. When the child does not engage the text, it is interpreted as the child's motivational problem. There is an alternative interpretation.

Most teaching practices incorrectly assume that there is a direct correspondence between the adult's and the child's understanding of the reading task. Competent adult readers understand that reading is a way of obtaining information about the world, and therefore read for a purpose. Adult readers experience reading as a useful tool, and understand how to integrate prior knowledge and experience into the goal of making the text meaningful.

Children with little exposure to reading and literacy do not have adult readers' conception of the task. As a result, they do not have the same understanding, and therefore do not have the same motivation to approach the task. One way of compensating for this 'lack of motivation' is to add teacher-supplied external reinforcement as a means of engaging the child in the task. Although this is one means of providing assistance, and is used in the KEEP programme as well as many others, a more natural way of approaching this problem is also emphasized at KEEP.

'Motivation' is embedded in reading comprehension lessons as children are assisted to create meaning – and motivation – through collaborative interaction with the teacher. The KEEP comprehension lessons are in the form of 'instructional conversations'. In these conversations, teachers rely mainly on *responsive questioning* to assist children to integrate their knowledge and experiences with their emergent understanding of the text. Through conversational dialogue, teacher and children jointly create meaning from the text. Unlike most reading comprehension lessons in the United States (Durkin, 1978–79; Tharp and Gallimore, in press), these conversation-like lessons do not focus strictly on literal text details. Teachers are explicitly trained to 'pull' the students as deeply into the text as possible, moving from details to higher levels of comprehension. What drives the task for the children is the opportunity to bring their personal experience into the lesson and to compare their emergent interpretations of the text against those of peers; gentle probing of their reasoning by the teacher assists them to create and express increasingly more competent and sophisticated renderings of their experience and of the text. As the 'conversation' unfolds, the children develop the 'larger context' for why they are engaged in the activity – and the context which many low achieving students lack.

Through teacher assistance, the students are able to use higher order comprehension strategies, just as the young girl was able to 'use' a memory stategy through collaboration with the father in our homely example. They are performing – in collaboration – at a level higher than they could achieve alone. In terms of our presentation, this is the zone of proximal development where learning and development are most rapid and certain.

The 'instructional conversation' (Tharp and Gallimore, 1988) has profound cognitive and motivational consequences. Arranging for assisted performance to occur, through the instructional conversation and responsive questioning, is far from simple. It requires major structuring of the school environment. The KEEP reading programme is one example of such a structure, which is briefly described in the next section. Following a brief description of the KEEP programme we present a detailed example of the instructional conversation and responsive questioning.[4]

The KEEP Reading Programme

Each day at the KEEP school, small groups are taught reading comprehension by the teacher. The daily comprehension lessons last about 20 minutes for each group of four to six children. These groups meet with the teacher while the other 25 children are working in the peer learning centres. At each centre, there is teacher-assigned work tailored to each child's instructional level, which is determined by a reading objectives/criterion referenced testing system (Crowell, 1979).

The usual reading programme elements are taught, including decoding, and sight vocabulary. A major distinction is the emphasis on comprehension, which is the focus of instruction for two-thirds of a two-hour language arts period, including three-fourths of the time in the teacher-instructed small group, and 50 per cent in the independent learning centres. It is the emphasis on comprehension that greatly increases both the amount of responsive questioning, and the opportunities for teachers to engage in regulatory questioning.

The daily face-to-face lessons taught by the teacher have many Socratic qualities, with the teacher relying heavily on questions which demand various levels of cognitive processing, from recall of literal details to inference and prediction (Crowell and Au, 1979). The teacher's questions are responsive and built upon pupil contributions 'in flight'. Although the teacher is guided by instructional objectives, pre-planning is often abandoned when an unanticipated but more productive line of discussion emerges.

The teachers are, however, guided in their questioning by an explicit strategy of text processing that teaches children to weave together old and new information (Tharp, 1982). This is achieved by a sequence of operations: the hypothesizing of themes or schemata likely to be relevant to the upcoming text; the calling-up of information stored in memory; the perception and categorization of emerging text material; and the comparative/contrastive relating of memorial material with text material. This sequence is rapid, and recurs in cycles over advancing portions of the text.

Even casual observation of a KEEP comprehension lesson quickly reveals that rapid-paced teacher questions characterize the sessions. Most sessions with beginning readers start with questions that seek to activate children's existing knowledge. The aim of such questions is to help the children develop from their own experience a way of comprehending the story-to-be-read. Although the teacher knows the story and students, it is not always obvious what understandings the children have available to process the text. The following excerpts from reading lessons illustrate how performance is assisted in the daily reading lessons.

Integrating Prior Experience and Text to Create Meaning

During a KEEP reading lesson, a teacher was introducing a story about an immigrant girl. The immigrant girl, named Pilar, had recently arrived in the United States from Mexico. Pilar wants to be called 'Polly'. Action in this story is motivated by Pilar's embarrassment by her Hispanic name, her father's use of Spanish, and his attendance at a high school to learn English. This theme of embarrassment is crucial to understanding the text, but the children do not perceive it.

The teacher began the lesson in the routine way: before the text was introduced, she asked the children questions to call up and assess their relevant previous experience with the major elements of the text-to-come. She asked directly for personal experiences of embarrassment. This elicited no response. The teacher offered some possibilities of embarrassments, but the line of questioning proved futile: one boy mentioned that his mother was fat – but neither he nor any of the others in the group reflected any concern. It seemed clear that 'embarrassment' was not a word or concept they could use to understand Pilar's motivation.

Therefore the teacher decided to relate an incident from her own childhood – her mother was sick and could never participate in normal activities. She described some times when she had felt embarrassment about her mother's lack of participation. This disclosure produced more silence. Though frustrated, the teacher persevered; her next effort did assist the children to understand Pilar's motivation.

> Teacher: What would my friends say if they found out my mother was always sick?
> Clara: Tease you!

This exchange sparked active participation by most group members, with Clara leading. The discussion included a digression on the morality of using violence to deal with those who tease. For these Native Hawaiian children being teased aroused strong feelings, and once they interpreted Pilar as fearing 'teasing' by peers, it was possible for them to understand the story beyond its literal details.

Through assisted performance, the teacher led the students to consider Pilar's plight in terms of the subjective feelings she might have about having a Hispanic name, or having 'immigrant' parents. There is no indication that these Hawaiian students appreciated that a problem might arise from being immigrant or being different. But is is also clear that through leading questions, it was possible for them – with the teacher's help – to link the character's motivation with one which they could appreciate.

This is an observable version of what probably transpires in the mind of the mature reader – either (1) starting with personal knowledge to organize text: or (2) starting with the text, and relating it to personal knowledge. It is exactly this correspondence which makes reading an enjoyable and understandable activity for competent readers. That is, the motivation for reading derives at least in part if not wholly from such activity on the part of the reader. This flexible, bi-directional, interactive processing is something beginning readers are capable of only if the strategic aspects are provided through assisted performance in the zone of proximal development. At this point, then, what ultimately will be 'in the mind', is now discernible in its elementary form in the interaction of teacher and pupil. Through the use of responsive questions, the child's and adult's understanding of the task has now been moved closer together, and the 'motivation' for continuing the task has now become embedded in the task itself.

Responsive Assistance in the Acquisition of Specific Academic Skills

Making a task meaningful for students is accomplished by assisting them to weave text information with their previous schematic knowledge. In order to comprehend in this way, readers must also be able to process the text itself accurately. Assisting them to get the facts of the text is also essential, and that requires strategies for retrieving information from the text. Teachers are inclined to ask about literal details of stories (Hao, 1980; Durkin, 1978–1979; Zetlin and Gallimore, 1980). Such questions as: What is the boy's name? What colour is the ball? can have both assessment and assisting functions for beginning readers. Although reading instruction in KEEP attends to these basic skills, it is always done with the overall goal of assisting comprehension. With skilful responsive questioning, both goals can be served.[5]

As an example, a teacher begins the instructional conversation with her reading group about the text they have just read with a question about a literal detail:

Teacher: How will Jaspar make music?
Child: A guitar.

After this one question at the detail level, the teacher switches to the 'problem' in the story and commences a series of questions designed to assist the children's processing toward higher levels:

> Teacher: Okay, he (Jaspar) doesn't have $29.95. What does that have to do with the problem? Why is Amy mentioning this?
> Children: (no response)
> Teacher: When I–we–talk about a problem, why does this ($29.95) come to mind?

The teacher is regulating the performance of the children so that they make use of the details they remember, rather than merely demonstrate that they recall details. One result is longer responses, with more implications:

> Teacher: What does his mother say when he (Jasper) went (to ask for money for a guitar)?
> Amy: He – he said – his mommy – he went up to his mommy and he said he needed somethin' and his mommy – his mommy looked down at his shoes and maybe she said, he need new shoes.

Text questions focused exclusively on details of the story are typical of the comprehension lessons observed in a control school, in Honolulu (Hao, 1980), in Illinois (Durkin, 1978–1979), and in a school for trainable mentally retarded (Zetlin and Gallimore, 1980; 1983). Detail is also used in KEEP lessons, but it is mostly with younger learners, or when the teacher judges that students are not comprehending because they have missed details. The detail sequences are more appropriately regarded as efforts to repair miscomprehensions.

To construct questions that inquire beyond simple details, teachers must study the stories they use. Teachers we have observed who rely almost exclusively on literal detail text questions tend to omit this step in their preparation of reading lessons. They use the detail questions to assess children's comprehension at this lower level, and content themselves with correcting errors of fact. Unfortunately, this omits assistance in a child's zone of proximal development, where it is required. Over-reliance on detail questions is incompatible with the instructional conversation and the collaborative development of meaning. In its worst form, it becomes traditional recitation which assesses what students have comprehended, but does not assist them to develop an understanding or teach them the strategies of comprehension. Recitation tests, but it does not teach.

Assisting Students to Relate Experience to Text

Once children's previous schema have been activated, or new schema have been created in their joint discussions, and once the text details have been marshalled, the two need to be woven together to create the new cloth of comprehension.

Questions can be asked that assist children to develop meanings by seeing connections between experience/knowledge and story content (text). The interwoven knowledge forms the basis of revised or new schema. To illustrate these questions, and how they function to assist comprehension, we will focus on a single lesson from a KEEP first-grade class (Macmillan, Boggs and Au, 1980).

In this lesson the children are reading the story 'Freddy Finds a Frog'. The children are attempting to understand an interaction between Freddy and Mr Mays. Freddy has asked Mr Mays what he would do with a frog. Mr Mays say he would take the frog fishing. Freddy laughs, and says, 'Frogs can't fish'. Mr Mays clarifies: he means to use the frog for bait. Freddy runs away, horrified. The children had trouble reconciling some of the facts because they did not appreciate the double entendre contained in the statement, 'I would like to take the frog fishing'.

> 1 Teacher: What did Mr Mays say he would do with the frog?
> (Clara: He would take . . . Lotte: water, um fishing)
> 5 Teacher: Do frogs like to go fishing? (Group: Nooo. Some additional reactions, when Teacher repeats the question, one yes, several no's).
> 11 Teacher: Why don't they like to go fishing? (several opinions, don't like water, don't like flies, don't like fish, and finally, Lotte says, 'They use for da bait')

This sequence of questions, including an extended discussion of bait and the long narrative by Lotte on using crayfish for bait, exemplifies asking for relationships between experience and the text itself. Question 1, above, is of course a detail text question. Questions 5 and 11 are relationship questions. They call for the children to combine both experience and text information: for example, they may not have known that frogs are used for bait (some students and the teacher say they did not know), but since one or more knew about bait and baiting hooks, they were able to incorporate new information and relate it to their existing schemas.

Having explored the 'frogs as bait' idea, the teacher resumed by asking the children to guess how Freddy felt about Mr Mays' suggestion. Note Clara who repeats what seems like a contradiction of her peers' interpretations (utterances 78, 80 and 82).

> 62 Teacher: How do you think Fr–how does Freddy feel about using the frog for bait? (63 Amy: Sad: 64 Vergie: inaudible) '
> 65 Teacher: Does he like that idea?
> 66 George: No-o-o:
> 67 Teacher: Clara____?:
> 68 Sammy: No-o-o.

69 Teacher: How does he feel about that? (70 Amy: He's sa-a-ad: 71 Unhappy)

72 Teacher: He might be unhappy or sad, why?

73 Sammy: Because he didn't want–he didn't want to–He–he wanted to keep the frog.

74 Teacher: How come Mr Mays told him that? Is Mr Mays a mean man?

75 George: No-o-o-o-o. (rolling)

76 Teacher: Why did he suggest using the frog for bait? 77 Amy: He couldn't think of any—

78 Clara: But Freddy laughed.

79 Teacher: O-o-o-h, that's the first thing that came to his mind.

80 Clara: But Freddy laughed.

81 Teacher: Good!

82 Clara: But Freddy laughed (looks at book)

83 Lotte: ?

84 Teacher: Did Freddy think it was funny?

85 Sammy: No-o-o

86 Amy: I would

87 Lotte: No-o-o

From utterance 62 to 77 it appears comprehension is proceeding smoothly, if not in large jumps. Several of the children can easily understand Freddy's dismay, and think of appropriate labels for the reaction. At utterance 74, the teacher shifts the topic, presumably to explore the children's comprehension of Mr Mays' motivation. But Clara, who has been silent throughout the discussion of Freddy's reaction, raises an objection (utterance 78) to the other childrens' suggestions that Freddy was sad or unhappy with Mr Mays' proposed use of the frog.

However, the teacher continues on with the question of Mr Mays' motivation (utterance 79), which prompts Clara twice to repeat 'But Freddy laughed' (utterances 80 and 82). Clara's persistence is rewarded when the teacher in utterance 84 asks: 'Did Freddy think it was funny?' Two children say no: one says, 'I would put it in a pond.' Clara says nothing. The teacher then embarks on the following exchange, in an effort to get the children to understand the double entendre and how that can account for Freddy's having laughed at the suggestion of using his frog for bait.

89B Teacher: Clara, why did you say Freddy laughed?

89C Teacher: Okay, read that part that you s-said when Freddy laughed

90 Clara: 'I would take it fishing, Freddy laughed.' 91 Teacher: Kay, who says, 'I would take it fishing'? 92 Sammy: Mr Mays.

93 Vergie: Mr Mays

97A Teacher: C—, why did Freddy laugh?

98 Amy: Because maybe he didn't—

97B Teacher: Lotte?

97C Teacher: Amy?

98 Amy: —Maybe he didn't know that—

99 Amy: —Maybe he didn't know that he was going to use the frog.

100 Teacher: No-o-o-o, he laughed for another reason Lotte, who can read that?

101 Lotte: Because – cause Mr Mays didn't know what to do with the frog. That's all he could think was – because – because he didn't – he didn't know that he could use frogs was for bait. That's why Freddy laughed.

The Repair of Comprehension

In Utterance 89C (above) the teacher begins to repair the miscomprehension – she instructs Clara to read from the text, to get the story details in order, to determine what was said and who said it. But by utterances 98 and 101, it is clear that further repairwork is needed: no one has stated clearly why Freddy laughed.

102A Teacher: Okay, wait – okay, wait a minute. (Sammy puts down his hand, looks at book)

102 Teacher: That's not the reason Freddy laughed

103 Sammy: Frogs can't fish.

104 Teacher: Right! Okay, Mr Mays said, 'I don't have a frog, but if I did, I'd take it fishing,' and Freddy thinks, 'Ha, going fishing with a frog – the frog's sitting with a fishing pole?' – (while quoting Mr Mays, enacts 'thinking' and fishing pole on shoulder) (Lotte looks at Teacher momentarily, then at book) (Amy watches Teacher).

105 George: No-o-o-o-o (rolling)

106A Teacher: That's pretty funny.

106B Teacher: So Freddy laughs, he goes 'frogs can't fish, they can't sit there with a fishing pole.' But Mr Mays really meant, 'Un-uh (negative), I would use that frog as—

108 Teacher: Bait.

George(?): Bait

109A Teacher: Right the frog would be his bait.

109B Teacher: And then, did Freddy laugh, Clara?

110 George: N-o-o-o-o

111A Teacher: N-o-o, he didn't think that was too funny.

In utterance 103, Sammy says, 'Frogs can't fish.' This prompts the teacher to 'explain' the sequence of events by re-enacting the events, first posing as Mr Mays (thinking with fishing pole on shoulder), and then acting out Freddy's presumed and humorous image of the frog with a fishing pole. After her performance, the teacher asks: 'And then did Freddy laugh?' (utterance 109B), to which even Clara now says: 'Nooo'.

The long exchange about why Freddy laughed was begun by the teacher to repair a relatively major failure of comprehension by the children. It became obvious that repair work was needed because the children did not understand that Freddy's laughter was due to his initial misunderstanding of Mr Mays' phrase 'take the frog fishing'. Freddy got the point, and ran away horrified; but the children still don't get the point.

From the context it appears that the beginning of the repair sequences (89B) the teacher herself was not quite certain what it was the children missed. Thus, part of the long exchange from 89B to 109A is investigatory. She immediately (89C) suggests a strategy for resolving the question by asking Clara to read from the text 'the part that you said when Freddy laughed'. Quite aside from this particular instance, the training of the children to check back to the text source represents teacher provision of strategic assistance – in effect, one of the options or strategies to use when there is miscomprehension is to reread the text.

Clara's response to the reading request introduces yet another possible confusion (90). Clara read the two sentences in such a way that one might think it was Freddy who said, 'I will take it fishing.' The teacher's next question (91) is aimed at clarifying the fact it was actually Mr Mays who said he would take it fishing. And her next question (97A) in context sets up the sequence: that it was Freddy who laughed after Mr Mays' statement. The responses which follow 97A show that the children are still struggling to understand and that they are continuing to use a text-search strategy for obtaining ideas. There is little indication here of using personal experience, although one child offers a speculation (99) that would not explain Freddy's laughter. The teacher persists.

Eventually in 103, a piece of information is provided which the teacher seems to regard as the key, as it prompts her to provide a summary of relevant text (104). However, it is not clear the children understand yet what 'going fishing with a frog' implies, and why Freddy thought it was funny. In the subsequent sequence, the teacher finishes by establishing that once Freddy realized what Mr Mays really meant, it was no longer funny in the least.

During this repair sequence, the teacher used questions to get the children to (1) get the facts straight as to who said what and (2) to appreciate the sequence of events and statements of the characters. As a 'repair' strategy, this is common, effective, and often sufficient to provide understanding of a text, when combined with the use of personal or conceptual knowledge. Here it was insufficient because the children did not appreciate the double-meaning of Mr Mays' statement. An alternative strategy might have been to guide the children through an analysis of the statement and of double entendre in general. It is likely these second graders are well experienced with double entendres and the often humorous consequences of them in discourse, given the narratives by children from similar backgrounds recorded by Watson-Gegeo and Boggs (1977).

These transcript excerpts provide examples of the assisting function of teachers' questions. The children are cognitively and linguistically capable of understanding, but at age six still rely on assisted performance to array and sequence ideas, knowledge, and facts.

When children struggle to comprehend some aspect of a story, with sensitive teacher assistance, they are gaining practice with a fundamental task, one that forever confronts the mature reader who reads to learn sometimes new and difficult concepts and information. It is practice on such comprehension problems, with the assistance of a teacher, which provide the child opportunities to learn to use a variety of processing strategies in flexible ways: to test personal ideas and perceptions against peers: and which allows the teacher opportunities for regulation of processing at the frontier of a child's ability and understanding (cf. Rogoff and Gardener, 1985). In the zone of proximal development, comprehension questions are a principal means of assistance available to teachers in their efforts to teach would-be comprehenders.

In these excerpts, we have also seen the 'tailoring' of teacher contributions to the level most useful to the students at a particular point in the discussion. In studies of adult–child, dyadic interaction, this adjustment of assistance to the less experienced partner's level is a principal aspect of assisted performance (Tharp and Gallimore, in press). Such adjustment to the learner's level has been termed by other authors as 'semiotic mediation' (Wertsch, 1985) or 'scaffolding' (Wood, Bruner and Ross, 1976). In this process, the teacher provides assistance at a level from which the student can benefit at the particular point in the activity in which they are engaged. When the student is successful, the teacher provides 'broad' assistance, which provides minimal direction and leaves maximal responsibility to the student for that portion of the activity (Schneider, Hyland and Gallimore, 1985).

When such assistance is not responded to appropriately, the responsive teacher may switch to 'narrow' help, providing more specific direction; the teacher is thereby assuming a greater share of the responsibility for the overall activity. This means the activity is in the zone of proximal development. The student or child can perform some aspects, but a complete performance is possible only if the more capable partner fills in what the less capable cannot yet manage. When narrow assistance is successful, the adult typically switches to broad assistance once again. The student gradually learns how to carry out activities independently, learning both the steps necessary to carry them out and the fact that activities are made up of series of steps.

The Nature of Assisted Performance and Responsive Teaching:
General Issues

In this final section, we conclude with three general issues that are of concern to educators attempting to adapt teaching practices to incorporate the notion of assisted performance.

1   Does assisted performance have to exactly parallel what is found in the natal culture?
2   Can assisted performance be adapted to various ethnic/linguistic groups?
3   How are the means of assisting performance best learned by teachers?

1 *The natal culture as the basis for assisting performance*

An important element of KEEP success appears to have been the close attention to the everyday cultural practices of the students as the basis for adjusting teaching practices (Tharp *et al.*, 1984). This raises an interesting question: Must assisted performance exactly parallel the natal culture in order to be effective? Must classroom patterns of assisted performance strictly imitate the patterns of the home culture?

In fact, the KEEP experience suggests not (Jordan, 1985). Patterns of assisted performance can be effective even if they do not duplicate natal culture patterns. While the KEEP peer learning centres are an example of assisting performance in a way that is similar to the natal culture patterns, the KEEP comprehension lesson represents a departure from the home patterns of assisting performance. For example, the pattern of assistance reflected in the lesson excerpts presented earlier is unlike the pattern of adult–child interaction in the natal culture (Jordan, 1977). In fact, the manner in which the KEEP teachers interact has seldom been observed in Hawaiian homes (Gallimore, Boggs and Jordan, 1974; Weisner, Gallimore and Jordan, 1986; Weisner, Gallimore and Tharp, 1982). The comprehension lesson is much more like the interactions described by many researchers as typical of middle-class literate caregivers and their children (e.g. Ochs, 1982).

Thus, some assisted performance in the KEEP programme is culturally familiar, and some relatively unfamiliar. The relatively familiar interactions of the peer learning centre assist performance – but so do the unfamiliar interactions used by the teachers in the daily comprehension lessons.

These data suggest a general principle: assistance should be offered in those contexts most likely to be accepted by the child. Children may be assisted in ways that are similar to their experience; they may also be assisted in ways that depart from their experience. How and by whom performance is assisted is less important than that performance occurs and thereby development and learning proceed.

2 *The use of assisted performance in various cultural settings*

How well do the KEEP results extend to other groups in other settings? Do the notions embedded in the concept of assisted performance apply just as well to other cultures and low-achieving groups? Could they be successfully used with special education students such as mentally retarded students, for example? Our answer is yes.

Although KEEP was developed in a specific cultural context, the theoretical basis of assisted performance is based on a broad theoretical framework. Moreover, similar results have been reported for Hispanic students in Southern California by Schneider, Hyland and Gallimore, (1985); and for Navajo Indians in the Southwestern United States (White, Tharp, Jordan and Vogt, in press; Tharp, 1984, 1985; Vogt, Jordan and Tharp, 1987; Jordan, Tharp and Vogt, 1985).

Evidence for the value of assisted performance with special education students is already available (Brown and Campione, 1986; Palinscar, 1986; Zetlin and Gallimore, 1980; 1983). There is every reason to expect the learning and development of these students to be enhanced by teaching which is collaborative and designed to assist performance in the zone of proximal development. Certainly, the performance of mentally retarded and learning disabled students improves with collaborative assistance in everyday settings: discrepancies in performance by such students across different contexts was the beginning point of the chapter (see studies cited earlier). Application of assisted performance practices to special education students is an area ripe for research and practical experimentation.

3 *Assisting teachers to provide assisted performance*

Although the concept of assisted performance appears easy and perhaps even simplistic at first glance, experience indicates that it is difficult to put into practice. Traditional teacher training methods are likely to be ineffective in changing established teaching patterns into those required to assist performance in students' zones of proximal development.

These cautionary conclusions are based on the attempts at training teachers to assist student performance, by engaging in instructional conversations and using responsive questioning. Training studies were part of 15 years of research and development conducted at KEEP (Tharp and Gallimore, 1979; 1982; in press). In brief, this work indicated that ordinary programmes of in-service development produced few lasting changes in teacher behaviour. Workshops and university courses, for example, were effective only for the introduction of vocabulary and concepts, and for arousing interest and motivation to participate (MacDonald and Gallimore, 1971).

To learn teaching practices that assisted performance required exposure to models (live and tape demonstrations of assisted performance), practice with children in actual classrooms, and feedback (viewing of video recordings soon after teaching a lesson) (Tharp and Gallimore, in press; Gallimore, Dalton and Tharp, 1986). Weekly coaching meetings with a consultant were essential, in order that lasting changes in teaching were gained from models, practice, and feedback. For many individuals, the weekly sessions were needed for up to a year, with a minimum of at least several months.

The majority of teachers receiving this time-intensive training experienced extended periods of frustration and difficulty (Gallimore, Dalton and Tharp, 1986). To reduce reliance on conventional recitation was more difficult than most assumed. In fact, many of the teachers assumed they were already using and practising assisted performance in the zones of students' proximal development (Hyland, Gallimore and Schneider, in press). It took several sessions of video feedback (after watching models) for them to appreciate how far from the assisted performance ideal they in fact were functioning. At this point they needed to learn not only a new set of teaching standards, but also how to analyse their own performances and make corrections.

Teachers who learn to critically attend to self, and to personal technique and knowledge, enter a transition in their professional development. The impact of greater attention-to-self, and to one's knowledge and pedagogy, initiate a change process which begins for some as a highly stressful experience (Gallimore, Dalton and Tharp, 1986; Tharp and Gallimore, in press). Many teachers described a transition from initial confusion to a stage in which they 'heard in their head' the voice of the models they had watched; they found themselves 'mouthing' words of expert practitioners they had watched. Teachers sometimes reported feeling uncomfortable with this imitation yet it seemed to be a necessary step for moving beyond recitation. In time, the 'voices of the models' gave way to their own more confident inner voice (Gallimore *et al.*, op. cit.). Finally, for some teachers even their own inner voice began to fall silent as the skills of assisting performance were internalized, and automatized.

The teachers often described the difficulty of calibrating the level of assistance a child requires in the instructional conversations. This task requires, so the teachers report, listening carefully and constantly thinking about what a student is trying to say, what the context is, what the student knows and has experience with. It is this demand to think about students' utterances that makes continuation of 'inner speech' a functional activity, long after other aspects of assisting performance have been internalized and automatized (Gallimore *et al.*, op. cit.). Teachers say they must continue indefinitely to 'talk to themselves' as a reminder to listen, reflect, ask themselves questions about the meaning of child utterances, and consider alternative interpretations of the text that might relate to child utterances.

The teachers have learned to respond, as middle-class parents do, by tailoring their responses to the students' utterances (Ochs, 1982; Schneider *et al.*, op. cit.). And as parents do, teachers assist language development, as well as text processing, as a concomitant of the instructional conversation (Speidel, in press). As they assist comprehension, teachers expand and elaborate student utterances, in ways that are later observed in the speech of the children. Speidel's work suggests substantial parallels between the 'responsive teaching' of literate parents, and the teachers at KEEP who have learned to assist performance in the instructional conversations. One of the remarkable ironies of the KEEP research was the discovery that teachers had to be trained to interact with students as they did during the 'bedtime stories' they all read at home with their own children (Heath, 1982; Ochs, 1982).

One more element is required, in addition to the pedagogical skills of assisting performance. The teacher must be well grounded in the academic knowledge which is being taught. We believe the importance of the teachers' knowledge of the subject matter cannot be stressed enough. Even beginning reading teachers – the focus of the KEEP research – must have an intellectual grasp of the literary qualities of primers, if they are to teach in the zone of proximal development. Those that approach stories as no more than the literal details on the pages of the primers make no significant progress, and remain wedded to recitation and other forms of teacher-dominated interaction.

When the internalization occurs, and the inner voice becomes a self-regulating function during interactive teaching, the teacher approaches the ideal of teaching – assisting performance in children's zones of proximal development. The teacher has approached a point of knowing what to teach (substantive knowledge) and knowing how to teach (pedagogic knowledge). At this point, teachers report that they feel more professional, that they have learned to function in ways that match their original conception of teaching, prior to entering the profession. Most of them report that the painful process of training was justified by the effects on their teaching, their increased job satisfaction, and the benefits to their students.

Once they have acquired these skills, teachers can capitalize on the basic principle which we developed at the beginning of this chapter: *The performance of retarded and learning disabled individuals often improves when they can perform in collaboration with more competent and assisting others. It is the occasion of such collaborations that learning and development are most rapid.*

Notes

1   The research reported here was supported by the Kamehameha Early Education Project (The Kamehameha Schools/Princess Bernice Pauahi Bishop Estate). Additional support was provided by the Sociobehavioral Research Group, Mental Retardation Research Centre, UCLA, and by National Institute of Child Health and Human Development grants to

Ronald Gallimore. The authors are grateful to many colleagues who have contributed to the research reported here. Sandra Kaufman provided helpful editorial assistance for which we express our appreciation.

2   Mildly handicapped refers to students who are mentally retarded, learning disabled, significantly under achieving, and behaviour disordered (Macmillan, Keogh and Jones, 1985). In general, these students demonstrate lowered academic achievement, but are not characterized by physical or organic difficulties.

3   The reasons why some ethnic minority students have this problem are a matter of controversy. For example, the cross-cultural literature suggests that the understanding of the task and consequently the goals of the activity may be very different for the tester and testee. But whatever the explanation, children who do not readily command these strategies are handicapped in conventional classrooms, and on many standard tests.

4   Although we have featured responsive questioning, questions are only one means of assisting performance. They are the most natural part of the instructional conversation, and the most frequent, but they are not the only form of assistance. Tharp and Gallimore (in press) have identified five other forms of assistance, in addition to questions. These include modelling, feeding back, contingency managing, instructing, and cognitive structuring in addition to questioning. Instructional conversation is also not the only context in which assisted performance occurs; however it appears to be a powerful one for mildly handicapped and low-achieving students.

5   The discussion in this section is an elaboration of the Experience–Text-Relationship method (see, e.g., Au, 1979; 1981; Tharp, *et al.* 1984).

References

Au, K. H. (1979), Using the experience-text-relationship method with minority children, *The Reading Teacher*, **32**(6), 677–9.

Au, K. H. (1981), The comprehension-oriented reading lesson: Relationships to proximal indices of achievement, *Educational Perspectives*, **20**, 13–15.

Boggs, S. T. (1985), *Speaking, Relating, and Learning: A Study of Hawaiian Children at Home and at School.* (Norwood, New Jersey: Ablex Publishing Corp).

Brown, A. L. (1974), The role of strategic behavior in retardate memory, in N. R. Ellis (ed.), *International Review of Research in Mental Retardation*, Vol. 7, pp.55–111. (New York: Academic Press).

Brown, A. L. (1978), Knowing how, when, and where to remember: A problem of meta-cognition, in R. Glaser (ed.), *Advances in Instructional Psychology*, Vol. 1. pp.77–165 (Hillsdale, N.J.: Erlbaum).

Brown, A. L. and Campione, J. C. (1986), Psychological theory and the study of learning disabilities, *American Psychologist*, **41**(10), 1059–68.

Calfee, R. R., Cazden, C. B., Duran, R. P., Griffin, M. P., Martus, M. and Willis, H. D. (1981), *Designing Reading Instruction for Cultural Minorities: The Case of the Kamehameha Early Education Project* (Report to the Ford Foundation). Cambridge, MA: Harvard Graduate School of Education, and Honolulu: Kamehameha Schools/Bishop Estate. (ERIC Document Reproduction Service No. ED 215 039).

Carver, C. S. and Scheier, M. F. (1981), *Attention and Self-Regulation: A Control-Theory Approach to Human Behaviour* (New York: Springer-Verlag).

Cazden, C. B. (1986), Classroom discourse, in M. C. Wittrock (ed.), *Handbook of Research on Teaching*, 3rd edn, pp.432–64 (New York: MacMillan).

Ciborowski, T. and Price-Williams, D. R. (1974), *A Study of Cued Free Recall Learning among Rural Hawaiian Children using Standardized Norms* Tech. Rep. 71 (Honolulu: Kamehameha Early Education Project, The Kamehameha Schools).

Cole, M. and Bruner, J. (1971), Cultural differences and inferences about psychological processes, *American Psychologist*, **26**, 867–75.

Crowell, D. C. (1979), *The Kamehameha Reading Objective System* (Honolulu: Kamehameha Schools/Bishop Estate, Center for Development of Early Education).

Crowell, D. C. & A. U, K. H. (1979), Using a scale of questions to improve listening comprehension, *Language Arts*, **56**, 38–43.

Durkin, D. (1978–1979), What classroom observations reveal about reading comprehension instruction, *Reading Research Quarterly*, **14**, 481–533.

Edgerton, R. B. (1967), *The Cloak of Competence* (Berkeley: University of California Press).

Erickson, F. and Mohatt, G. (1982), The cultural organization of participation structure in two classrooms of Indian students, in G. Spindler (ed.), *Doing the Ethnography of Schooling* (New York: Holt, Rinehart & Winston) pp.132–74.

Figueroa, R. (in preparation), *The Assessment of Hispanic Children's Intelligence* (University of California, Davis).

Fischer, K. W. and Bullock, D. (1984), Cognitive development in school-aged children: conclusions and new directions, in W. A. Collins (ed.), *Development during Middle Childhood: The Years from Six to Twelve* (Washington, D. C.: National Academy Press) pp.70–146.

Friedman, M., Krupski, A., Dawson, E. T. and Rosenberg, P. (1977), Metamemory and mental retardation: Implications for research and practice, in P. Mittler (ed.)., *Research to Practice in Mental Retardation: Vol. II, Education and Training pp.99–104* (Baltimore, Md.: University Park Press).

Gallimore, R. (1981), Affiliation, social context, industriousness, and achievement, in R. Munroe, L. Munroe and B. Whiting (eds), *Handbook of Cross Cultural Human Development* (New York: Garland Press) pp.689–715.

Gallimore, R. and Au, K. H. (1979). 'The competence/incompetence paradox in the education of minority culture children', *The Quarterly Newsletter of the Laboratory of Comparative Human Development*. 1, 3, 689-715.

Gallimore, R., Boggs, J. W. and Jordan, C. (1974), *Culture, Behavior and Education: A Study of Hawaiian-Americans* (Beverly Hills, CA: Sage Publications).

Gallimore, R., Dalton, S. and Tharp, R. G. (1986), Self-regulation and interactive teaching: the impact of teaching conditions on teachers' cognitive activity, *Elementary School Journal*, **86** (5), 613–31.

Gallimore, R. and Howard, A. (eds) (1968), *Studies in a Hawaiian community: Na Makamaka O Nanakuli*, Pacific Anthropological Records No. 1 (Honolulu: Princess Bernice Pauahi Bishop Museum, Department of Anthropology).

Gallimore, R., Lam, D. J., Speidel, G. E. and Tharp, R. G. (1977), The effects of elaboration and rehearsal on the long-term retention of shape names by kindergarteners, *American Educational Research Journal*, **14** (4),471–83.

Gallimore, R., Tharp, R. G. Sloat, K., Klein, T. and Troy, M. E. (1982), *Analysis of Reading Achievement Test Results for the Kamehameha Early Education Project: 1972-1979*, Tech. Report No. 102 (Honolulu: Kamehameha Schools/Bishop Estate, Center for Development of Early Education).

Hao, R. K. (1980), *Comparative Data on Reading Programs: KEEP and Kalihi Public Schools*, Working Paper (Honolulu: Kamehameha Schools/Bishop Estate, Center for Development of Early Education).

Heath, S. B. (1982), What not bedtime story means: narrative skills at home and school, *Language in Society*, 11 (2),49–76.

Howard, A. (1974) *Ain't no Big Thing: Coping Strategies in a Hawaiian-American Community*. (Honolulu: University Press of Hawaii).

Hyland, J. T., Gallimore, R., and Schneider, P. (in press), Knowing what they teach and teaching what they know: improving teaching in eighth grade U.S. history classes, To appear in L. C. Solomon (ed.) *From the Campus to the Classroom: The Practical Application of Educational Research*.

Jordan, C. (1977). *Maternal Teaching Modes and School Adaptations in an Urban Hawaiian Population*, Tech. Report No. 67 (Honolulu: The Kamehameha Schools/Bishop Estate, Kamehameha Educational Research Institute).

Jordan, C. (1978a), *Peer Relationships among Hawaiian Children and their Educational Implications*. Paper presented at the annual meeting of the American Anthropological Association, Los Angeles.

Jordan, C. (1978b), Teaching/learning interactions and school adaptations: the Hawaiian case, in *A Multidisciplinary Approach to Research in Education: The Kamehameha Early Education Program*, Tech. Report No. 81 (Honolulu: Kamehameha Schools/Bishop Estate, Center for Development of Early Education; revised version of a paper presented at the annual meetings of the American Anthropological Association. Houston, Texas, December 1977).

Jordan, C. (1981a), *Educationally Effective Ethnology: A Study of the Contributions of Cultural Knowledge to Effective Education for Minority Children*, Doctoral dissertation, UCLA (Available on microfilm from University Microfilms Library Services, Ann Arbor).

Jordan, C. (1981b), The selection of culturally compatible teaching practices, *Educational Perspectives*, 20 (1),16–19.

Jordan, C. (1983), Cultural differences in communication patterns: classroom adaptations and translated strategies, in M. Clark and J. J. Handscombe (eds), *TESOL '82: Pacific Perspectives on Language, Learning and Teaching* (Washington, DC: Teachers of English to Speakers of other Languages) pp.285-294.

Jordan, C. (1984), Cultural compatibility and the education of ethnic minority children, *Educational Research Quarterly*, 8 6(4), 59–71.

Jordan, C. (1985), Translating culture: from ethnographic information to educational program, *Anthropology and Education Quarterly*, 16, 106–23.

Jordan, C., Tharp, R. G. and Vogt, L. (1985), *Compatibility of Classroom and Culture: General Principles, with Navajo and Hawaiian Instances* (Working Paper, Center for Development of Early Education, The Kamehameha Schools, Honolulu 96817).

Kaufman, S. (1988), *Retarded Isn't Stupid, Mom* (Baltimore: Paul H. Brookes Publisher Co.).

Laboratory of Comparative Human Cognition (1982), Culture and intelligence, in R. J. Sternberg (ed.), *Handbook of Human Intelligence* (New York: Cambridge University Press) pp.642–719.

Langness, L. L. (1987), *Theodore V. Barrett: Life Story and Biography*, Unpublished manuscript, Sociobehavioral Research Group, Mental Retardation Research Center, University of California, Los Angeles 90024.

MacDonald, S. and Gallimore, R. (1971), *Battle in the Classroom* (Scranton PA: Intext).

MacMillan, D. I., Keogh, B. K. and Jones, R. L. (1985), Special educational research on mildly handicapped learners, in M. C. Wittrock (ed.), *Handbook of Research on Teaching* 3rd edn., (New York: MacMillan), pp.686–724.

MacMillan, G., Boggs, S. and Au, K. H. (1980), *A Discourse-Annotated Transcription of a Model KEEP First Grade Reading Lesson (Teacher-Claire Assam). (Report # 94)* (Honolulu: Kamehameha Early Education Progam).

Ochs, E. (1982), Talking to children in Western Samoa, *Language in Society*, 11, 77–104.

Palinscar, A. S. (1986), The role of dialogue in providing scaffolded instruction, *Educational Psychologist*, 21 (1 and 2), 73–98.

Phillips, S. (1972), Participant structures and communicative competence: Warm Springs children in community and classroom, in C. Cazden, D. Hymes, and V. John (eds), *Functions of Language in the Classroom* (New York: Teachers College Press) pp.370–94.

Phillips, S. (1983), *The Invisible Culture: Communication in the Classroom and on the Warm Springs Indian Reservation* (New York: Longman).

Rogoff, B. (1982), Integrating context and cognitive developmentally, in M.E and A.L. Brown (eds), *Advances in developmental psychology* Vol.2 (Hillsdale, NJ: Lawrence Erlbaum Associates) pp.125–70.

Rogoff, B. (1984), Adult assistance of children's learning, in T.E. Raphael (ed.), *The Contexts of School-Based Literacy* (New York: Random House).

Rogoff, B., and Gardener, W. (1984), Adult guidance of cognitive development, in B. Rogoff and J. Lave (eds), *Everyday Cognition: Its Development in Social Contexts* (Cambridge: Harvard University Press) pp.95–116.

Rueda, R. and Mehan, H. (1986), Metacognition and passing: strategic interactions in the lives of students with learning disabilities, *Anthropology and Education Quarterly*, 17 (3), 145–65.

Rueda, R. and Mercer, J. (in preparation), *Labeling Linguistic Minorities* (University of Southern California & University of California, Riverside).

Sabsay, S. and Kernan, K. T. (1983), Communicative design in the speech of mildly retarded adults, in K. T. Kernan, M.J. Begab and R. B. Edgerton (eds), *Settings and Behavior of Retarded Persons* (Baltimore: University Park Press) pps.283–94.

Schneider, P., Hyland, J. T. and Gallimore, R. (1985), The zone of proximal development in eighth grade social studies, *The Quarterly Newsletter of the Laboratory of Comparative Human Cognition* 7 (4), 113–19.

Scollon, R. and Scollon, S. (1981), *Narrative, Literacy, and Face in Interethnic Communication*. Norwood, N.J.: Ablex Pub. Corp.

Speidel, G. E. (in press), Conversation and language learning in the classroom, in K. E. Nelson and A. van Kleeck (eds), *Child Language*, Vol.6. (Hillsdale, NJ: Lawrence Erlbaum Associates).

Speidel, G. S., Gallimore, R., Kobayashi, L. and Hao, R. (1983), Contextual cues in transfer of learning, *Quarterly Newletter of the Laboratory of Comparative Human Cognition*, 5 (2), 40–3.

Tharp, R. G. (1982), The effective instruction of comprehension: results and description of the Kamehameha Early Education Program, *Reading Research Quarterly*, 17 (4), 503–27.

Tharp, R. G. (1984), *A Cross-Cultural Comparison of Educational Effectiveness: Navajo and Hawaiian Instances*. Paper and Chair, Symposium at the Meetings of the National Indian Education Association, Phoenix, November.

Tharp, R. G. (1985), *Wholism and the 'Observational-Learning Complex': A Comparative Study of Comprehension Instruction Among Navajo and Hawaiians*. Meetings of the National Indian Education Association, Spokane, October.

Tharp, R. G. and Gallimore, R. (1979), The ecology of program research and evaluation: a model of evaluation succession, in L. B. Sechrest (ed.), *Evaluation Studies Annual Review*, Vol.4, (Beverly Hills, CA: Sage Publications), pp. 39–60.

Tharp, R. G. and Gallimore, R. (1982), Inquiry processes in program development, *Journal of Community Psychology* 10, 103–18.

Tharp, R. G. and Gallimore, R. (in press), *Rousing Minds to Life: in Social Context of Teaching, Learning and Schooling* (Cambridge: Cambridge University Press).

Tharp, R. G., Jordan, C., Speidel, G. E., Au, K. H., Klein, T. W., Calkins, R. P., Sloat, K. C. M. and Gallimore, R. (1984), Product and process in applied developmental research: education and the children of a minority, in M. E. Lamb, A. L. Brown and B. Rogoff (eds), *Advances in Developmental Psychology*, Vol.III, (Hillsdale, New Jersey: Lawrence Erlbaum & Associates) pp.91–140.

Torgeson, J. K. (1977), The role of nonspecific factors in the task performance of learning disabled children: a theoretical assessment, *Journal of Learning Disabilities*, **10**, 27–34.

Tucker, J. A. (ed.) (1985), Curriculum-based assessment (Special Issue). *Exceptional Children*, **52** (3), 193–304.

Turner, J. L. (1980), Yes, I am human: autobiography of a retarded career, *Journal of Community Psychology*, **8**, 3–8.

Turner, J. L. (1983), Workshop society: ethnographic observations in a work setting for retarded adults, in K. T. Kernan, M. J. Begab and R. B. Edgerton (eds), *Settings and Behavior of Retarded Persons* (Baltimore: University Park Press), pp.141–71.

Vogt, L. A., Jordan, C. and Tharp, R. G. (1987), Explaining school failure, producing school success: two cases, *Anthropology & Education Quarterly* **18**, 276–86.

Vygotsky, L. S. (1956), *Izbrannie Psibhologicheskie Issledovania* (Selected Psychological Research) (Moscow: Izdateel'stro Akademii Pedagogicheskikh Nak).

Vygotsky, L. S. (1960), *Razvitie Vysshikh Psikhicheskikh funktsii.* (The Development of Higher Mental Functions) (Moscow: Izdatel'stvo Academii Pedagogicheskikh Nauk).

Vygotsky, L. S. (1962), *Thought and Language* (Cambridge, MA:MIT Press).

Vygotsky, L. S. (1978), *Mind in Society: The Development of Higher Psychological Processes*: M. Cole, V. John-Steiner, S. Scribner and E. Souberman (eds and trans.) (Cambridge, MA: Harvard University Press).

Vygotsky, L. S. (1981), The genesis of higher mental functions, in J. V. Wertsch (ed.), *The Concept of Activity in Soviet Psychology* (Armonk, NY: Sharpe).

Vygotsky, L. S. (1985), *Izbrannie Psibhologicheskie Issledovania* (Selected Psychological Research.) (Moscow: Izdateel'stro Akademii Pedagogicheskikh Nak, 1956). Transl. and quoted in Wertsch, J. V. and Stone, C. A. The concept of internalization in Vygotsky's account of the genesis of higher mental functions, in Wertsch, J. V. (ed.) (1985), *Culture, Communication and Cognition: Vygotskian Perspectives* (New York: Cambridge University Press).

Vygotsky, L. S. (in press), *Collected Works Vol.2*, Minick, N. (trans.) (originally published 1934; New York: Plenum).

Watson-Gegeo, K. and Boggs, S. T. (1977), From verbal play to talk-story: the role of routines in speech events among Hawaiian children, in S. Ervin-Tripp and C. Mitchell-Kernan (eds), *Child Discourse* (New York: Academic Press).

Weisner, T. S., Gallimore, R. and Jordan, C. (1986), *Unpackaging Cultural Effects on Classroom Learning: Hawaiian Peer Assistance and Child-Generated Activity* (Los Angeles: University of California, Department of Psychiatry & Biobehavioral Sciences).

Weisner, T., Gallimore, R. and Tharp, R. G. (1982), Concordance between ethnographer and folk perspectives: observed performance and self-ascription of sibling caretaking roles, *Human Organization* **41** (3), 237–44.

Wertsch, J. V. (1978), Adult-child interaction and the roots of metacognition, *Quarterly Newsletter of the Laboratory of Comparative Human Cognition*, **2** (1), 15–18.

Wertsch, J. V. (1979), From social interaction to higher psychological process: a clarification and application of Vygotsky's theory, *Human Development*, **22**, 1–22.

Wertsch, J. V. (1981), *The Concept of Activity in Soviet Psychology* (New York: M. E. Sharpe).

Wertsch, J. V. (ed.) (1985), *Vygotsky and the Social Formation of Mind* (Cambridge: Harvard University Press).

Wertsch, J. V., Minick, N. and Arns, F. A. (1984), The creation of context in joint problem-solving, in B. Rogoff and J. Lave (eds), *Everyday Cognition: Its Development in Social Contexts* (Cambridge: Harvard University Press) pp.151–71.

Wertsch, J. V. and Stone, C. A. (1985), 'The concept of internalization in Vygotsky's account of the genesis of higher mental functions', in J. V. Wertsch (ed.), *Culture, communication and cognition: Vygotskian perspectives* (New York: Cambridge University Press), pp.162–179.

White, S., Tharp, R. G., Jordan, C. and Vogt, L. (in press), Cultural patterns of cognition reflected in the questioning styles of Anglo and Navajo teachers, in D. Topping, V. Kobayshi and D. C. Crowell (eds), *Thinking: The Third International Conference* (Hillside, NJ: Lawrence Erlbaum Associates).

Wood, D. J. (1980), Teaching the young child: some relationships between social interaction, language, and thought, in R. Olson (ed.), *The Social Foundations of Language and Thought* (New York: W. W. Norton & Co.) pp. 280–96.

Wood, D. J., Bruner, J. S. and Ross, G. (1976), The role of tutoring in problem solving, *Jounal of Child Psychology and Psychiatry*, **17** (2), 89–100.

Zetlin, A. G. and Gallimore, R. (1980), A cognitive skills training program for moderately retarded learners, *Education and Training of the Mentally Retarded*, **15** (2), 121–31, reprinted in J. Jacobs (ed.), *Mental Retardation: A Phenomenological Approach* (Springfield, IL: Charles C. Thomas).

Zetlin, A. G. and Gallimore, R. (1983), The development of comprehension strategies through the regulatory function of teacher questions, *Education and Training of the Mentally Retarded*, **18** (3), 176–84.

Chapter 4

Skill Generalization and Children with Learning Difficulties
David Sugden

When skills are being learned either incidentally or through some form of instruction, it is hoped that they can be used in situations other than the one in which they were originally learned. This simple statement describes the process of transfer or generalization, and hides a multitude of complexities involved in the nature and approaches to the teaching of this skill. The aim in this chapter is to elaborate on the above statement, working through each aspect of the generalization process. First there is a description of the process itself, what it involves, the various levels that can be included, and the problems that children face in school if they have difficulty with generalization. Second, there is an examination of cognitive skills and generalization within them. Third, an outline of a recently conducted study involving generalization is presented. Finally, guidelines for promoting effective generalisation will be offered with suggestions as to how they can be incorporated into the classroom situation.

Nature of Generalization

Description of the Process

Consider a child learning to read. The child has to quickly recognize that the same prose may vary slightly from text to text. The layout of the page may vary; the type may be smaller or larger or may even be different altogether as in the variations of letters such as 'a', 'g', 't', 'y', or indeed almost all the alphabet. The context in which reading takes place is also different: an English reader is not set out in the same manner as instructions on a card in craft design technology. Yet the child has to recognise that modifications of the same skill are required in order to complete the task. This is a fundamental requirement not only of our education in school, but similar situations are present outside school. When children listen to people talking, at school, at home, on the television, radio, at the cinema, they are again faced with generalization problems. They need to be able to generalize from different voices, emphases, and accents in order to extract meaning from verbal language.

In the performance of motor skills, we are faced with a similar situation. Motor-skill problems constantly provide novel situations in which children have to adapt previously learned responses. Skills of everyday living such as working a washing or vending machine will necessitate generalization because of the slight variations in each of the machines. Simple operations such as the working of a switch may be a stumbling block, because one switch may need a twist while a flip was required in the original learning situation. The sporting arena also provides numerous examples of the generalization process. A basketball player working on a skill in practice has to be able to bring that skill to the game situation. Similarly young tennis players attempt to generalize their skill training to a competitive match. A golfer who has learned a particular shot with both feet level and the recommended distance apart will have to adapt this swing when on a slope, or when the backswing is shortend because of an overhanging branch. The ability to perform skills across all appropriate situations in an environment involves producing different variations of a class of responses in different situations. The chapter by Connell provides detail of this process.

Social skills provide another arena where generalization can be viewed. At a very simple level a child learns to say 'thank you' after having received a gift or when someone has helped them. This generalizes to a great number of situations involving shopping, travelling, and even to saying 'no thankyou' when the appropriate situation arises. At a different level, a child showing behaviour difficulties may be helped by a tightly structured teaching environment. Eventually however, the child has to be able to generalize the appropriate behaviour to situations that are not as tightly organized. The chapter by Galvin will elaborate upon this.

A final important, but not so obvious example is in cognitive skills. A child aiming to remember certain items may perform various operations to facilitate this process. He or she may group the information so that like items are organized together, or may elaborate the information by placing it in the context of a short story. Both of these processes will facilitate retention. Generalization occurs when the child can recognize a number of similar situations that would benefit from this process.

The preceeding examples illustrate the different forms of generalization, stressing that it is a fundamental requirement both in and out of the school situation. Without it we would be severely hampered in our daily lives. If we had to start again every time we came to a novel situation, we would only have a tiny fraction of the repertoire of skills we possess. Our teaching techniques have had tremendous success with teaching individual skills. We task analyse the skill, learn each component part and then place it back into the wholistic setting. However, it is obvious that we have not enough time to do this with all skills across all situations. Therefore generalization is a necessity.

So far the process of generalization has been described in global terms as though it were a unitary concept. Upon closer examination, the process can be broken down into at least three component parts. First, there is the learning of the particular skill, such as a forehand drive in tennis, the elaboration of a picture into a story, the reception of a compliment or an initial blend in reading. Second, there is the retention of this skill over time. Most definitions of learning would differentiate between a temporary occurrence and the more stable permanent performance, which is necessary for the generalization process. Third, there has to be a recognition of the situations in which this skill can be used. The child has to analyse the learning situation, recognizing the demands a skill will place on their personal resources.

Children with Learning Difficulties

Children with learning difficulties are identified because they have problems with a variety of skills in and out of the school situation. These skills can be cognitive, linguistic, social, motor, adaptive or a host of others. As in Chapter 1, the description of children with learning difficulties is made in terms of skills, and is based upon their performance on tasks they are required to perform in the school environment. Organic impairment and socio-economic status are important descriptors, but performance on skills is the crucial variable for diagnostic assessment and programme development.

In general terms, how do children with learning difficulties perform in the classroom? First, they do not reach the same *level* of performance as other children. For example, they do not progress as far in mathematics often having difficulty with basic addition, subtraction, multiplication and division. Reading is often below that which would be expected for their chronological age. There are great variations in the attainment levels of children with learning difficulties, and there are problems of accurate identification. But in spite of this most professionals would place level of learning as a primary characteristic of children with learning difficulties.

Second, children with learning difficulties very often learn at a slower *rate* than other children. Typically our learning is characterized by fast initial progress followed by a slowing down as learning progresses. Learning curves depicting this are known as negatively accelerated, indicating that the rate of learning slows down after the initial burst. Another type of curve involves very slow learning in the beginning and then a speeding up in the rate as learning progresses. This curve is known as a positively accelerated curve and is typically seen on very difficult tasks and in children with learning difficulties. In both cases, there is difficulty with the early part of the task as the relevant cues are difficult to select. This will have an obvious effect on the rate of learning.

A third and fundamental characteristic of children with learning difficulties, and the one that is central to this chapter, is their problems with *generalization*. They do not appear to make the same links as other children and often stay in a fixed mode of responding. Campione and Brown (1981) note that the children do not appear to have 'flexible access' to cognitive structures that enable them to learn more efficiently. The skill appears to be welded to the context in which it was first learned. It is not the case that these children never generalize; we do have examples of them doing so. However, in directed learning situations, they do not appear to make spontaneous generalizations across time, material, situations and persons as readily as other children. Teachers report that the children learn material in isolation, not connecting it to other learning. Thus the process which is arguably central to effective functioning both in and out of school appears to be less fully developed in children with learning difficulties.

Generalization and Cognitive Processes

Strategies and Control Operations

In Chapters 1 and 2 there was an outline of how human behaviour can be explained in terms of cognitive processes, and in all cognitive processing models, the concept of memory has played a major role. By the middle 1960s, there was interest in the memory capabilities of children with moderate learning difficulties. Most researchers at that time were working under the short-term, long-term memory paradigms, which are not nearly as popular today. However they found that children with learning difficulties had a deficiency in working or short-term memory in which information was held for a short period of time while it was being used, and then either forgotten or stored more permanently. During this short period of time, various mnemonic strategies are employed such as rehearsal, organization, visual imagery, verbal elaboration and directed forgetting. A number of classic studies found children with learning difficulties to be deficient in the spontaneous production of these strategies (Belmont and Butterfield, 1969; Ellis, 1970; Brown, 1974). There was no suggestion that these children never used such strategies, only that they were not as spontaneously produced as in other children.

Rehearsal overwhelmingly has been the most popular strategy to teach, and this simply involves giving overt or covert attention to a particular piece of information that has recently been presented. Every day we use this strategy to remember telephone numbers, directions for travel, shopping lists, and instructions, by repeating the information either out loud or silently. Laboratory experiments and everyday experience tell us the same thing: this strategy aids retention. Kail (1984) has suggested that there are at least two questions concerning age-related changes in rehearsal.

The first involves the age at which we find the first evidence of rehearsal, and the second surrounds its developmental progression. From studies on remembering pictures and words, it seems that rehearsal appears at around 7 years of age, when it is used in a quite rudimentary manner, but children become increasingly proficient from the age of 9 or 10. With age, children also become more flexible in their usage of rehearsal, such as re-ordering into groups and points to remember which facilitate rehearsal. For younger children, rehearsal appears to consist of rote repetition of words or pictures in a list; adolescents modify the rehearsal process to the structure of the material to be remembered.

Kail (1984) has also suggested that of the other strategies, some can be used for the storage of information, while others are more beneficial to the retrieval of information. Grouping strategies are used for the storage of information, and usually involve organizing the to-be-remembered material into some grouping that will aid in the retention of the material. This is quite a sophisticated strategy and is usually seen later than rehearsal. Retrieval strategies have been said to involve qualities akin to those of Sherlock Holmes (Flavell and Wellman, 1977). When a memorizer knows the information is available, he or she waits, and then deliberately searches for related information that is close to the desired material. This search strategy is seen in about a third of 6 year olds, three quarters of 8 year olds, and 90 per cent of 11 year olds. This rise in usage is accompanied by a similar rise in the number of items remembered. The older children also use the strategy in much more efficient and flexible ways.

The ages quoted above as to when children acquire particular strategies appear to be unduly pessimistic. We all have everyday examples of preschoolers remembering items very well indeed. So what is happening? Kail (1984) has suggested that 3 and 4 year olds do not apply strategies to material that is school-based such as remembering words or numbers, but do so in their relevant world of finding toys or books etc. It is as though the developmentally young child is dependent upon relevant context for the appropriate production of strategies. These strategies are uncomplicated, but they do develop into the sophisticated flexible, verbal and semantic strategies we see in later years.

The evidence from studies involving children with learning difficulties points to them using strategies such as these less often and less efficiently than their peers (Belmont and Butterfield, 1969; Brown, 1972; 1974; Campione and Brown, 1977; Ellis, 1970). After these deficiencies were found, it was a natural progression to attempt to teach them, and from the early 1970s to the present time, many training studies have been reported. The early training studies showed some success (Butterfield *et al*, 1973; Turnure and Thurlow, 1973). By a carefully structured programme, using task analysis, repetition and lots of time, rehearsal could be produced by individuals who previously did not employ it. To evaluate such a teaching programme, two important criteria need to be examined.

implication

First, it is important that the strategy is durable; that its effects will be retained over a substantial period of time. It is no use teaching a strategy, and then find that its effects are limited to a few days. Second, the effects ought to generalize. The question of durability was easily resolved with a number of studies showing individuals still proficient on a strategy six months after originally being taught (Brown, *et al.*, 1974; Burger *et al.*, 1980). Generalization was a different matter.

Although some of the early studies were successful, doubts were raised about their practicality in schools, first because of the time involved, but more importantly because the children did not generalize the strategy. They could perform the strategy when requested, but when they were given a different task closely related to the one on which they had learned the strategy, they failed to employ the strategy in this new situation. They had learned the strategy in the first instance because when they were placed back in the original situation, they immediatley adopted the strategy again. The strategy was locked into one situation: the children had failed to generalize a cognitive strategy, just as every day we see children failing to generalize mathematics strategy. This is a failure in control operations, or executive control. The child has the strategy but has difficulty in identifying the situations in which this strategy would be effective.

Thus although impressive maintenance effects have been found, the results on generalization are not so encouraging. It is as though the children have tunnel vision with regard to the strategy: it appears to be welded to the situation in which it is learned. In order to remedy this situation, we should not teach a routine aimed at a specific task, but should use a more general programme involving strategies, their use and control. This teaching approach started to be used with some success in the late 1970s, and our project, which will be described later, incorporated this principle.

From our work on normal children, and those with learning difficulties, it does appear that in order for a child to be able to generalize a cognitive strategy such that it affects all of the information they receive, they have to be competent in two areas. First, they need to learn the strategy and be comfortable with it. This strategy must be maintained over time, and should be taught in such a way as understanding of it is a priority. This leads to the second area, in which they have to learn when and where to apply this strategy for optimal usage. This second aspect is obviously the key area to generalization and to explore it a little more we need to examine the concept of metacognition.

Metacognition

In the last few years this has become a popular term in psychology and often it has been misused in an educational context. Wellman (1983) notes that it is a fuzzy concept, being a cover term referring to a family of knowledge about memory and cognition. It has a developmental progression, and has a positive, though ill-specified role in the performance of cognitive and memory tasks. Flavell (1971) notes that metacognition involves thinking about one's own perceiving, understanding and memory, with some of these labelled metamemory, or metaperception, but with metacognition remaining the superordinate term. He then distinguishes between metacognitive knowledge and metacognitive experience. The former is relatively stable information about cognition, usually knowledge about ourselves, the task we perform, and the strategies we employ. Thus there is more to being competent in the strategies described above. Once the strategies have been learned, metacognitive knowledge is that which determines which situations are suitable for which strategy.

Flavell (1985) believes that metacognitive knowledge is not qualitatively different from any other kinds of knowledge, in that it grows with maturation and experience, can be activated automatically, and can be flawed. Metacognitive knowledge serves as a base for metacognitive experiences which are task based and usually deal with progressing towards the goal of a particular activity. During reading, individuals may realize that by rehearsing, they will be better able to remember the dates or names in the prose. They may also realize that key sentences often in bold type may help. Each component of metacognition can prompt each of the others. These concepts have been used widely in psychology, and their use has spread into education in tasks such as reading (Garner, 1987).

Learning and memory are directly related to each other, and very often difficult to separate. Learning is an internal process denoting some kind of change as a result of experience. An internal process obviously cannot be seen, and so we use behavioural measures calling upon memory to determine if learning has taken place. When a child begins a learning situation, metacognitive processes are involved in three spheres. First, the child must realize that situations exist in which there is a need to remember. Again there are developmental progressions in the process of a child acknowledging that previous information is relevant to the task on hand. This general point is also a starting point for the generalization of a skill.

Second, there is the manner in which a child diagnoses the objective of a task, and selects the best way to achieve that objective. Here the child has to assess the difficulty of the task, and in effect to perform his/her own task analyses. This is a fundamental difference between cognitive approaches and those which are more behavioural in nature. In the latter, the teacher performs the task analysis from her or his diagnosis of the task. This may be quite correct from the teacher's viewpoint, but totally wrong from that of the child. When analysing a task, a child has to assess his or her own personal resources and relate these to the perceived demands of the task. A process of evaluation is involved with the linking of various strategies to predicted performance.

After this has taken place the child has to select a memory strategy likely to achieve the desired goal. This again is a process that lies in the heart of generalization. A child can perform a strategy which leads to increased performance on a particular task, but may not choose to use it again in a similar situation. It may be that the child does not realize that the strategy was responsible for the increased learning. As shall be stressed later, a key feature in teaching for transfer is keeping the child fully informed as to why he or she has performed well; in this case because he or she has used the appropriate strategy.

The third metacognitive process that is involved in learning is that of monitoring the information that is being acquired. The monitoring process can be broken down into stages. First the child has to determine the extent to which they have learned something. Preschoolers do this with only minimal success, but by 7 years of age, children are quite competent. The next stage is how they allocate attention to the various parts of the learned material, and whether this is the most efficient. For example, is more attention given to material that is well known, or that which is not? It is more efficient to give attention to the latter, and again developmental differences are seen with 7/8 year olds concentrating on unlearned material, while 5/6 year olds concentrate on the learned material.

The above processes make up what is called metacognition. When we use this in memory tasks it involves an awareness that a situation calls for remembering. It involves choosing skills that are used to diagnose the difficulty of a memory task and allocate the appropriate strategy. Finally it involves monitoring the effect of that choice on the memory task. These abilities are required on any task that is to be learned; thus they become crucial to a task that involves the use of previous learning: that is a task involving generalization.

Teaching Verbal Elaboration in Schools

Recently, we took some of our ideas and put them into a school situation (Sugden and Newall 1987). We chose to teach the strategy of verbal elaboration which involves transforming information into one's own frame of reference such that it can be easily remembered. The strategy is also called semantic elaboration, and this really describes what the child is doing. Information is taken in by the child and is elaborated by giving it meaning. This meaning is obviously related to the child's own schema surrounding the particular subject matter. So if a child sees a picture or listens to a story about a girl and her dog, that child can elaborate and even modify the story into his or her own frame of reference that facilitates memory. To do this, the child has to recognise that the story can and needs to be actively transformed or elaborated, and this will be beneficial to its being remembered. It is not enough to be able to perform the strategy. If this strategy is to be particularly useful, the child will use it across a range of subject matter in a variety of contexts. This is generalization and the child has to recognise these multiple situations, all of which would benefit from this strategy.

The strategy is language-based and ideally lends itself to the classroom situation. It involves the child's talking with another person, in this case a teacher, who takes the child beyond what he or she would achieve without this help. We decided to teach it over a long period of time, going beyond the usual short-term learning experiment that often characterizes this type of study. Thus the teaching was done weekly over a period of six months with the children being assessed at various stages of the programme. Long-term effects were then measured up to a year after the programme had finished.

Our overall aim was to help children use the strategy of verbal elaboration in a variety of settings so that they learn more efficiently. We selected children with poor memories and who appeared to have a passive approach to learning in that they seemingly did not use strategies on information that was presented to them. Our sample was 15 children out of a possible 40 from two special schools, and these 15 were chosen because they had the poorest memories in the group, together with an apparent lack of mnemonic strategies. They had a mean chronological age of 120 months with a mean reading age of 87 months.

The children were assessed on four occasions: at the beginning, mid-point and end of the teaching session, and 9 months after the teaching programme had finished. Three different modes of assessment were used: first, remembering pictures presented in various ways to determine if strategies were being used; second, answering questions on prose material that was read to the children; finally, inventing a verbal story, and answering questions on it. Thus our modes of assessment ranged from fairly tight quantitative analysis to more open-ended and less structured methods.

Our aim was to teach verbal elaboration in such a way that it transferred across tasks and materials, and to do this, we had quite specific characteristics in our programme. First, the children were actively involved; they were not just allowed to be passive recipients of environmental stimuli but were required to expand information that was presented to them. Second, the process had been subjected to a task analysis and the various components were introduced sequentially. Finally, there was strong teacher involvement and support in the beginning, but this was reduced and eventually eliminated by the end of the six-month teaching period.

The following is an illustration of a child who completed all of the programme. The child was first taught verbal elaboration using pictures, as it was thought this would be more stimulating and did not place any demands upon reading ability. The teacher first explained what she was going to do and then showed a pair of large brightly coloured pictures. She took one of the pictures, say a pair of running shoes, said what is was, and then told a story about the picture. She did this with a number of pictures and then asked the child to do one. Thus the child had to say what the picture was and then tell a story about it.

In order to help the child, various enabling questions were asked: What type of shoes are these? When would you use them? Why are they like that? Do they help you to run faster? Would they be good for other activities? The plan was for the teacher to reduce this prompting, eventually expecting the children to go through the questioning on their own. This type of questioning is explained more fully in Chapter 3 by Gallimore *et al*. A child can only progress so far on their own, and then with skilful assistance can reach a different level. Vygotsky (1978) uses the term 'zone of proximal development' which describes the difference between what the child can achieve alone, and what can be done with assistance. The child is not able to answer overall questions such as 'Can you describe this picture?' or 'Tell me a story about these two pictures'. Neither can the child break the task down into sub-questions. However, the child can answer smaller unit questions when devised and asked by someone else. Eventually we are aiming for the child to generate his or her own questions and answer them; this is the essence of verbal elaboration.

After several pictures had been used, the next step was the invention of a story which linked two pictures together. For example a picture of running shoes followed by a picture of a cool drink could be linked by a story about running, being hot, and needing a drink. Many examples were used and the teacher support was gradually withdrawn until the children themselves could go through the whole process of self-questioning and generating a story. At the beginning of each session, there was a recap of work done in the previous session. Another strategy that was employed involved the teacher showing just one of the pair from the previous session, and then asking if the children could remember the other one and the story that went with the pair. By the end of the seventh session, most of the children were competent in using this strategy, with one or two of them still requiring the occasional prompt.

In the next phase, words were introduced to accompany the pictures. The pictures were kept as an aid to the children, but they were eventually dropped, when we realized that the children were elaborating the words without reference to the pictures. By the end of the first term, the children could use verbal elaboration with both words and pictures, and could link pairs of pictures of words by the invention of a story. During the second term there was an extension of the work done in the first term, and we increasingly required the children to go beyond the information that was actually presented. Story invention was one way in which this was done, with the teacher beginning a story and the children extending it. Again lots of examples were given so that the children could generalize over a wide range of subject matter. Once the children carried on the teacher's story, they would then be asked questions about the story they had invented. Increasingly we were looking for the flexible allocation of learned skills into new situations.

The results showed that some success had been achieved in our original aim. If an overall score was taken comprising tests of visual and prose recall, the children had an original mean of 21, out of a possible 48, which rose to 28 at the end of the training, and to 32 nine months after the programme had finished. Scores on most parts of the test increased rapidly by the end of the first term, and followed by either a slowing down in the rate of improvement, or as in one case by a plateau effect. The prose test changed throughout the test occasions because the children could easily answer the level we initially gave them after they had completed the first term's work. Thus we increased the difficulty level of the questions, and the actual number was increased.

On average by the end of the teaching sessions the children were answering correctly two-thirds of a longer and more difficult test, compared with between one-third and one-half correct in the first two tests. Different items were used each time the test was given. A further test was given involving answering questions to stories the children had generated. They were given a sentence, and then had to produce a story to follow on from that sentence. After the completion of the story, the teacher asked the children a number of questions about the story. On the first testing session, it was often difficult to generate enough questions because of the sparseness of the invented story. After the teaching sessions all children generated a story with enough detail to generate six questions, and some of them were so complex that many more could have been asked.

Qualitative evaluation of the children also took place. They were observed in every teaching session with notes made about their approach to learning, and comments were received from the class teacher. During the first teaching sessions, the children did not appear to be actively involved in the learning process. They had little idea how to approach the tasks we gave them. They did not actively transform the information and it was as if the material as opposed to the child was the important partner in the learning process. At the end of the programme this situation was reversed with most of the children dominating the material, and placing it into a framework they had imposed. This was noticeable in the recall of pictorial and verbal items: many of the children started to organize items into natural groups which made recall easier. We did not actually teach this although we did make the children aware of such groupings. Tape recordings of the children's invented stories allowed us to analyse the more involved and complex stories. Finally, class teachers made unprompted comments about many of the children's eagerness to speak in class and their improved verbal skills.

Overall the results were encouraging. Gains were made that were statistically significant, and these gains maintained over a nine-month period, with no further direct teaching on the skills. Results from the paired presentation of pictures mirrored the overall scores, with fast improvement followed by a plateau effect together with long-term retention. Memory of individual pictures only improved after the second testing session, suggesting that a strategy for remembering these was a little harder to generate, or as the children during the teaching sessions were practising with paired items, it may have taken time for the training effects to generalize to individual presentations. No improvements were seen on the organized presentation suggesting that there are limits to the transfer that can be generated. It appears that there may be a class of events to which a certain cognitive skill can be applied. The results from the verbal presentations and invented stories were very encouraging. More difficult items in greater numbers were retained, and the children were inventing longer and more complex stories. This did lead to a slight deterioration in memory performance on the last test, but we feel that it was due to the complexity of the stories rather than any deterioration in memory.

We were pleased with the results, and it does appear that a cognitive strategy can be taught to generalize across material, and be robust over time. However, it still does not weaken the proposal that for children with moderate learning difficulties, improvement in generalization is a major objective in their education. The qualified success on this particular study was obtained only after great thought in designing the programme, followed by careful teaching. Also there were still one or two children in the group who did not spontaneously use the strategy. They had improved from their original scores, but they could not really be described as having flexible access to these strategies.

Guidelines for Teaching Generalization

Our work in the schools has been based upon the results of research studies over the last 15 years. These studies have shown that generalization can be achieved, but this achievement is hard won and has to be weighed up against the expenditure of energy and resources. Brown and Campione (1986) note:

> Regardless of one's theoretical bias, which class of learning theories one espouses, etc., the central problem remains the same – how to persuade learners to use the fruits of past learning in novel domains; how to induce the flexible use of acquired knowledge. (p. 258)

Brown and Campione are fond of using the term 'flexible access' to describe generalization, indicating that the mature learner is characterized by the ability to make information available and utilize it in a variety of settings. In order to achieve true generalization the child has to break away from the 'welding' of a skill to a particular situation. This has to be replaced by flexible use of the skill across contexts. From their work they have produced guidelines that they believe will induce this flexible access.

When teaching pupils it is usually an aim to foster independent learning, and dialogue with pupils to achieve this includes the comprehension fostering activities of summarizing, questioning, clarifying and predicting. Brown and Campione (1986) believe these four activities can be brought into the daily dialogue of the classroom, and often involves the pupils' attempting to teach other pupils. The teacher assigns a passage to be read by him or herself and indicates that he or she or one of the pupils is to do the teaching. After the passage has been read the teacher (pupil or classteacher) summarizes the content and then starts to ask questions. These are the summarizing, questioning, clarifying and predicting activities, and should be embedded in as natural a dialogue as possible with students and teacher giving each other feedback. Within this framework, we can pull out the recommendations for promoting generalization.

A first recommendation would be standard whatever theoretical background one came from, and that is that the skill area must be understood to a depth that affords detailed task analysis. Brown and Campione (1986) call this 'know your domain' and stress that if the teacher has difficulty in seeing the relationship between two skills then certainly the learner will not see it. If he or she has a thorough knowledge of the skill area, then s/he can design teaching situations which form a representative sample of the occasions when the skill can be employed. Some skills may have components in common, and may be generalizable. However, at first glance these components may not be obvious, and it is only with a thorough knowledge that the links can be seen and made available to the pupils. The activities of summarizing, questioning, clarifying and predicting were chosen from a task analysis of what is involved in reading comprehension. These serve the purpose of enhancing comprehension, while also acting as a monitor to the learner as to whether understanding is occurring. Thus the overall recommendation is that the teacher knows the 'domain' so well that he or she can break it down in a number of different ways, and can illustrate a variety of ways in which skills link with each other.

The second recommendation requires the teacher to know the individual learner. This is not just to know which books the child can or cannot read or what level they are at, but involves the recognition that the same level of performance is very often obtained in different ways by two children. When faced by a novel task, different children will select different parts of the task to direct their attention. It is important to diagnose the types of errors children make rather than concentrating solely on the correct performance. This is illustrated when the child is learning to read and the teacher performs some type of miscue analysis. Errors that are typically seen include omissions, repetitions, reversals, hesitations, substitutions, additions, and children will differ in the type that they make. They will also differ on the level of the error they are making.

Some children when faced with an unknown word will be guided purely by the physical shape of the word and make a phonographemic error, by saying for example 'window' instead of 'went'. The word is semantically and syntactically incorrect but looks similar to the original. Other children will make errors that are syntactically correct but not semantically. So they will substitute 'buy' for 'bring'. They are both verbs but substituting them would not make sense. Finally there are children who make errors even though the word is semantically correct, such as substituting 'desk' for 'table'. Error patterns give us great insight into the way the child is approaching the task, and must be taken into account when trying to induce generalization. Similar error analysis can be made in the mathematics area; for example in addition the concept of 'carrying' can induce a number of different types of errors.

Miscue analysis and mathematics are obvious examples when examining errors, but there are other ways even though some are not as easy to translate into the educational context. We have a long history of the study of learning styles in psychology, with many bipolar scales such as field dependence–field independence, and reflectivity–impulsitivity, and we have only to watch children approach a novel task to see these styles in action. For example, some children may learn a task by proceeding cautiously making fewer errors as they progress, whereas other children may work faster, continue to generate novel responses, but not reduce the number of errors. Follow this by an analysis of the type of errors each child is making and the teacher is really getting to know the learning style of the child and how each one is processing information to aid them on a particular task. This has obvious implications for how the task will be presented and organized in order to facilitate generalization.

Brown and Campione's (1986) third recommendation is that the teaching of a particular skill should be done in as many settings as is possible. It seems pretty obvious that if lack of generalization means that the child will only use a skill in the context within which it was learned, then teach the skill in a variety of contexts. This is where teaching skill becomes particularly evident. It is obvious that there is not enough time to teach a skill in every possible situation in which it may be used. Thus the teacher has to select a sample of skills that cover the whole range of possibilities that the child may face. When we were teaching verbal elaboration (Sugden and Newall, 1987), we used single pictures which were changed frequently; we used pairs of pictures which again were frequently changed; we used single words, followed by verbal presentation of a story; and finally we used story invention. All of these were aimed at providing a sample of situations that the child would normally experience such that they could use the strategy over all of them.

Across the teaching situations there should be a common factor or rule (in our case it was verbal elaboration), and this factor must be made explicit to the children. It is asking too much to expect the children on their own to see the links between the various situations. It must be pointed out to them what is the aim, and why these situations are linked. In this way we are directly teaching generalization. It is always useful to put in examples where the particular strategy is not useful. The training situation can be built up in this way so that eventually a range of situations is presented, and the children have to determine which ones would be facilitated by the particular strategy that had been learned.

Support for multiple settings or variable practice comes from a variety of sources, including the influential schema learning theory applied to motor skills. This basically states that in order to increase retention and facilitate generalization, practice on a variety of examples within a particular class of events is much more potent at all stages of learning than practice on one single instance (Schmidt, 1975). An extension of this is the concept of contextual interference, which is established by practising, in no particular order, several different but related tasks during the practice session (Battig, 1979). The learner is lured into producing more distinctive and elaborate cognitive processing strategies which will facilitate retention and generalize to related tasks. In non-handicapped individuals, we have strong evidence for the efficacy of schema learning and contextual interference (Battig, 1979; Goode and Magill, 1986; Lee and Magill, 1983). In children with learning difficulties the evidence is available, if not quite as strong (Edwards *et al.*, 1986; Porretta, 1982). There are still many questions to answer about multiple settings. For example, how 'wide' should the settings be? Obviously, we want to generalize to as many contexts as possible, but aiming for width may sacrifice the linking process. This is particularly important with children who have problems making such links in the first place.

A fourth recommendation has been labelled 'expert scaffolding' by Brown and Campione (1986). This refers to an expert, usually a teacher or parent, but it could be a peer, who guides the novice learner through the learning situation. Initially this person takes the major role, showing the child what to do, and serving as an effective model. The children are encouraged to watch and then participate in a social situation before attempting the task on their own. In this way, responsibility is initially with the group for the task, and only when this is established does the individual take it on their own. Thus there is high support in the first instance with this support being gradually reduced so that the child takes over. In our study (Sugden and Newall, 1987), the teacher was the expert and first showed the children what to do by presenting a picture and telling a story about it. This she did several times with different pictures before she took pairs of pictures and related them by means of a story. When the children attempted to perform the task, the teacher gave support by means of 'enabling' questions. She steered the children into the strategy of verbal elaboration by her questions.

In the beginning the teacher models the required behaviour, making it overt, concrete, and explicit. As the children became more proficient she asked fewer questions, only moving in when the child appeared to be having a problem. In their chapter, Gallimore *et al.* use the idea of 'assisted performance' in much the same way. Using concepts from Vygotsky, they describe unassisted performance as reflecting the child's current level of functioning, and assisted performance as the next or nearest step of development to come. They conclude their chapter with the basic principle:

> The performance of retarded and learning disabled individuals often improves when they can perform in collaboration with more competent and assisting others. It is the occasion of such collaborations that learning and development are most rapid.

A fifth recommendation directly follows the 'expert scaffolding', and requires the children to be responsible for their own learning; that is they become skilled in self-management. First the children should be aware of the aims of the programme and should be fully informed all the time. They should be shown that the skill actually works for them, and eventually we would like them to be in control of their learning so that they can set goals, work out a plan to achieve those goals, monitor their own progress and evaluate the results. It is in the issue of self-management and awareness that the study of metacognition has become a focal point in educational psychology. The fourth and fifth recommendations very much work together. As the teacher gradually reduces the support, then the child is taking over more and more of the responsibility for his or her own learning, and recognizing the what and why of his or her actions.

As the children are progressing towards competence in a particular skill the teacher provides direct feedback concerning the effectiveness of their learning. Obviously the teacher is selecting strategies to teach that she believes will work, and are effective. However the children are often unaware about the effectiveness. For example if they are unaware that they are using the new skill and it is working for them, they are unlikely to maintain it when the social pressure is not present. Thus qualitative explicit feedback should always be part of the teaching procedure. The feedback is always geared towards the level of the child, such that he will be able to progress gradually to full competence. Reinforcement in terms of praise will also be given, but it is not a sufficient condition for this type of learning to occur.

It is clear that lack of spontaneous generalization is a fundamental characteristic of children with learning difficulties, and this problem is not an easy one to solve. However, the results of research over the last twenty years are starting to bear fruits in terms of specific guidelines for pedagogy. If these guidelines are all employed and incorporated into a structured programme aimed at specific remediation, then there can be cautious optimism for their effectiveness.

References

Battig, W. F. (1979), The flexibility of human memory, in L. Cermack & F. Craik (eds), *Levels of Processing in Human Memory* (Hillsdale, NJ: Erlbaum).

Belmont, J. M. and Butterfield, E. C. (1969), The relations of short term memory to development and intelligence, in L. Lipsitt and H. W. Reese (eds), *Advances in Child Development and Behavior*, Vol 4 (New York: Academic Press).

Brown, A. L. (1972), A rehearsal deficit in retardates' continuous short term memory: keeping track of variables that have few or many states, *Psychonomic Science*, 29, 373–6.

Brown, A. L. (1974), The role of strategic behaviour in retardate memory, in N. R. Ellis (ed.), *International Review of Research in Mental Retardation* (New York: Academic Press).

Brown, A. L. and Campione, J. C. (1986), Training for transfer: guidelines for promoting flexible use of trained skills, in M. G. Wade (ed.), *Motor Skill Acquisition of the Mentally Retarded* (Amsterdam: North Holland).

Brown, A. L., Campione, J. C. and Murphy, M. D. (1974), Keeping track of changing variables: long term retention of a trained rehearsal strategy by retarded adolescents, *American Journal of Mental Deficiency*, 78, 446–53.

Burger, A. L., Blackman, L. S. and Tan, N (1980), Maintenance and generalisation of a sorting and retrieval strategy by EMR and nonretarded individuals, *American Journal of Mental Deficiency*, 84, 373–80.

Butterfield, E. C., Wambold, C. and Belmont, J. M. (1973), On the theory and practice of improving short term memory, *American Journal of Mental Deficiency*, 77, 654–69.

Campione, J. C. and Brown, A. L. (1977), Memory and metamemory development in educable retarded children, in R. V. Kail and J. W. Hagen (eds), *Perspectives on the Development of Memory* (Hillsdale, NJ: Erlbaum).

Campione, J. C. and Brown, A. L. (1981), Inducing flexible thinking: the problem of access, in M. P. Friedman, J. P. Das and N. O'Connor (ed.) *Intelligence and Learning* (New York: Plenum).

Connell, R. E. (1988), Cognitive processes and motor behaviour, in D. A. Sugden (ed.), *Cognitive Approaches in Special Education* (Lewes: Falmer Press).

Edwards, J. M., Elliott, D. and Lee, T. D. (1986), Contextual interference effects during skill acquisition and transfer in Downs' Syndrome adolescents, *Adapted Physical Activity Quarterly*, 3, 250–8.

Ellis, N. R. (1970), Memory processes in retardates and normals, in N. R. Ellis (ed.), *International Review of Research in Mental Retardation*, Vol 4 (New York: Academic Press).

Flavell, J. H. (1971), First discussant's comments: what is memory development the development of?, *Human Development*, 14, 272–8.

Flavell, J. H. (1985), *Cognitive Development*, 2nd edn. (Englewood Cliffs, N. J.: Prentice Hall).

Flavell, J. H. and Wellman, H. M. (1977) 'Metamemory', in R. V. Kail and J. W. Hagen (eds), *Perspectives on the Development of Memory and Cognition* Hillsdale, N. J.: Laurence Erlbaum Associates.

Gallimore, R., Tharp, R. G. and Reuda, R. (1988), The social context of cognitive functioning in the lives of mildly handicapped persons, in D. A. Sugden (ed.), *Cognitive Approaches in Special Education* (Lewes: Falmer Press).

Galvin, P. (1988), Behaviour problems and cognitive processes, in D. A. Sugden (ed.) *Cognitive Approaches in Special Education* (Lewes: Falmer Press).

Garner, R. (1987), *Metacognition and Reading Comprehension* (Norwood, N. J.: Ablex).

Goode, S. and Magill, R. A. (1986), Contextual interference effects in learning three badminton serves, *Research Quarterly for Exercise and Sport*, 57, 308–14.

Kail, R. (1984), *The Development of Memory in Children*, 2nd ed. (New York: Freeman).

Lee, T. D. and Magill, R. A. (1983), The locus of contextual interference in motor skill acquisition, *Journal of Experimental Psychology: Learning, Memory and Cognition*, 9, 730–46.

Porretta, D. L. (1982), Motor schema formation by EMR boys, *American Journal of Mental Deficiency*, **87**, 164–72.

Schmidt, R. A. (1975), A schema theory of discrete motor skill learning, *Psychological Review*, **82**, 225–60.

Sugden, D. A. and Newall, M. (1987), Teaching transfer strategies to children with moderate learning difficulties, *British Journal of Special Education*, **14**, 63–7.

Turnure, J. E. and Thurlow, M. L. (1973), Verbal elaboration and the promotion of transfer of training in educable mentally retarded children, *Journal of Experimental Child Psychology*, **15**, 137–48.

Vygotsky, L. S. (1978), *Mind in Society: The Development of Higher Psychological Processes*: M. Cole, V. John-Steiner, S. Scribner and E. Souberman (eds and trans.) (Cambridge, MA: Harvard University Press).

Wellman, H. M. (1983), Metacognition revisited, in M. T. H. Chi (ed.), *Trends in Memory Development Research* (Basel: Kager).

Chapter 5

Instrumental Enrichment: A Cognitive System
Jacqueline Rutherford

When we deliberately attempt to influence existing cognitive structures so as to maximise reception, learning and attention, we come to the heart of the educational process. (Ausubel, 1966, p.172).

'Look at the cat. What does the cat say? Who else has a cat like this one . . .', the communications which take place between child and adult are rarely seen as being more than a vehicle for the exchange of information. Yet in these interchanges we find the bases of many sophisticated thinking skills, and, through participation in them, the adult helps the child to establish those processes which will enable him or her to cope with far more complex situations and experiences. Taking the example given, we see that the adult unconsciously guides the child through various processes, beginning by focusing attention on a particular item, which he or she conveniently labels, thereby affording it greater significance than peripheral items. He or she expects a response from the child, possibly encourages recall of a previous experience, requests that the child make an association between visual and auditory memory, so that a response to the original stimulus is extracted.

Throughout the interaction, the adult carries an expectation of participation on the part of the child which will indicate understanding, even if only in the form of eye movement or pointing. As these expectations are fulfilled, further exchanges are modified. This may result in the child's being pushed forward into more complex areas, such as anticipation, hypothesizing, classifying, or in the revision or consolidation of the original points.

Fine decisions such as these determine the nature of the interchanges which arise as adults or older siblings communicate with young children. The result is a process of mediation through which the child's contact with the environment is shaped by another person. It is this process, along with a belief that all children regardless of ability or background are open to cognitive modification, which lies at the centre of Feuerstein's Instrumental Enrichment Programme.

Nature of the Programme

Historical Perspective

During the 1950s and '60s, the population of the newly founded State of Israel underwent many significant changes. Among these was the need to absorb into its populace waves of immigrant Jews from areas such as North Africa and the Middle East, all with cultures very different from those of their new home. Many of these young immigrants were taken under the wing of the Youth Aliyah movement and it was here that they encountered Reuven Feuerstein.

Feuerstein was required to undertake the intellectual examination (using standardized clinical assessment techniques) of these young people in order that they might be quickly integrated into their new communities. During this examination, he found that many of his subjects, if scored on the standard IQ test he was using, would be classified as mentally retarded. The significance of this was highlighted when comparisons were made between the results of different cultural groups, and the discrepancies which existed were sufficient to generate unease as to their validity. Feuerstein concluded that the tests being used were inadequate, having evolved as a result of psychologists emphasizing product rather than process. Within the context of the immigrant population where cultures were so variable, this was clearly proving to be an unacceptable means of measuring either ability or potential. Of the three methods presented to him as possible modes of assessment, psychoanalysis, the behaviourist approach and the psychometric approach, Feuerstein found nothing which met with his own ideas about cognition, rather

> direct attention to the operation of the mental processes responsible for the mastery of any content area or skill is still assiduously avoided, and, although the 'black box' is occasionally tampered with, the 'lid' on cognition has not been lifted (1980, p.6).

Feuerstein also stressed the idea of cultural deprivation, believing this caused many of the areas of failure exhibited by those undergoing assessment. Feuerstein and his colleagues operated the premise that the kind of interactions that occur within a family, are established by much broader cultural influences. Removed from those influences – for reasons such as a particular cultural group undergoing traumatic changes and 'fragmenting' as a result, or cultural problems within a particular individual or family 'blocking' the normal routes by which values and attitudes are transmitted – the child may fail in the development of many cognitive skills. Examples of such failure may be:

1   An inability to draw comparisons between items or events.
2   Poor logical reasoning skills.

3   An inability to differentiate between incoming stimuli so that perception of a problem is blurred with no significant features standing out.
4   Poor spatial and temporal organizational skills so that events are seen in isolation, bearing no relation to past or future occurrences.

To encompass many of these weaknesses, Feuerstein uses the term 'an episodic grasp of reality', where each new situation encountered by the subject is seen as being novel, and the individual makes no attempt to relate it to previous experiences. For many who have taught children of low ability, this must be one of the most consistent problems which has to be faced. There are many children for whom a variety of instances or examples does not lead to generalization. Such children seem to lack the ability to formulate 'rules' which they can transfer across to novel situations. What Feuerstein suggests is that had teachers been a little less concerned with content areas and afforded more attention to the processes involved, development of those skills necessary for transfer could have been encouraged.

Learning Potential Assessment Device

Feuerstein maintains that through intervention, gaps such as these can be remedied, but first it is necessary to assess precisely those areas which are inadequately developed. The Learning Potential Assessment Device (LPAD) is designed to pinpoint any area of cognition which is causing poor performance, and also determine learning potential.

In three respects the LPAD differs most significantly from standardized tests of intelligence. First, it is essential that there is rapport established between the tester and the subject. The whole procedure is a dynamic occurrence, and is concerned with the nature of the interaction between the two parties involved. The apparent level at which the individual is functioning is only of partial interest. In addition the tester must try and establish how much the subject is open to modification; to what extent can his or her performance be changed and improved upon within the confines of the assessment situation.

> we would suggest to take as the most important criteria . . . his capacity to become affected, to become modified through planned investment (Feuerstein, 1987).

This results in the second major difference, a swing in emphasis to look at process rather than product. Through operating a test–teach–test formula it becomes possible to monitor both the rapidity with which new skills are acquired, and the ease with which subjects transfer newly acquired skills to problems apparently dissimilar from the original one.

> I would define intelligence as the capacity of the individual to use acquired experience by adapting to new situations (Feuerstein, 1987).

The subject is taken through progressively more difficult tasks until the tester has enough information on which to base his assessment. This prompts the third major deviation from a standardized testing procedure, that of interpretation of results. Questions which the examiner might ask cover areas such as:

1　How rapidly does the child focus on the basic principles being taught?
2　What is the capacity of the child to grasp the rule or principle being taught; how rapidly can he transfer that rule across to novel situations?
3　What is the amount and nature of the investment needed on the part of the tester before the child is able to grasp basic principles?
4　What is the particular preference of the child as to mode of presentation; for example, does she respond better for instance to verbal, pictorial, or numerical input, and how readily is she able to move through different modes of presentation?

Examples such as these clearly indicate that stress is on process rather than product. They also illustrate how sensitive and skilled the examiner needs to be in order to observe every slight change in behaviour and determine its significance. The degree of skill required, along with the fact that the test takes 3–5 hours to administer has meant that its usefulness has been seen by many as questionable; indeed the week's training course offered in this country contains very little information regarding the LPAD. However, an understanding of the format and methods used during the process of assessment is useful in implementing the programme itself. Just as with the LPAD, the teaching situation requires flexibility and a readiness to participate in a dynamic process of learning.

In order to standardize the interpretation of results, Feuerstein and colleagues devised the 'cognitive map'. Broadly speaking this divides the thinking into areas or processes, all of which can be modified by a structured input. Very much simplified, the various dimensions which make up the 'map' can be broken down into input, elaboration and output stages.

The input stage is concerned with the quantity and quality of the information gathered from the initial display of stimuli with which the subject is presented. How much information can be extracted and how useful does that information become? Examples of deficiencies in this area may be seen as the individual being unable to:

1　Realize the problem; all too often children embark on finding a solution to a problem without having realized what exactly is required of them.
2　Consider more than one source of information at any one time resulting in a fragmented overview which inhibits perception of the whole problem.

3   Extract only the significant information and discard what is irrelevant.
4   Retain information in short-term memory long enough for it to be related to items in more permanent storage.

Failure in areas such as these determines the nature of subsequent processes; if the information gathered is inadequate or inaccurate, it is more likely to lead to confusing and conflicting outcomes. Drawing an analogy with computer systems, the more accurate and extensive the information which is in store, the greater the capacity for cross referencing and new material to be generated. In many learning situations, low ability children are expected to build on information without ever having to indicate how efficiently they have absorbed the information necessary for that process of elaboration to take place.

Realizing that it is within the input area that an adult can exercise greatest control, many modern programmes of instruction for children with learning difficulties specify the nature of materials to be presented in great detail. It might be argued that in limiting the incoming material to such an extent many of the processes which should be taking place at the input phase are in fact made redundant. For example, there is no need for the process of selection to take place if that process has already been eliminated through total control having been exercised by the adult. Feuerstein maintains that deficiencies in the input and output phases are less inhibiting than failure to elaborate. However, if the child is given too refined a presentation of material, might it in fact inhibit elaboration, in that the greater the significance of the information as it is absorbed the more likely that the child will be able to incorporate it into his existing structures.

Too many of the teaching programmes which are used with slow-learning children dictate precisely the information to be learned and also the exact response required before further learning can take place. Little scope remains for such areas of learning as discrimination, exploration, comparison, and consideration of differing sources of information, all of which are features of the input phase of the Feuerstein model. Similarly areas such as inference, hypothesis testing, perception and definition of the problem, which should occur in the elaboration phase often become redundant. The learner is simply required to move rapidly to the output phase and give the precise response when requested.

In the output phase the individual is required to communicate the product of the elaborative phase. The Instrumental Enrichment programme is designed to encourage the child to formulate his thinking into a form which is sufficiently coherent as to be understood by others.

Feuerstein also stresses the 'level of efficiency'; this area unites the previous three and brings them to a point of automatization. Feuerstein (1980) maintains that:

the less automatic the question, the greater is the vigilance required to master all of its components, and the less efficient the handling of the task (p.111).

Central to the undertaking of any part of the assessment procedure or subsequent programme of intervention is the belief that in any of the above areas, it is possible to foster change, and that once a change has occurred, the direction of cognitive development is altered. Although Feuerstein worked closely with Piaget for several years, and many of the principles upon which his work is based coincide with those of Piaget, it is in the area of initiating change in cognitive development that differences are most apparent. Feuerstein argues that if the progression towards the formal operational level of functioning is automatic, why are there so many discrepancies and why do so many of us fail to achieve it? He maintains that it is not enough for the individual to be subject to and experience a wide variety of stimuli in order that appropriate response be developed.

Into that equation it is necessary to interject another human factor, that of the second person. The equation thus becomes stimulus–human factor–organism–response, the second person acting as a mediator through which the child is able to perceive and make sense of an otherwise confusing array of incoming information. The mediating agent (often parent, but equally well older sibling or teacher) guides the individual through the stages of input, elaboration and output, encouraging development of new skills, consolidation of those in the process of acquisition, and practise of those established. The mediator's role might include:

1   The selection of stimuli; implicit in this is the intention of the mediator in that by directing the child to specific stimuli the likelihood of the required goal being achieved is increased. A filtering process takes place whereby the child's attention is drawn to that which is seen as being most relevant.

2   Scheduling of stimuli so that the order in which they are absorbed is meaningful in that the individual is able to establish links between the immediate, past and future events.

3   Conveying a sense of competence so that the individual feels to be in control and able to succeed with minimum interference.

There are many more interactions which Feuerstein suggests offer children the opportunity of a mediated learning experience, and having interpreted the results of the LPAD, it is possible to establish which areas it would be most useful to concentrate on. The vehicle on offer is a structured programme designed to link in with those areas defined by the assessment procedure. However, while many aspects of Instrumental Enrichment are carefully structured, the whole purpose of mediated learning experience is to produce 'an independent thinker' able to generate and use new information. Therefore it is with the mastery of these skills that the programme is concerned.

The Structure of the Instrumental Enrichment Programme

Teacher and pupil materials for this course of instruction can be supplied only to those who have undergone a period of training. It is also worth noting that the programme was never intended to be an end in itself, it is simply the first step towards other aspects of learning and the curriculum.

Essentially there are fifteen 'instruments' in the form of tear-off worksheets, each designed to foster particular skills, related to the cognitive deficiencies established in the assessment procedures. In addition there is a teachers' guide to each instrument. The tasks within each area are highly structured and carefully sequenced so that they become progressively more difficult with a gradual reduction in given cues. There is a great deal of overlap and mutual reinforcement as concepts and skills are re-encountered in different situations. The mastery pages which occur at intervals throughout the instruments encourage a self-monitoring system which is considered to be an important aspect of the programme. Although originally designed for use with adolescent subjects, the Schools Council and other reports suggest that the age range could be extended.

In the first of a two year programme, four instruments are covered: organisation of dots, orientation in space, comparisons and analytic perception. The skills required for the 'dot' instrument cover those which are necessary for all other areas and so it is suggested that all pupils begin with this instrument. The level of the reading required for the completion of these early instruments is minimal. Also they bear no relation to the type of subject matter the learner is likely to have encountered previously. It is expected that these two factors will increase the likelihood of success.

It is normal for pupils to work on two instruments concurrently, this way the likelihood of transfer and reinforcement is increased. The areas covered by the second year are those of comparisons, analytic perception, categorization, temporal relations and family relations; at any time the instrument 'illustrations' may also be used. (Further details of the instruments may be found in 'Instrumental Enrichment', Feuerstein, 1980).

At different times pupils tackle problems either individually or in small groups; at all times discussion provides the central core. This being the case, the suggested structuring of each lesson remains constant. Firstly there is an introductory discussion time of approximately fifteen minutes, followed by a period of individual work time when students would complete specific tasks. Finally there is a return to the dialogue mode in order to encourage transfer of the skills which have been used into other areas of the curriculum of student experience. This is referred to as bridging in the context of Instrumental Enrichment. At all times the teacher works on the assumptions that:

1   The student will retain new information more successfully if he or she has been active in the process of acquisition.

2   The process of learning not only involves the acquisition of information, but also an appreciation of the processes involved as the learning takes place.

3   The usefulness of the information is dependent on how efficiently the student has been able to relate it to existing knowledge or experience.

Using a Work Sheet

Possibly one of the easiest ways to understand the use and content of the programme is to exemplify the kind of teaching strategies and areas covered using one particular work sheet. Figure 5.1 (OD1) represents a scaled down version of the first work sheet in the instrument Organization of Dots. This is the first area that the pupil undertakes when starting on the IE programme.

A superficial appraisal of Figure 5.1 might suggest that the skills it teaches bear little relation to the content of a school curriculum and that there is little to be gained from learning how to join together dots that a good puzzle book could not provide. In fact, Feuerstein would argue that the skills necessary to complete this instrument successfully are fundamental to the rest of the problem-solving situations in which we might find ourselves. When using the work sheets in the Organisation of Dots section of the programme, a teacher would be expected to guide the student so that he or she was able to fulfil the following expectations.

1   Impose structure on an apparently random array of information.
2   Recognize items of information which are more useful than others.
3   Recognize that certain information provides a means of self-monitoring so that the whole process becomes more of an independent activity.
4   Establish a common vocabulary through which ideas can be communicated.
5   Hypothesize about possible courses of action in order to establish those most likely to lead to success.
6   Listen to other people's ideas and opinions and be prepared to modify his or her own as a result.
7   Justify his or her own ideas.

There are many more general principles which provide the framework within which the lesson takes place. Overriding all of this is the fostering of an awareness of the actual processes themselves; it is not enough that the student makes sense of the information on the page, he or she also has to be guided towards recognizing the processes involved as these take place. This generates an understanding of the means by which all new problem situations can be tackled. The specific nature of the skills being used allows for the student to practice using them in subsequent work sheets and to transfer them to other areas of his or her experience.

Figure 5.1 Scaled-down version of the first work sheet in the instrument Organization of Dots (OD1).

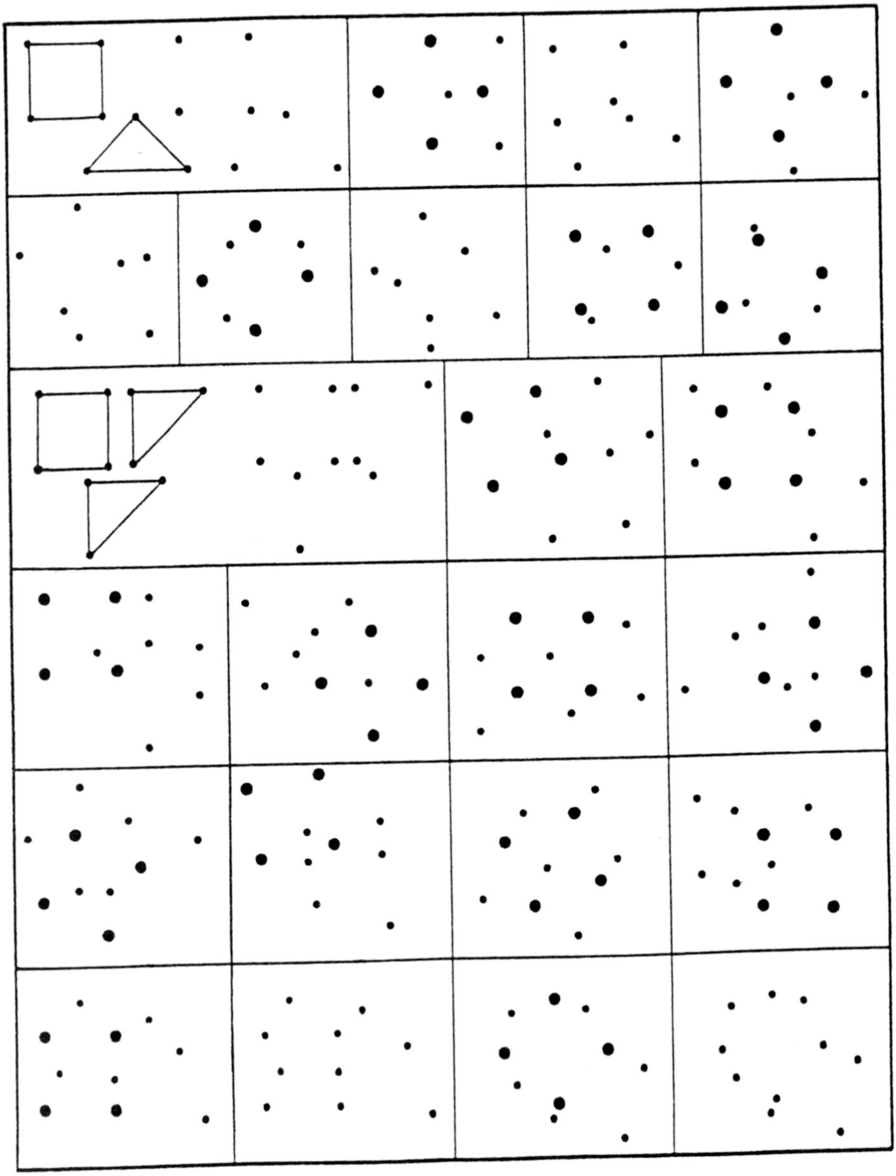

Table 5.1 is designed to give some indication as to the possible content of work relating to the particular sheet. It should be stressed that the time factors involved are largely unpredictable and the material in the chart could cover a few lessons or weeks of work. In fact although there are three broad areas – discussion,

individualized work, and bridging or generalization – there is enormous overlap, and bridging in particular should occur throughout the lesson. During the discussion the teacher is expected to use open questions whenever possible, be receptive to pupils' responses, be prepared to modify his or her objectives as a result, and guide the pupils towards making connections with their own experiences. It is a dynamic process and as such very difficult to formalize. The organization of dots chart is meant merely to give some indication as to possible avenues.

For many teachers one of the most difficult aspects of using the programme is the change in teaching technique which it demands. The child is no longer seen as a passive recipient but there is a two-way process taking place and the teacher has to encourage and be responsive to all the feedback generated. It may mean that the nature of the lesson takes quite significant swings away from the original planned course, and the teacher has to be prepared to go with that.

One of the main points of an IE lesson is that the pupils absorb what is presented to them into their own experiences, that they 'make the connections'. Some of these connections may be far removed from the original objectives decided upon by the teacher, yet he or she has to be prepared to respond to their significance. It is also necessary for the teacher to retain his or her original objectives, and possibly draw the students back towards them if the direction taken by the group becomes too obscure. With this in mind, clearly all the objectives given on the chart serve merely as indications of possible lines of development. However, there are certain aspects of the activities covered which run throughout the whole programme and on which it might be useful to elaborate.

1 Accuracy

Precision in use of language and presentation of work is an important feature of all of the instruments. Feuerstein sees impulsivity as being characteristic of many of the less able children he dealt with. He regards it as symptomatic of such factors as a poor self-image, an expectation of failure, an inability to ingest all of the elements of a piece of information, and poor memory facilities. The accurate presentation of work is seen to be significant in that it stresses the need to operate within specific structures and is likely to lead to an improvement in many of those areas previously mentioned. The design of the programme also encourages a dramatic extension of vocabulary; in an attempt to establish the importance of accuracy when communicating information, children are encouraged to use words which many teachers of less-able pupils would find surprising.

They are also encouraged to use their new found vocabulary in the abstract, in that they are trained to hypothesize and constantly question both their own speculations along with those of other pupils. This need to push children away

Organization of dots   Sheet 1

Teacher objective	Method (dialogue and discussion)	Pupil response
Pupils define problem by deduction and inference using materials given	– Is there a problem? – Why do you think that . . . .? – Is there anything that gives us information? – Is there information which might be more useful	– States definition of problem – States the information which is most useful – Explore why parts of the information might be more useful than others
Pupils learn a common vocabulary to use in order to complete the work sheet	– Describe what is on the page – What could we call the shapes – How could we describe the way the page is set out? – Why might it be useful for us all to use the same – names – labels?	– Accurate use of vocabulary such as a square, triangle, frame, row, horizontal, vertical, etc. – Ability to locate particular items easily using reference terms established by group – Stating other situations where labelling might be useful
Pupils work out the formula of a plan which they can use to complete the work sheet	– When might you use a plan? – What is a plan; are there things you need to make a plan? – Teacher translates pupil responses into main elements of planning behaviour	– States stages involved in planning named activities – Extract features of plans which are common – Transfer common planning attributes to work sheet problem
Pupils define the properties of a square	– Is this shape the same as this one? – why not?	– States attributes of a square

Pupils define the properties of a triangle	– As above – How might solving the problem be easier now that the shapes have names? – Are there things about the shapes which might make solving the problem easier . . . ?	– States attributes of a triangle – Names other instances when accurate labelling is useful – States instances when it is necessary to focus on certain aspects of a situation and ignore others
Using a plan as a guide pupils decide on particular strategies to follow	– Can anyone suggest a starting point, why? – What do other people think about that idea? – Where could we go from there? – Is there a way of knowing if we are right? – Are there other situations when you might use a drawing or picture to check what you have done – Is that a useful way of checking why . . . ?	– States relevant features which provide a starting point – Systematically considers different starting points – Considers sequence of procedures and states that which is most likely to be successful – Use self-monitoring skills during independent work – Devise a situation or complete a task where there is only a picture to provide necessary information
Pupils learn the four rules which apply to the work sheet	– Practically illustrate the four rules – and test pupils understanding before individual work begins	– Complete specified sections of the sheet using the areas covered – State other instances where rules are used etc . . . .

from a 'concrete level of operations' is central to the philosophy which underlies IE. Feuerstein argues that in far too many instances of special schooling, children are presented with concrete examples of a problem and then left to operate within that level. If the child is to profit from the mediation of a teacher or parent then surely he or she should be guided on towards the next operational level. Only one of the instruments used in the first year recommends the use of concrete examples to illustrate teaching points.

2   Developing Appropriate Strategies

This covers an enormous area; first, the child has to learn that there are 'means' by which many problems can be solved. Second, he or she has to learn how to extract the information which allows him or her to formulate those means. Having formulated appropriate strategies the child then has to develop flexibility such as the ability to switch routes or restructure strategies. Feuerstein refers to a failure in this area as 'blocking'; many teachers must have experienced working with a child where an apparently minor change in the information given can result in a totally blank look, as though the problem was completely novel and had never been seen before. Alternatively the child who thinks he or she has understood the problem, embarks on a particular line of attack, and when that fails, assumes that the problem is insoluble rather than changing tack and trying a different approach. This illustrates the 'episodic' way of seeing the world mentioned earlier, and verifies the need to generalize in the abstract, so that events are not seen simply as isolated trial-and-error processes.

3   Automatization

To become sufficiently skilled in a particular area so that the processes involved reach a level of automaticity, requires a great deal of practice. The design of the IE programme is meant to ensure that this occurs. Through repetition, the cognitive skills used reach the level whereby they can be used without conscious thought. In many problem-solving situations, most of us arrive at a solution without being aware of the means by which we travelled there. It is only when faced with a particularly difficult or unusual problem that we actually begin to break down and recognize the various stages necessary to set about solving it. What seems to happen with many less able children is that they are not aware of the strategies available to them. Neither are they sufficiently well practised in the use of these strategies, and they have not realized that not only do they have the means to solve a problem, but that it is to their advantage to do so. So many children seem to learn because it is necessary that they complete a task in order to satisfy a need extrinsic to themselves. The Instrumental Enrichment programme attempts to transfer that need to an intrinsic level. The child is encouraged to reach a level of awareness whereby he enjoys using the thinking skills he or she is learning not because of any end-product, but because s/he can see the intrinsic value of developing those skills.

4 Self-monitoring

There is an enormous bank of evidence to indicate that optimum performance requires not only the acquisition and use of information, but also an understanding of the processes involved, and how they relate to each other. Without the ability to direct one's own thought processes, the links between processes are difficult to establish. In all of the instruments, pupils are given means by which they can check their own work without having to approach the adult. In earlier instruments mastery pages ensure that self-monitoring takes place.

During the individual work period when the child is actually employed in completing the work sheet, all of these skills will be required. During this time, it is recommended that the teacher moves around the work area helping individual children to work out their problems. It is also useful if pupils help each other in this way since understanding an interpretation of a problem and giving appropriate explanations or guidance can also be extremely productive. Often, pupils may be required to work in small groups. Throughout the whole of each teaching session, the process of bridging should occur. This is defined as the generalization of what has been learned to other experiences the child may have had. Referring to the chart, examples might be the advantages of accurate labelling, planning, not leaping to conclusions, and so on. For many teachers it is the most difficult aspect of the programme. Bridging should always be child-centred; new information will be far more readily accommodated if it can be related to the child's own perspective. As has been stated, this means that the teacher has to be very receptive and flexible in his or her own perceptions of the information under discussion.

> The materials of IE demand that you ask different kinds of questions of the learner, so that the materials and experiences of the teacher and the learner become a kind of continuing interaction. (Feuerstein, 1980).

Evaluation

What evidence is there available to substantiate the claims made as to the effects of intervention using the Instrumental Enrichment Programme? There have been research projects carried out in many countries and within many different age and ability ranges. It is therefore not surprising that clear-cut results are hard to find. Looking at some of these projects there would seem to be three areas in which major inconsistencies occur: teaching programme variables, assessment procedures and the training programmes made available for instructors. Through concentrating on these three areas and drawing information from a variety of projects it is hoped to illustrate the difficulties of assessing such a programme.

Most of the evaluative information has been produced from four areas: the Israeli projects, North American research, work with deaf and hearing-impaired students and the Schools Council project carried out here in Britain. The document *Making up our Minds* which was published by the Schools Council in 1983 provides much of the evidence as to the use of IE in this country, although work is currently taking place in Oxfordshire and Somerset which is likely to add to this. Work with the deaf/hearing impaired groups is included because it provides a large proportion of the research available, and is possibly most positive in its perspective.

Teaching Programme Variables

Ideally the writers of the programme require that it be undertaken by a stable group of pupils for a two-year period. The Israeli report published in 1977 specifies that the group instructed in Instrumental Enrichment numbered some 218 subjects aged 12–14 years and performing 3–4 years behind their peers. There was also a control group who were given the equivalent amount of time as the IE group allocated to additional input. In this experiment each group received additional tuition for 1 hour a day for a period of two years. Due to there being National Conscription in Israel, tests carried out at the end of the two-year period were able to be repeated two years after that by the Army.

Contrast with this, reports from Nashville where students only completed one year of the programme, in total about 50 hours of tuition, or the British experiment where some of the schools within the five areas dropped out after one year and others were allocated only about one hour a week to the programme. The Yale University project established an equivalent control group as did most of the experiments carried out with hearing-impaired students, but this was unusual in Britain and Canada.

Assessment Procedures

Use of standardized tests

Looking at the kind of intellectual measures chosen, we find that they extend over a wide range, examples such as Primary Mental Ability Tests, Ravens Standard Progressive Matrices, WISC, and The British Ability Scales. Overall, while there were changes in results, these were often so small as to be without significance. Most of the increased scores noted occur in areas relating to those groups concerned with numerical content, spatial relations and abstract reasoning.

Arguably, many of the tests used could be seen as being closely linked with the content of the programme itself. Several items in the LPAD are revised from the Ravens Matrices and critics have observed that the gains which occurred were in precisely those areas practised and taught by the programme. For instance there were virtually no gains observed in those tests with a strong verbal content. Bradley (1983) maintains that even with the Israeli and American research, which is probably 'tighter' than most other examples, there was so much lacking in the format of the research procedure that the results become suspect.

In a different vein, work with the hearing impaired has produced some encouraging results. Jonas and Martin (1984) have produced numerous papers documenting the use of IE programmes with deaf and hearing impaired students, mainly adolescents. Results range from 'trends towards improvement' in areas such as the ability to carry out comparisons, and reflectivity (1984) to the IE group being almost three times higher on the Ravens Progressive Matrices (1984).

Transfer Across the Curriculum

The means of assessment varies from the administration of a special battery of tests designed to cover twelve areas of the curriculum (as devised by the Israeli and American researchers), to the use of, for instance, the Edinburgh Reading Test here in this country. One of the first questions which must be asked is how reasonable is it to expect changes in cognitive performance which are supposedly fostered by the programme to be reflected in other areas of the curriculum in such a short time span? It is worth noting that in many instances subjects were tested before completing the recommended two-year period of teaching. Where particular tests were devised, how closely did they reflect the content of the normal curriculum? Also, how much information was made available regarding whether such changes were unusual or just what would be expected given the period of time covered?

Possibly in this area of transfer more than any other the evidence for positive gains are lacking. In spite of having devised the twelve tests used in America and Israel, the only significant improvements were found to be in the areas of geography and the Bible. One of the standard problems encountered by teachers of low-ability pupils is the problem of transfer. It has been found that while children can be trained to develop specific skills, they need not necessarily use these skills when presented with similar problems out of context, i.e. in the ordinary lesson situation. Our education system tends to measure success in terms of product and usually in comparison with other children. If IE was to be adopted as a viable part of the school curriculum, the evidence suggests that many changes are required. These would include a little less concern with product and more awareness of process; people looking more closely at areas like the means taken to find a solution, how flexible the pupil was, how open to suggestion, etc. Also possibly a tightening of curriculum content so that the links between a programme like IE and other lessons might be more clearly established.

One of the keys to the lack of evidence of success of IE to transfer into other areas must surely lie in the area of 'bridging'. This is undoubtedly the weakest area of the whole programme in that it is so dependent on the individual teacher's interpretation of each lesson content. It is also limited because it is contained in a curriculum which is increasingly becoming less flexible. For the teacher, the process of bridging into other areas of the child's experience is difficult enough, but to cross into other subject areas requires either a very good understanding of the content of those areas and/or very close liaison with her colleagues. In addition, it requires a degree of flexibility, whereby all parties are prepared to and have the facility to capitalize on any particular points or opportunities which may arise in either the IE or subject lesson. Ideally IE lessons should not be seen as divorced from the rest of the school day, but as a means to access and enhance all the other lessons in which the child participates.

Attitude, Behaviour and Motivation

It is within the area of attitude, classroom behaviour and motivation that there is some ground to be gained. Again the tests used covered a sizable range, from the Classroom Participation Scale, and the Piers Harris Self-Concept Scale in America and Israel, to the Coopersmith Self-Esteem Questionnaire and general teacher observation in this country and with the hearing-impaired groups. Yet again criticism has been levelled at the extent of the assessment devices used, and this throws into question the validity and reliability of many of the results.

Ultimately, it is probable that those which hold most conviction are the questionnaires completed by the teachers and the pupils themselves. Here there is undoubtedly evidence of improvement in areas such as application, motivation, general work habits and classroom behaviour. Many of those involved in the various experiments cite this area as being that in which there is most to be gained from using the programme. Both from the students' and teachers' points of view, there are many reports indicating that IE lessons became some of the most enjoyable in their school day.

Training Programmes for Instructors

Finally, what differences are there in the kind of training and follow-up sessions which were made available to the IE instructors? In Israel and America, teachers were given extended training courses in both the use of the programme and in the assessment procedures upon which it is based. Thus training amounted to up to 180 hours with additional sessions to instruct in the use of mediational teaching style. There were also regular follow-up sessions provided where instructors could meet with each other and other professionals to discuss any problems they had encountered and exchange ideas about materials.

In Britain the training course consists of a $4\frac{1}{2}$-day workshop run by the American distributors of the programme. In some instances, depending on locality and how many teachers within a particular area were involved in using IE, follow-up sessions were organized. In certain areas of the country, Somerset for instance, there has been greater commitment on the part of the LEA in terms of finance, time and personnel. Additional teachers along with educational psychologists have been assigned to gather information, and to provide feedback and support to those involved in the scheme. However, this is unusual, for most teachers who attend the training week, feedback is minimal and they are faced with:

1   Convincing their colleagues that the time from the curriculum allocated to IE is worth while.
2   Additional work in terms of preparation of lessons and materials along with feedback and consultation with other members of staff in order for successful bridging to take place.
3   The use of a teaching style and technique which is quite possibly novel to them, with very little opportunity to evaluate how successful it is proving to be.
4   The problems of maintaining a consistent group of students for a period of two years.
5   Little opportunity to liaise with colleagues involved in teaching the same programme.

Possibly because of these kinds of problems, many of the teachers who start using the Instrumental Enrichment, unless they happen to work within one of the areas where it has been taken on board with greater commitment, fail to return to complete the second year's training course which would qualify them to teach the next four instruments of the programme.

Given that Instrumental Enrichment has been evaluated on a variety of samples with anything from 50 to 150 hours' tuition, on a range of different tests used to measure the efficacy of the result, following a number of different instructor training programmes, it is not surprising that the results are inconclusive. In addition, in education it is rare to find any initiative that has unequivocal supportive evidence. Even such large-scale projects as Follow Through have been rife with arguments about tests, methods and criticisms of methodology. (Anderson *et al.*, 1978; House *et al.*, 1978; Wisler *et al.*, 1978).

Despite the different results, there are encouraging studies performed under controlled conditions which illustrate the possibilities for Instrumental Enrichment. Shayer and Beasley (1987) reviewed the American and Israeli research and followed it with a small-scale investigation of their own performed under optimal conditions. The American and Israeli studies as previously mentioned showed only modest overall gains. As with other evaluation studies, only a small part of the Feuerstein model was tested. Shayer and Beasley (1987) devised their own investigation using 12–14 year olds in a special school for moderate learning difficulties. Both an experimental and control group were set up from random samples, and the experimental group received three hours a week of IE over a twenty-month period, giving a total of 150 hours' teaching. Both pre- and post-tests were used consisting of Thurstone Primary Mental Abilities Test, a battery of 12 Piagetian tests, and various tests of achievement. Help from Feuerstein also enabled the Learning Potential Assessment to be given. A number of subjects from both groups were 'lost' and the results are on six children from each group.

The wide range of pre- and post-tests gave detailed and often-conflicting results. The effects on achievement were very modest, leading Shayer and Beasley to conclude that if this were the only criterion, it would be difficult to justify the considerable effort and expense which IE involves. However, they also argue that these tests are not appropriate for evaluating IE because they are subject-based, and IE does not attempt to teach academic content. The same is true of the crystallized intelligence tests such as Thurstones PMA which embodies many of the general achievements of schooling and work skills.

On the other hand there should be effects on any problem-solving activities reflecting the emphasis of IE on metacognitive activities. One measure of this was the Vygotsky concept of 'zone of proximal development'. This is the difference between what the child can do alone, and what he or she can do with the help of more capable others. For the experimental group over the training period this had been raised from 9.5 years to 11.2 years, while for the control group it was raised from 10.5 to 10.7 years. In the control group there was a gain in unassisted performance of 12 months with 23 months in the experimental group. A similar differential was found on the Piagetian battery with the IE group having a relative increase over the control group of 20 months mental age in 20 months.

The authors summarize the results of their work and that of others by stating that there is good evidence that IE has a substantial effect on the meta-cognitive abilities of pupils, and their ability to approach novel tasks. Because of this they feel the programme is justified in time and expense. However, there is scant evidence to show that this translates into school achievement. Finally, the authors make a number of suggestions for the future use of IE. First, they argue that IE may retrospectively influence a pupil's learning, so that previous lack of success in, say, reading can be covered again at a higher level of functioning and at greater speed. Second, there has to be more detail on the bridging part of the programme:

> we believe that what is needed here is not just improved inservice training, but further research leading to a better description of how bridging is developed. (Shayer and Beasley, 1987, p.17).

Third, they argue for more content-free learning materials to be generated that are not restricted by copyright. Finally, they feel there is no reason why the methods should not be applied to academic areas such as science.

There can be little doubt as to the thoroughness of Feuerstein's analysis of those deficiencies which are likely to result in a child exhibiting learning difficulties. What is in question is:

1   How necessary is it for ordinary classroom teachers to have an understanding of that analysis in order to use the IE programme to greatest effect.

2   Does the evidence so far produced provide sufficient justification for the amount of effort required to implement the programme within the normal school curriculum?

On both counts the answers must be inconclusive; there are clear indications that the greater the understanding regarding the theories upon which the programme is based, the greater the improvement in and enjoyment of the teaching process. Those teachers who were involved in the process of assessment in order to establish specific areas of failure clearly had an advantage when it came to planning their teaching programmes. This was one area in particular where the British programme was very weak.

Regarding incorporating the programme into the curriculum, justification can only arise if it becomes apparent that the child's abilities in other areas improve. Here things become slightly more complicated; in terms of specific subject areas there is little to suggest that transfer takes place. However, with respect to the affective side of learning, the area which often defies measurement, there is enough to suggest that it would be foolhardy to dismiss IE out of hand. Many teachers and pupils, through using the instruments in the programme, discovered more about the process of teaching and the nature of learning than they had in many years of being in the classroom. Such close analysis of lesson content and the interactions involved, must be beneficial; possibly if the same amount of detail had been put into the 'bridging' aspect of the programme, results would have been more convincing. As it is, given the areas IE sets out to teach, given the almost impossible task of assessing change in those areas, and given a general inexperience in looking at these areas, there is still more than enough evidence to suggest that the Feuerstein programme should not be ignored.

References

Anderson, R. B., St Pierre, R. G., Proper, E. C. and Stebbins, L. B. (1978), Pardon us, but what was the question again?: a response to the critique of the Follow Through evaluation, *Harvard Educational Review*, **48**, 2, 161–70.

Ausubel, P. (1966), 'Meaningful reception, learning and the acquisition of concepts', in Klausmeier and Harris (eds) *Analysis of Concept Learning* (New York: Academic Press).

Bradley, T. B. (1983), Remediation of cognitive deficits: a critical appraisal of the Feuerstein model, *Journal of Mental Deficiency Research*, **27**, 79–92.

Feuerstein, R. (1980), *Instrumental Enrichment: An Intervention Programme for Cognitive Modifiability* (Baltimore: University Park Press).

Feuerstein, R. (1986), Instrumental Enrichment. Address to Association of Educational Psychologists Conference, Blackpool.

House, E. R., Glass, G. V., McLean, L. D. and Walker, D. F. (1978), No simple answer: critique of the Follow Through evaluation, *Harvard Educational Review* **48**,2, 128–160.

Jonas, B. and Martin, D. S. (1984) in Martin D. S. (ed.), International Symposium on Cognition, Education and Deafness.

Narrol, H., and Bachor, D. G. (1975), An introduction to Feuerstein's approach to assessing and developing cognitive potential, *Interchange*, **6**, 1, 1–16.

Sharron, H. (1987), *Changing Children's Minds* (London: Souvenir Press).

Shayer, M. and Beasley, F. (1987), Does Instrumental Enrichment work? *British Educational Research Journal*, **13**, 2, 101–7.

Sternberg, R. J. and Bhana, K. (1986), Synthesis of research on the effectiveness of intellectual skills programmes: snake-oil remedies or miracle cures?, *Educational Leadership*, **44**, 2, 60–7.

Weller, K. and Craft, A. (1983), *Making Up Our Minds: An Exploratory Study of Instrumental Enrichment* (London: Schools Council).

Wisler, C. E., Burns, G. P. and Iwamoto, D. (1978), Follow Through redux: a response to the critique by House, Glass, McLean and Walker, *Harvard Educational Review* **48**, 2, 171–185.

Chapter 6

The Development of Language and Communication
Diane Shorrocks

Rice and Kemper (1984) have referred to language learning as a 'commonplace miracle'. This description is perhaps a good place to start since it seems to embody two ideas that are of some significance in child langauge research. It is 'commonplace' in that the vast majority of children accomplish the process with speed and apparent effortlessness and 'miraculous' since we really don't have an adequate explanation of how it happens. What is clear, however, is that our ability to use language to good effect is an important factor contributing to success and failure in the education system. We use language to exchange ideas, gain information, relate to others, think, plan and generally order and classify our experience. As such it enters constructively into most activities in school.

Before setting out my aims for the chapter, some definition of terms is called for. *Language* can be defined as a code or conventional system of signs for representing objects, events and experiences in the world. *Speech* is just one of the many possible vehicles for using this code, others being signing, writing etc. *Communication* involves the exchange of ideas and intentions, but being a competent communicator involves more than just producing and comprehending sequences of the language code.

My aim in this chapter is to provide a framework for the analysis of children's language development, based on the study of those who seem to be progressing in 'normal' ways. I hope to make this as comprehensive as space will allow and to try to ensure that it is soundly located in up-to-date theory. Only when such a framework is available does it become possible to carry out the detailed and accurate diagnosis of the precise nature of the language difficulties experienced by some children. By providing, in addition, some of the theoretical discussion on which the conclusions are reached, along with suggestions for follow-up reading, more creative and individually based help and development programmes potentially become possible. With a fuller understanding of the basic rationale of some of the processes of language learning, not only can these individual children who may be experiencing difficulties be helped, but our more general policies for language development in school can be further considered. In more precise terms, in developing the framework, I shall aim to do the following:

1   To convey a richer notion of what it is to be a competent language user.
2   To emphasize that the whole process takes longer than is sometimes thought, even for the 'average' child.
3   To challenge the idea that there is a single path that all children take towards mastery of language.

The chapter has three main sections. The first deals with some examples of parent–child conversations during the early stages of language learning to set the scene and raise some preliminary questions. The second gives a descriptive developmental account of the various aspects of language and communication, which are treated separately here, but in reality interact closely with one another. The third section deals with explanations of the process, homing in on what appears to be the beginning of a consensus view in the research.

Communication in the Early Stages

I shall begin in the time-honoured manner by considering some examples of children's talk. Here, Mark (aged 14 months) and his mother are playing together on the floor with a variety of toys, including a Ladybird picture book. This has thirty or so pages all with the same format – a full-sized coloured picture of an everyday object on the right-hand page and its name in large print in the centre of the left.

In this short episode, a skilled language user is attempting to introduce the idea of conversation to a novice. How does she set about this? In this case, the book itself sets a kind of 'format' for the exchange (Ninio and Bruner, 1978) and within this framework she asks questions, makes statements and generally creates 'openings' which Mark sometimes takes up and sometimes not. When he fails to join in, she supplies the answer. She has quite an impressive range of tactics up her sleeve – many ways of asking questions, supplying labels when she deems it necessary and generating excitement when she knows a favourite picture is next. But perhaps most subtle of all, having elicited a 'pussy-cat' response from him, she proceeds to ask more questions about this picture, knowing his interest in the subject matter and something of his speech 'repertoire'.

But what of Mark? How does he contribute to the exchange? Firstly, he initiates the episode by handing mother the book then looks on with interest as she begins to turn the pages. His first verbal contribution in this naming game comes with the picture of the ball. What is interesting is that the sounds he

Context	Mother	Child
Mark picks up book and gives it to Mother, looking up at her.		ah /ɑ:/
	What? Oh, you want the book now Do you want me to read it to you?	
Mother takes book and begins turning the pages	What's that?	
No response	It's a watch, tick-tock	
She turns the page	That's a spoon	
No response		
She turns the page	Ball!	
		uh uh /ə/ /ə/
	Ball	
Mother turns page	and what's that?	
		uh uh /ə/ /ə/
	Car?	
Mother turns page	Spoon	
She turns page slowly full of 'expectation'	Ah, wait till you see this one Look, what's that?	
		a butede /ə/ bã t/ə/ də/
She smiles at him	A pussy cat, yes!	
Mark points to the picture		dar /da:/
	What does the pussy-cat say?	
		uh oo uh da /ə ũ: /ə/ d/a/ i duh dee /i d/ə̃/ di:/ a sa der duh /ʌ/ s/ə/ d/ɜ:/

produces bear little resemblance to the adult form yet the mother accepts his attempt and seems to confirm it with her answer. The same pattern of sounds comes for 'car' too and this she also accepts. With the picture of the cat, however, Mark's attempt is really quite creditable. The overall intonation pattern of the words is present even though the actual sounds do not exactly match the adult version.

If we were to comment on the conversation as a whole, perhaps its most notable characteristic is the orderly way in which it is conducted. At no point do mother and child speak at the same time (though sometimes this happens in their conversations just as it does among adults) so the idea of turn-taking seems to be fairly well established even though Mark does not always take up his turn. What is also clear is that with very limited linguistic means at his disposal, Mark can participate in a conversation – a conversation that is being created by both of them, even though most of the 'management' appears to be coming from the mother at this stage.

One further point can be made based on this extract, which concerns methodology. This information on children's developing language and conversation skills was collected in the homes of the children over a long period of time and recorded on tape with accompanying notes about the context of each remark. I was present during the actual events and could then listen to the playback of the recording at a later point in the day. On many occasions, I, like the mother judging from her responses, felt that some of the things the child said were fairly clear and 'word-like' at the time. Listening to them again later however, some of these were much less clearly interpretable.

A good example of this is Mark's 'pussy-cat' in this conversation. What this points to is the importance of expectations and surrounding context which appear to predispose the listener to 'hear' certain things. This is why an accurate version of the child's utterances is given in phonemic form alongside the 'everyday' version. It is an important point for researchers and others dealing with children in educational contexts to note. Several writers (Newsome, 1978; Wells, 1985) have suggested that this 'reading in' of meaning and the assumption that the child has something to say may be significant in encouraging the child gradually to extend and elaborate these meanings, guided by the more skilled communicator.

Now let us consider a further conversational exchange that occurs during the same play session when mother and child are playing with a large plastic ball with holes of different shapes over its surface into which plastic pieces can be slotted. The ball can be pulled open to release the pieces. Nearby are some small plastic doll-like figures.

Here there appears to be more negotiation about the nature of the activity: the mother begins by trying the shape-fitting game but Mark has other ideas. Acceding to this she provides an ongoing commentary, offers advice and builds on some of the moves begun by the child (calling to the figure). When attempting to draw his attention to an object, she tries a range of strategies – 'look, look', repetition and questioning. His actions and gestures are being constantly interpreted by her.

Context	Mother	Child
Mother picks up the ball, pulls it open and empties out the shapes	Shall we get them out for you? Look!	
Mark picks up one of the doll figures	Put them in there	
He pushes the figure into one of the holes	That's right	
	Turn it round	
It falls out	Oh, it's fallen out the bottom	
Mother puts it back in	Where's he gone?	
	Call him – oo oo, oo oo	
Mark look towards the window	Oh no, we aren't calling out there	
She points to the ball	oo oo, oo oo	
Mark looks into it		oo oo /ũ:/ /ũ:/
	Anybody at home?	
Mark picks up the dog figure		a buh /a/ b/ə/
	Put the puppy-dog in	
Mark pushes it in then picks up 'man' figure and pushes it in	And the man too	
Mark peers into the ball		duh duh
	Yes, do you want to get him out	/d/ə/ d/ə/
She pulls ball open	Put your hand in and get him out	
Mark takes figure out and plays with it		
Mother picks up another		
figure and shows him	Look at this	
	What is it	
	Look at this, look	
	Look at him smiling at you	
	Look. look.	

In verbal terms, Mark's participation is small, yet he is clearly involved in and comprehending the exchange (when the mother 'calls' to the figure he looks to the window – apparently a location of other 'calling'). What seems to be happening is that in the context of this game, which again is being mutually created by both of them, different kinds of communication are appropriate.

There is little verbal output from Mark but he is listening and understanding. If we were trying to make an assessment of his language abilities at this point, the issue of the influence of context and communicative appropriateness would need to be carefully considered. Wells (1985) also points out that context has a considerable influence on the nature and amount of conversation that occurs.

The final example of conversation between Mark and his mother occurs 10 months later when Mark is approximately two years old. Once again they are looking at the picture book.

Context	*Mother*	*Child*
Mother turns to orange-juice page	What's that?	
		mook /m uːk/
	No, it's not milk	
		dun doo /d/ã/n d/u/i/
	Orange juice	
Mark holds his finger up to mother She looks at it and wipes it		oosa /u/ː s/ã/
	That's just sugar It's come off There you are	
Mark looks at his finger		iz gon /iz g/ã/n/
	Yes, it was off your sweets Blow it off – it'll be alright	
Mark blows his finger Mother turns to picture of telephone	What's that?	
		toli /tãli/
	A telephone Who talks on there? Who talks on that?	
Mark point to picture		tway /twẽi/ kway /kwẽi/ a kway /ə/ kwẽi/
	I don't know what you're saying	
Mark turns page to tree picture	Yes	twee /twĩː/
		tyee /tjĩː/
	Yes	

Context	Mother	Child
He turns page again to balloon picture		bloom /blu:m/ bloon /blu:n/
	Oh, do you like them?	
		uh bwoken /e bw/əʊ/k/ə/n
	It's broken is it? You've got a balloon, haven't you?	
Mother turns page to duck picture	What's that? Ah, look!	
		uh for boon /ə/ f/ɔ:/ b/u/n/
	What is it?	
There is a small noise from tape recorder		noys /n/ɔ:/jz/
	Yes it is	
Mark looks and listens		iz go way /iz g/əʊ/ wei,
	It's gone It's nothing – don't worry	
Mark looks up at mother and repeats		uz bam /əz b/ã/m/ weez man /wi:z m/a/n/ erz man /ɜ:/rz m/a/ ur iz man /ɜ:/r iz m/a/
Mother looks puzzled	Where's the man? I don't know what you mean	
She turns to boat page	Oh, what's that?	
		bowt /b/əʊ/t/
	Good	
Mark tries to turn page but mother resists She points to fork picture	Wait a moment	
	Oh, what's that? Do you know what that is?	

Context	Mother	Child
Mark still trying to turn to next page		wor kweem /w/ɔ:/ kwɪːm/
	Pardon?	wur kweem /w/ə/ kwĩːm/
	Ice-cream, no! You don't eat ice-cream with a fork!	
She realizes he is talking about the next page – a lollipop	Oh there! Yes, you're right	

In the space of ten months much progress has been made and considering the same kind of activity on both occasions allows us to highlight some of the changes. The mother still uses comparatively short phrases and simple constructions (the mean length of her contributions in the first session is 4.6 morphemes and 4.98 morphemes in the last), but she now extends the discussion around some of the topics–

'Who talks on there?' – having set the topic of the telephone.
'It was off your sweets' – in the 'sugar' episode.

The whole exchange is more clearly being managed by both of them with the turn-taking format even better established. It has much less of a 'display' character and more of a sense of meanings being genuinely exchanged and negotiated. More conversational sophistication can be demonstrated by the mother, so that she can now deny the truth of some of Mark's comments. She also takes up his comments even if they don't seem directly relevant and thus potentially helps him to develop his own topics and extend his meanings.

As far as Mark is concerned, many points need to be made about his progress. He now has a much broader command of the sound system of the language and, in grammatical terms, he produces two- and three-word combinations. He clearly has messages to convey and more linguistic tools at his disposal to achieve this. He initiates topics in varied ways, sometimes by his actions, sometimes verbally and sometimes both (specific examples are the 'finger' and 'noise' themes). When his mother denies the truth of his statements he seems to understand and deal with this in appropriate ways (the 'juice' sequence).

However, he is not always understood, a problem adults have too when engaged in conversation. But at this very early stage he has ways of dealing with it

– the beginnings of conversational repair strategies of a certain kind. In the 'telephone' sequence he has three attempts at making her understand, each one subtly different from the last and the final one more elaborated than previous ones. His mother acknowledges she does not understand so he gives up and moves on to the next picture. A similar thing occurs in the 'noise' sequence, but here he has four goes at conveying his meaning, each one again different and leading to a more elaborate and differentiated final attempt. While not advocating the deliberate misunderstanding of children's communications in order to foster this, it is clear that when such events happen, within limits they may provide the motive for further advance.

Taking the findings based on all of these extracts together several key points emerge.

1 Many of these skills would not have been revealed if we had taken the child's remarks in isolation and indulged in a more directly linguistic analysis or a straightforward calculation of the changing and increasing length of the child's utterances. Such measures may help us to record a child's progress to some extent but they miss key interactional aspects of communication which may be providing the context and the motivation for development. In the case of one frequently used measure – Mean Length of Utterance (MLU) – there are considerable problems in deciding what are the 'morphemes' (the unit of measurement used) in the utterances of very young children. To count morphemes (often equivalent to words but also including sub-parts of words which change meaning – e.g. plural endings or past tense markers in words) requires the researcher to interpret and put a gloss on what the child is meaning in order to arrive at a 'version' of the words that can be counted.

Even if the counting can be achieved with some validity, it is not clear after the earliest stages how useful simple length of an utterance is as a guide to language proficiency. As Wells (1985) argues, the length of what children say often decreases once a certain level of linguistic competence is achieved and mastery of more complex forms allows for the condensing of what is said.

It is important, therefore, to consider children's utterances in their conversational context, since this is the context in which language is both learned and used. Young children are learning about conversation and through conversation and this should surely, therefore, provide the framework in which we evaluate their progress and diagnose their weaknesses.

2 The particular mother–child pair referred to here has evolved communication strategies in relation to one another which might be termed 'negotiatory' since the mother openly queries the child's meanings and the child, in turn, has begun to evolve strategies for responding to this. Other mothers and children in the same study (Shorrocks, 1981) create rather different patterns however: some take up virtually everything the child says even when it is clear that the meaning is ambiguous and others ignore much of what the child says unless the meaning is

obvious and the child very insistent. These maternal communication strategies must always be considered in relation to the particular characteristics and progress of the child.

3 The kind of analysis which has been used in these extracts shows that even at this early stage children have a great deal of implicit knowledge about language and the communication process. But we can only gain insight into their understanding if we have in mind a rather broader view of what it is to be a skilled communicator and are therefore predisposed to see rather more of the richness in such early behaviours. It is too easy not to recognize these dimensions and therefore underestimate the child's performance as a communicator.

Knowing a Language

Since we have now demonstrated the need for an understanding of what skilled communication involves, what do we know when we can effectively use a language?

Phonology

We know the basic sound of our language and the ways in which these can be combined. Not all languages have the same range of sounds (think of the 'clicks' in some South African languages) and we obviously learn the particular 'subset' used in our own language. Once we have experience and therefore implicit knowledge of this we can recognize that certain words are not from our language if they contain combinations of sounds not found there.

Semantics

We know that particular combinations of sounds have meaning – that is, words refer to items, events or experiences in the world. In languages with which we are not familiar, however, the sounds and words are often indistinguishable. Only experience of the language gradually enables us to 'hear' word and sound boundaries. The best evidence of this is to listen to a conversation in a foreign language with which we are not familiar.

Syntax

We know how to combine words into larger units and thus create phrases or sentences. We do this, not by storing all possible sentences in our memory (an impossible storage problem for the brain) but by knowing (implicitly) the rules of combination. Because we have a knowledge of words (perhaps many thousands in our working vocabulary) and also know how to combine them in order to create meanings that others who know our language can understand, we can produce endless numbers of new yet comprehensible sentences.

Pragmatics

We know how to use language appropriately in different contexts and social situations. As we saw with Mark and his mother, speech to certain people requires certain characteristics (registers) – talk to small children, 'formal' talk to our boss as opposed to informal chat etc. We also know how to manage conversations and how to present what we say in ways that will fit in with what has just been said or implied. We know when to make information explicit in conversation and when to assume or presuppose that the information is already mutually understood. We know how to 'read' the hidden intentions behind some remarks (indirect requests, sarcasm) and when language is being used in figurative or metaphorical ways ('I could eat a horse' is not usually intended to be interpreted literally!).

These various kinds of knowledge combine to produce skilled communication although it has to be said that we know little about the variations in skill levels among adults under some of these headings. Nevertheless, provided we bear this in mind, we potentially have a better framework for deciding and appraising the kinds of skills children need to develop. It is to recent research on the development of these skills in children that we now turn, under the headings just outlined.

The Development of a Knowledge of Language

Learning the Sound System

The various sounds in all human languages are produced by controlling the flow of air through the throat and mouth areas. This is the aspect of language studied by among others speech therapists seeking to understand and remedy articulatory problems in speech. But it is an aspect of language development that is sometimes underrated in its significance. Often speech production problems are the cause of broader language delay since if a child could be better understood he or she might generate more productive feedback from others.

Current information on the learning of the sound system indicated that there are several issues to bear in mind (Grunwell, 1981).

1   There is much variation in the precise order in which the sounds are learned and the strategies employed, linked presumably to particular patterns of family usage.

2   The learning of new sounds is not an all-or-nothing kind of process, where a sound will be accurately and fully used from its first appearance. Rather it is a gradual process of extension into new words and parts of words.

3   The starting-point of coming to terms with the sound system is not easy to define. From birth, children (even deaf children) vocalize and

subsequently 'babble', but using sounds in a contrastive and controlled way is a different matter.

4 Producing sounds is all tied up with being able to hear and discriminate between sounds, but it is not clear how these two processes are linked. Being able to produce a sound must imply that it has been perceived and discriminated but the reverse is not necessarily the case since a child may be able to discriminate between two sounds it hears but not use the two in its own speech. Children produce a wide range of sounds in their early vocalizing and babbling, but later, when these sounds have to be produced in specific and often awkward combinations then a slow process of relearning has to take place.

5 As with many aspects of development, children actively construct a knowledge of the sound system, sometimes using highly individual strategies to do so.

Turning to the sequence in which sounds often seem to be learned, the first distinction to be made is between vowels and consonants. The vowel sounds are not 'discrete' in the way that consonants are and it is therefore difficult to trace their development but it is the 'received wisdom' that for the average child the vowels are mostly mastered by the age of 3 (Cruttenden, 1979). Consonants, however, present a different picture and their learning is often not complete until the early school years or later. Crystal (1976) suggests that the sequence is as follows, bearing in mind individual variation.

By 2 p b m n w
2½ t d k g ŋ (as in si*ng*) h
3 f s l y (as in *y*ou)
4 ʃ (as in *sh*ip) v z r tʃ (as in *ch*ew) dʒ (as in *j*uice)
5 Θ (as in *th*ink) ð (as in *th*is)
6 ʒ (as in mea*s*ure)

Average age estimates for the acquisition of English consonants.

Children's Strategies for Dealing with New Sounds

The earliest words often bear little resemblance to the adult form but over time the more accurate 'renderings' develop. In trying to come to terms with the difficulties of the system, children use simplifying processes and strategies, some of which have been found to be:

1 Unstressed syllable deletion - where the unstressed parts of words are omitted as in

'banana' – /na: n/ə/
'enough' – /n/ʊ/f/

2 Final consonant deletion as in

'cat' – /ka/
'bed' – /be/

3 Reduplication – where the first or stressed syllable of the word is repeated to make the second syllable of a two-syllable word, as in

'bottle' – /b/ɑ/ b/ɑ/
'pudding' – /p/ʊ/ p/ʊ/

4 Harmonizing consonants – where all the consonants in a word may be 'harmonized', in the sense of using consonants from groups that are produced in a similar way or place in the mouth as in

'dog' – /g/ɑ/g/
'potty' – /ɑ/ti/

This does not mean that the child is consciously aware of these strategies (although as teachers and parents it is useful to become aware of them) nor that they themselves are unaware of the difference between their version and the adult form. In fact, children often become irritated if the adult feeds back their own 'version' to them. They can obviously discriminate the difference but are literally unable to produce the proper form for themselves.

As we have already seen, knowledge of the sound system is still developing in the school years, even for the average child (Grunwell, 1986). New words are constantly being encountered and there is evidence (Aitchison and Chiat, 1981) that the kinds of strategies just outlined for the early stages are used later too. The kinds of experiences met at school, particularly the beginnings of reading, may encourage a more conscious awareness of the sound system. This awareness is often shown by children becoming more sensitive to rhyme, puns, language games and 'verbal' jokes.

Learning about the Structure of Language — Syntax

The syntax or grammar of a language is concerned with the ways in which words can be combined into acceptable phrases or sentences. One of the major problems in discussing this is that there is little agreement as to what is the most appropriate linguistic framework for analysing the developing structures. The solution adopted by Perera (1984) and Graddol *et al.* (1987) is to use a fairly traditional grammatical framework and both of these sources are to be recommended as straightforward introductions to the topic for those with little background in linguistics.

Perhaps the fullest information we presently have for the pre-school stages of development comes from Gordon Wells and his team who worked on the Bristol

Language Development Project throughout the 1970s and early 1980s. In this major study, language samples were collected from 128 children from a range of social backgrounds covering the pre-school years (from approximately 15 months to five years). The information was collected 'naturalistically', that is, a radio microphone was attached to each child for one day every three months and random 90-second episodes of speech were collected throughout this period. As such it represents a huge amount of data on the spontaneous speech produced by children in home settings during the pre-school years.

On the basis of this broadly based evidence, Wells (1985; 1986) has argued that there is a fairly predictable sequence in the development of the structures, meanings and functions of language. He has suggested five 'stages' up to the age of five and I have selectively summarized these in Table 6.1. I focus on three apsects in the Wells data, sentence and clause structure, the meanings expressed in noun phrases and the functions to which language is put. As the key indicates, these are designated (a), (b) and (c) in the table. It must be stressed that these 'stages' should not be interpreted in a watertight way since the whole process is more continuous than the term might suggest. There are no ages attached as so much individual variation was found to exisit in the rate at which children appeared to master these aspects. This variation in terms of age is, however discussed by Wells in Chapter 6 of his 1985 book for those wishing to take this further.

The sequence is from single-word utterances to longer and more complex sentences. With the development of the auxiliary verb system, questions and negative sentences become possible even though these functions have been used earlier. Without the full structural forms, however, the questioning or negating functions can only be conveyed by tone of voice and intonation. Wells suggests that throughout the course of development there is a tendency for meanings and functions to emerge before the grammatical structures through which they will eventually become fully expressed. In terms of the meaning relations in what the child says, the move is from being able to refer to objects, people and their locations towards being able to talk about causality, change and purpose. The tense system of verbs appears to be masterd in the sequence present, past then future and conjunctions are progressively used (first 'and' but later 'because' 'if' and 'so that') to join units together, thereby conveying longer and more complex ideas. Bearing in mind what was said earlier, however, the ability to use relative clauses within sentences, for example, may lead to greater economy of length.

The information on which this sequence is based was collected, as we have seen, from the spontaneous speech of children in 'natural' contexts. What this may be failing to capture, therefore, is what the child is fully capable of at the limits of its abilities at any point. Such information can really only be obtained by administering tasks designed to elicit the child's knowledge of specific structures

TABLE 6.1 The development of sentence structure: Meaning relations in sentences and language functions in the pre-school period. (Based on Wells, 1985 and 1986)

Notes: (a) Developing sentence structures.
  (b) Developing sentence meaning relations.
  (c) Developing language functions.

Stage		*Structures and meanings*	*Examples*
I	(a)	Mostly single word utterances	'there', 'more'
	(b)	Operator plus nominal	'there Mark'
	(c)	Wanting, call, ostension (showing)	'doda' (entreats) 'Mummy', 'dog' (showing)
II	(a)	Mostly two constituents: subject + verb	'it burn'
		subject + object/complement	'it hot'
		preposition + noun/adverb	'down there'
	(b)	Naming and classification Changing location	'coming', 'going'
		Attributes	'hot', 'big', 'nice'
	(c)	Questions	'where', 'wassat'
III	(a)	Mostly three-constituents: subject + verb + object/adjunct	'man dig down there'
		subject + auxiliary + verb	'I am going'
	(b)	Change in state	'you dry hands'
		Verbs of mental states	'know', 'listen'
		Reference to past events	'Mark did'
		Ongoing events	'Mark doing it'
	(c)	Questions developing but via rising intonation	'Helen still in bed mummy?'
IV	(a)	Longer and more complex forms	'I want Daddy take it to work mend it'
		Auxiliary verbs developing	'can', 'do', 'will'
		Interrogative sentences	'can I do it'
		Negative sentences	'I don't like it'
		Clauses within clauses	'Where's the pen what Pappa gave me?'
	(c)	Requesting permission	'can I do it?'
		Indirect requests	'shall I cut another one?'
V	(a)	Major sentence types established. Length of utterance now may be shorter because of embedded and relative clauses, pronouns, ellipsis etc. 'What' and 'when' questions emerge.	
	(b)	More differentiated expression of time – 'before dinner' 'until bedtime' and past and future reference.	
	(c)	Most of major functions now established – giving information, asking and answering questions, requesting, suggesting, offering, expressing feelings and attitudes. Conditional and hypothetical functions now added.	

and meanings. This gives information about their abilities 'at the cutting edge' as it were, rather than conveying regular and comfortable usage. The wider issue here is the question of when do we say a child 'knows' or can use a particular grammatical form or meaning? Is it when it first appears in spontaneous speech, when it is regularly used in a more or less correct way, or when the child can use the item in controlled elicitation tasks but not in spontaneous speech? There is no simple answer to these questions but it is important to be aware of this problem of definition when appraising children's language.

By the end of this pre-school period, for most children, 'the major linguistic systems are in place and a basic vocabulary of several thousand words has been acquired' (Wells, 1986 p.32). This does not mean, however, that syntactic development is complete: as we shall see much has still to be mastered well into the school years.

For this information we have to turn to other studies, well summarized by Perera (1984). The kinds of structures that are produced later include:

complex noun phrases used as subjects – 'all the recorder players in my class went out to the hall'

some of the auxiliary verbs – 'shall', 'may', 'ought to'

some adverbial clauses:
   (time) – 'he ran off when he saw the escaped tiger'
   (place) – 'they spent the day here in the dark wood'
   (manner) – 'moving with great caution they walked over the ice'

relative clauses beginning with 'whose' and 'whom' – the children whose birthdays are this week have to go to the office'

certain kinds of passive sentences – 'the car was overtaken by the lorry'

Throughout the school years, fluency increases and children are less likely to hesitate or 'get lost' in their speech. However, it is important to remember that, even as adults, we make grammatical errors in our speech, changing tense mid-sentence, subject and object not 'agreeing', and many others. Eavesdropping on conversations readily demonstrates this. It is perhaps also worth making the point that we are talking about children producing these structures in their speech: producing them in writing once they are introduced to literacy in school may be a different matter. Perera suggests that

it is clear, ability in writing grows initially out of a sound foundation of oral language and that, as children mature, the structures they use in their writing may, in turn, influence the development of their speech (1984, p.270).

Finally, several researchers have noted the fact that what frequently happens in the course of many aspects of language development is that children begin to use a new item or structure in correct ways but then, at a later point, revert to earlier, incorrect usage. Perhaps this happens because, in a situation where a great deal is being learnt at the same time on many fronts, a kind or processing 'overload' occurs and the least stable elements (maybe the most recently mastered) cannot be so effectively controlled. During periods of rapid language growth such instabilities of learning may occur, followed by development to new levels and more stable language performance.

The Development of Word Meanings – The Semantic System

This section concerns itself with recent work on how children acquire word meanings and develop a vocabulary. Learning the meanings of words is all tied up with the child's developing understanding of the world around and is therefore closely linked with the development of concepts. As Blewitt (1982) writes, 'words are tools for expressing and interpreting meaning. As such they both signify external objects or events and symbolise interior meanings or concepts' (p.140). Concepts are often defined as mental representations based on the similarities or differences between the various objects and events we encounter. Thus my concept of 'dog' will be defined by the common characteristics I have noted and experienced in my dealings with a variety of such creatures and will be differentiated from 'cats' and 'cows', for instance. This is not to suggest that all concepts will have straightforward verbal labels: some of our categories of experience will be less easily labelled (unusual objects, colours or sensations).

The first problem facing the child is to sort out the individual units/words from the stream of sounds they hear, after which they face the formidable task of producing the particular sound combinations. Even if the adults around are presenting the child with a carefully tailored 'input', the 'units' the child hears may not correspond to adult words. There is in fact accumulating evidence that children find this 'segmentation' issue difficult (Peters, 1983) and may treat phrases rather than words as the 'unit' ('allgone', 'wassat'). In these cases, the ready-made phrases may be used in specific and inflexible ways, indicating that the child does not comprehend the internal structure of the 'unit' being used.

Studies of the kinds of words that babies first produce reveal some interesting facts. As far back as 1973, Nelson coined the terms 'referential' and 'expressive' to characterize the different strategies and vocabularies developed by children. The term 'referential' applies to children whose primary need in using language seems to be to talk about things and thus label the world: 'expressive' children, on the other hand, use language primarily for social interaction. This gives rise to very different kinds of initial vocabularies, 'referential' children using mainly nouns and 'expressive' vocabularies consisting of words such as 'hi', 'thankyou', 'allgone' etc. Horgan (1980) found a similar distinction between children whom she labelled 'noun-lovers' and 'noun-leavers'. Both writers stress that these two groupings should be seen as two ends of a continuum, with few children being at the extremes and most somewhere in the middle but predisposed to one strategy or the other.

What these studies indicate is individual variation in this aspect of language learning too. Peters (1983) draws attention to the fact that the 'common pattern' view of the language learning process may be a result of the kinds of children studied in the early, highly influential work in the 1960s. Not only were these children mostly white, English-speaking, firstborn and middle-class, it seems likely that they were 'referential' as defined above. The speech of this group is often clearer than others and their rate of progress has been shown to be somewhat faster.

The implications of this for child language research are considerable. Peters takes the analysis of this individual variation further by considering children who appear to begin their production of language by using the longer, unanalysed phrases mentioned earlier. She calls this a 'Gestalt' strategy and contrasts it with an 'Analytic' one. Children using a 'Gestalt' strategy work in these larger units with the overall stress and intonation pattern of their speech having a phrase-like quality. For these children, the move then is to break down the 'units' into their constituent parts and so to use them more flexibly. A nice way of describing this strategy is 'knowing the tune but not the words'. Children using a more 'Analytic' strategy begin with the neat one-word utterances so often referred to in the literature and progressively combine these in the ways we saw in the last section.

Beyond these very early words, how and in what order do children master new word meanings? The fact that they don't learn all their vocabulary at once must indicate constraints either in memory and processing systems or in the inherent complexity of the word meanings themselves. Alternatively, the sequence in which certain words are learned may be the result of the adults around using some words more frequently than others. In order to try to find which of these explanations is most valid we first need to recognize that words are of different kinds, the usual distinctions being:

'substantive/nominal' words – nouns
'relational' words of different kinds:

>   spatial words (in, on, under)
>   size words (big/little, tall/short)
>   temporal words (before/after)
>   similarity relations (more/less, same/different)

Taking the idea of the complexity of different words first. In linguistic analysis, one influential theory (Clark, 1973) suggests that the meaning of any word is made up of a series of components or 'features' and that for 'simple' words there are fewer of these than for 'complex' ones. For example:

'boy' = male + non-adult
'brother' = male + adult/non-adult + shared parentage

The word 'brother' has more features involved in its meaning and is therefore more 'complex'. It is assumed that the adult system is structured in this way and that children learn the system by a process of building up correct meanings, feature by feature. Several ideas follow from this:

1   Early word meanings should be very general and often over-extended (applied too widely and inappropriately – all animals are 'dogs', for example) because only a limited number of features are being used.
2   The 'features' that are used first will be the most obvious ones for the child to perceive (colour, shape, movement).
3   Words that have fewer 'features' will be mastered before those that have more.
4   Where pairs of 'relational' words are involved, some of the pairs will be less complex than others ('big/little' have fewer features than 'wide/narrow'). However, within these pairs one 'end' is often easier than the other and will therefore be learned first.

All very neat and plausible, but open to critisism on two counts. First, it is not so easy to break down all word meanings in this clear-cut 'components' way even in the adult system and second, as far as children's mastery of the system is concerned, the experimental findings do not fully bear out the theory. For example, in children's learning of nouns, often more 'general' words, with fewer features are learnt later rather than earlier as the theory would predict (e.g. 'Collie' or 'dog' before 'animal'). With 'relational' words too, although some pairs are learned before others and some 'ends' of pairs learned earlier too, the research findings are by no means clear-cut (Blewitt, 1982; Carey, 1982).

The alternative explanation, that the sequence in which words are learnt is determined by the frequency with which adults use them to children is also not watertight. Studies that have looked at adult 'input' show that parents label objects at a variety of different 'levels' for the child – some at a very specific level ('Fido', 'Daddy'), others at an intermediate level ('banana' rather than 'fruit') and some at a more general level still ('car' rather than 'Ford Escort XR3i'). In fact, adults use more 'intermediate' level labels, yet children's vocabularies do not reflect these characteristics (Blewitt, 1982; Brown, 1958). We are therefore in the awkward position of having some well-conducted empirical work showing that (given individual variation) children learn certain words before others but no good theoretical explanation for this.

We also have to account for the fact that children's word meanings often do not 'match' those of the adult: sometimes they are wider, sometimes narrower and sometimes completely different! Kuczaj and Lederberg (1977) have shown that in their sample, children interpreted and used 'old' as if it meant 'big' or 'young' as if it meant 'small'. What is interesting about this is that there could be good grounds for the confusion in terms of adult use to children: in this case, the dominant adult use could encourage incorrect notions in the child.

Other factors that may influence the way in which children learn and infer word meanings could be the linguistic and non-linguistic contexts in which they experience new words. Children as young as 18 months when presented with an unusual doll and told either 'this is dax' or 'this is a dax' could make use of the linguistic information conveyed by the 'a' and respond appropriately to it as either a proper name or a noun. There is also some evidence to show that if children come to understand and use words in particular circumstances and contexts, then 'tapping' their knowledge for assessment purposes should take this into account.

The Development of the Pragmatic Aspects of Language

In an earlier section (p. 131) we saw what is meant by the pragmatic aspects of language: managing conversation, tailoring messages appropriately etc. Before considering the development of some of these dimensions throughout childhood, two general points should be made. Firstly, we do not have much information about the range of adult performance in these aspects, although we do recognize when adults too lack certain conversation skills. Secondly, what is defined as skilled communication may vary from culture to culture in terms of the structuring of information in conversational turns and differences in ways of speaking with regard to pitch and intonation. Work by Gumperz *et al* (1979) documents the mutual misinterpretations that can occur between English speakers and English-speaking Indians because of these cultural variations in conversational structure and style.

Conversation Management

We saw earlier with Mark and his mother that even by the age of 2–2½ years many skills of conversation management have been established – turn-taking, topic initiation and continuance and conversational repairs. What those examples show is the significant change from a stage where the adult is imputing meaning to ambiguous child contributions to the point where the conversation is more mutually created and socially adapted. Children appear to be socially motivated from birth, with the human face having special significance: they seem predisposed to respond to others. As they become more skilled conversationalists, the exchanges become longer and more varied (as we saw).

It is perhaps important to emphasize at this point that, even though we have so far considered the various aspects of language development separately, they should be seen in relation to each other, as indeed they are for the child. As the child's syntactic knowledge and vocabulary increases, for instance, then the range of choices and degree of message precision available at any point in conversation is also increased.

1   Turn-taking

We have seen that this is established early and it seems that intonation is an important signal at first (a rising tone indicating questioning and thus the need for a response, for instance). By the time most children enter school they appear to have mastered most of the turn-taking skills used by the adult, at least as far as talking to one other person is concerned. When trying to participate in larger conversations, in groups for instance as often happens in school, then perhaps more complex skills are involved which require further experience and learning. McTear (1985) suggests that turn-taking provides a good example of the dynamic processes in conversation since change of turn is indicated on a moment-to-moment basis.

2   Initiating topics

Speakers must gain the attention of the listener and then go on to provide information which will allow the topic to be developed. McTear (1985) lists some of the devices, both verbal and non-verbal, used by children in the early stages to initiate exchanges.

Non-verbal – pointing, looking, touching, showing, giving, eye contact, and moving towards the other person.
Verbal – naming, greeting, asking questions (once the intonational or structural means are available) whining, or screaming.

As knowledge of language increases, this becomes reflected in the increasingly indirect, subtle and precise ways that children both gain attention and provide the information which allows a conversational exchange to be developed.

3   Creating coherent dialogue

One important way of creating coherence in conversation is by the use of special linguistic devices which provide cohesive ties across contributions. Such devices include the use of pronouns (he, she, they etc.) across sentences and within sentences too, which allow the participants to cross refer to items already introduced, in an economical way. Another device is the use of discourse connectors ('in fact, 'mind you', 'on the other hand') which allow the responder to make links to the previous statement. Children use both these kinds of device in the pre-school years and continue to develop them later too. The earliest discourse connectors to be used are 'and' and 'but', followed by words such as 'well', 'sure', 'right' and 'anyway'. Let us not forget, however, that for children with perhaps limited communicative means at their disposal, repetition or partial repetition of an earlier contribution is a significant way of creating cohesion and coherence in conversation.

4 Request sequences

From the earliest stages children can make requests by a combination of gesture and vocalization. Often, the first use of linguistic forms for this are 'more' 'want + name' etc. By age 5–6, however, children are capable of producing fairly complete *indirect* requests and from as early as 4 years, can select 'polite' forms in certain circumstances. Comprehending as opposed to producing these indirect forms comes earlier, perhaps as young as 3. Ervin-Tripp (1977) puts it rather well when she says 'the wide use of tactful deviousness is a late accomplishment' (p.188).

5 Conversational repairs

We saw that at a very early stage, Mark could deal with one kind of problem in conversation, that of recognizing that he was not being understood and having strategies to deal with this. But to participate smoothly in conversation requires additional repair strategies – the ability to ask for clarification from one's partner and strategies for retrieving the flow of a topic after interruptions or when both partners have spoken at once. McTear gives some interesting evidence that even young children can monitor their own speech and their partner's and 'locate, diagnose and repair conversational breakdown' (p.200). They can correct the contributions of others for both content and pronunciation although for social reasons this might be expected to decline with increasing age and sophistication as it seldom happens among adults. They can also correct their own statements for pronunciation, grammar and vocabulary.

The Content of Conversations

One aspect of the content of conversations which is worth briefly mentioning is the work on referential communication. It is an issue raised by the work of Piaget who suggested that the thinking of children under the age of about 7 years is egocentric and that this prevents them from taking the perspective of another person. The implication is that this will fundamentally affect their ability to communicate messages that require this kind of 'decentring'. Experimentally, this has been tested by putting two children either side of a screen, provided with similar materials and asking them to provide verbal information that will enable the other person to select a particular item. Alternatively, children may be asked to give instructions to a friend, taking account of feedback from them.

Some of this work has asked questions about children's perceptions of who is to blame, speaker or listener when communication fails (Robinson and Whittaker, 1986). At around 5 years, they do not appear to understand the reason for the communication failure and therefore can rarely take action to solve the problem. By about 7, however, they have a more accurate idea of communication problems. Young children seem to judge that all speaker messages are adequate (even when they are not) but older ones can detect that the message content is faulty.

We appear to have arrived at somewhat contradictory findings. Even preschoolers, according to the work reviewed here, seem to possess considerable skill in taking turns, initiating and sustaining topics and repairing certain kinds of conversational problem. Yet the work just mentioned indicates that they find the construction of messages is difficult under some circumstances well into the school years. It could be that there is a distinction to be made between mastering the 'mechanics' and procedures of conversation management and mastering the detail of the content of messages at a more sophisticated level.

Conclusions: The Course of Language Development

1   From this review of developing language, what is immediately clear is that the whole process takes a great deal longer than is often suggested (see Durkin, 1986). Children are still learning about the sound system, structure, vocabulary and use of language well into the school years.

2   Although some writers of recent work still want to argue to some extent for much common ground in the route children take, there is an increasing amount of evidence of much individual variation in progress and strategies. The implications of this for evaluating the progress of children experiencing problems are clear.

3   What has also emerged is that in many aspects of language skill we have no clear picture of adult performance against which to judge children's progress. Such insights as we do have indicate that adults make mistakes of all kinds in their speech yet can recognize, if asked in experimental settings, when sentences are correct or not. Clark (1982) makes a strong plea for acknowledging this when trying to assess the abilities of children.

Explanations of Language Development

Describing the course of language development, as we have just been doing, is a comparatively straightforward task, even though we must recognize that our knowledge is incomplete in many ways. Explaining why and how the process happens is a different matter and historically there have been competing explanations.

In very broad terms, there have been those who suggest that it is an innate predisposition and others who would want to explain it in terms of environmental creation of the ability ('nature' versus 'nurture'). Chomsky, whose role in this debate has been of major significance, points to the importance of our view of language and linguistic analysis in influencing the explanations offered. Until Chomsky's own analysis of language, a 'generative' one first present in the 1950s, the dominant view in linguistics was a traditional/structuralist one which did not examine how the user used linguistic information (Chomsky, 1986). As a form of linguistic analysis, this dealing with 'surface strings' of words in an isolated kind of way was especially suited to the then dominant framework within psychology – a behaviourist one.

This approach (especially Skinner, 1957) stresses imitation, practice and selective reinforcement as the prime language learning mechanisms. The process is seen as the gradual accumulation of separate language items brought about by the parents modelling and reinforcing more accurate utterances. The major arguments against this (Chomsky, 1957) point out that the explanation is not in line with some of the observed facts of language learning. Children often use forms they cannot have heard ('I goed', 'mouses' etc.), parents seldom correct the form of children's utterances only their content and the whole process takes place at a speed which would not allow for conditioning or reinforcement to take place for every item.

I shall not go into further detail of this debate, except to consider briefly the psychological implications of adopting a different view of the nature of language.

As Chomsky (1986) argues:

> The study of generative grammar shifted the focus of attention from actual or potential behaviour and the products of behaviour to the system of knowledge that underlies the use and understanding of language (p.24).

Traditional/structuralist linguistics and behaviourist psychology view language as a collection of utterances which he calls 'externalized language'. This carries with it the assumption that language can be analysed independently of the properties of the mind/brain (his terms) that create it. 'Generative' approaches imply a shift to the study of 'internalized language' and to an analysis of the systems of mental representations which enable us to use language.

It is clear that this view of language is different and necessarily implies a mentalistic, cognitive approach, the one that presently dominates in psychology. This approach was implicit earlier in this chapter when we considered the communication between Mark and his mother. The various contributions were not analysed in stimulus – response terms: instead, notions such as meaning, intentions, goals and strategies that dynamically create coherent dialogue were used.

Chomsky, however, following up his critique of the behaviourist positions, also has a great deal to say about how language is learned by the child. He argued that the speed with which children learn language, bearing in mind the often ungrammatical and 'degraded' language that they must often hear, indicates that an innate capacity must be at work. This position was reached without benefit of empirical investigation and both of these claims can be questioned in the light of subsequent research. Even in his recent work he argues for a strongly innate component, but now in relation to the experiences of the child.

> One may think of this (language) faculty as a 'language acquisition device', an innate component of the human mind that yields a particular language through interaction with presented experience, a device that converts experience into a system of knowledge attained: knowledge of one or another language (1986, p.2)

In using the phrase 'through interaction with presented experience' it would appear that he would not necessarily be far from current thinking (e.g. Wells, 1985; 1986) although we would need to be much clearer about the implications of the terms 'interaction' and 'presented experience'. Wells (1985), in fact, reaches a similar conclusion having analysed the apparently general sequence of emergence of many language forms and meanings across a wide variety of children.

At the same time, however, he also acknowledges that individuals differ in the rate at which they progress and even some small variation in the sequence (1985, p.321). The previous sections have indicated that this idea of individual variation has come to the fore in recent research from several writers (Peters, 1983, MacWhinney, 1987). As we have already seen, children vary in the strategies they adopt in learning the sound system, vocabulary, to some extent syntactic structures and conversational pragmatics. So the problem is to account for both what is universal in language development and what is variable. It would be unproductive to regard these individual variations as just trivial deviations from a universal sequence.

Hardy-Brown (1983) makes an important point about keeping clear the distinction between 'universal elements' and 'individual differences' and their possible causes – heredity ('nature') or environment ('nurture'). To capture all possibilities we need the matrix shown overleaf.

The focus in much language research is on cells 2 and 3, equating universal sequences with inherited factors and variability with environmental influence. If we consider cells 1 and 4 however, the possibility of environmental influences giving rise to similarity (for example, child rearing ideologies and behaviour within cultural or subcultural groups) and genetically induced variability have to

ENVIRONMENTALLY INDUCED SIMILARITY	ENVIRONMENTALLY INDUCED VARIABILITY
GENETICALLY INDUCED SIMILARITY	GENETICALLY INDUCED VARIABILITY

be allowed for. MacWhinney (1987) discusses such inherited factors as individual differences in hearing acuity, memory and attention process and their potential influence in language learning.

Rather than being kept distinct in child language research, these dimensions are often confused, as for instance when children are studied interacting with their biological parents. The problem is that children of above average language ability are likely to be interacting with similar parents and vice versa so it is impossible to distinguish genetic from environmental influences. Only research which studies adopted children in relation to both their biological and adoptive parents can do this and so far not many such studies exist. The result of using only biological parents in research is potentially to inflate the importance of 'environmental' influences.

These are significant elements to keep in mind but they do presuppose that what is 'inherited' and what is 'environmental' can be easily distinguished. There are those who have argued strongly that this is no easy or particularly fruitful enterprise (Richards, 1977). Richards makes the point that the two are so inextricably intertwined that it becomes an entirely arbitrary decision where the line is to be drawn between them, which in turn presents difficulties in suggesting the precise nature of the 'interactions' between them. Bearing these criticisms in mind, we should perhaps shift the focus away from trying to decide how much each contributes in the developmental process to the question of how developmental changes are brought about within the interactions the child has with its environment. If we study the child at any point in its development, its thinking and behaviour will be the result of all earlier interactions with the environment and will go on to affect and contribute to subsequent experiences in that environment. Genetic factors are having an effect only very indirectly.

Sameroff and Chandler (1975) have suggested that a 'transactional' view of the developmental process best captures these mutual influences that continue over time. Their model stresses that the child is an active participant in its own development in relation to an 'environment' that has been partly created by the child in previous transactions. What is important is not an analysis of the individual elements of 'child' and 'environment' but of the on-going transactions between them and how these might serve to either develop or suppress potentials within the child. The effects of the environment on the child will be crucially influenced by what the child is able to perceive of that environment or chooses to respond to within it. There is no simple way in which we can think of particular 'inputs' to the child being related to particular 'outcomes' of behaviour or under-standings. This would fail to do justice to the complexity and subtlety of the mutual influences.

It is a model that can be applied to any aspect of the child's development but one which is especially appropriate to the explanation of language development. The communicative processes set up between children and those around will, as we have seen, be mutually created and sustained. The child does not come into the world a blank slate, empty-headed as it were, but rather as an adapting and communicating being. Infants seem predisposed to learn to talk and the environment, in the form of people around, provides the experiences that potentially allow these predispositions to develop.

In the last decade, much research has been carried out on the role of the environment in language learning, the 'contemporary nurturist' position (Kuczaj, 1986) where the 'environment' is always seen in relation to what the child too is bringing to the transactions. What has been discovered is that the language used by adults when talking to young children has special charac-teristics. Utterances are short, often structurally simple, contain much repetition and redundancy and are spoken at a higher pitch and slower rate than speech to other adults. These modifications have been called 'motherese' (although fathers indulge in them too!) and even chidren as young as 3 and 4 years make adjustments when talking to younger ones (Sachs and Devin, 1976). These general findings are reported in several studies (Snow, 1972; Cross, 1977) but there is not always agreement about the degree of 'fine-tuning' that is found in parent–child conversations over time, nor the exact role that the adult 'input' plays.

On the 'fine-tuning' issue, Wells (1985) has some useful points to make. He looked at variation in the frequency of parents' use of certain forms and meaning in relation to the children's use of these. On several but not all of the items he considered, the child's first use of a word or function was preceded by an increased usage by the parent. Longitudinal analysis such as this seem to provide some evidence that adult input is directly related to the child's progress for some linguistic items. To quote Wells himself,

> For this learning to take place, it is clearly necessary for the input of the child to contain a suffcient frequency of examples of what has to be learned. It may well be particularly helpful if the frequency of the more complex items is kept low until the point where the child is ready to

to learn them. A relatively sharp increase in frequency at this point would then render them particularly salient and encourage the child to pay particular attention to them (1985, p.378).

Much parental speech seems therefore to be fairly closely 'matched' to the child's abilities, but some may be a little in advance, so allowing the child to progress. As Brown (1977) suggests, productive communication with children 'is always the launching platform for attempts at communication on a more adult level' (p.15). All this does not imply that these moves are consciously or explicitly thought through by parents; it is more likely that they sensitively respond to changes in their children, using the child's apparent comprehension as cues. Parental input therefore seems to play an enabling role rather than a determining one. Scollon (1979) has taken up the question of exactly how this enabling might take place, especially for the learning of more complex structural forms. His suggestion is that, for instance, when the child is only using single-word constructions, over several 'turns' in conversation the child may gradually build up a more complex meaning, helped by the adult. He calls these *'vertical'* constructions and sees them as the first steps towards the later *'horizontal'* constructions the child will produce as a sequence of words within a single utterance.

The Linguistic Deprivation Debate

If we see linguistic transactions between the child and the environment as important in the language learning process, do children from different social backgrounds necessarily experience such 'enabling'? The issue of educational disadvantage and more particularly deprivation in terms of language experiences has been a major educational debate. The argument is that certain home backgrounds and lifestyles reduce children's chances of academic success, so that 'working class' children and certain ethnic minority children underachieve, partly as a result of an impoverished language experience in the early years. The early work of Bernstein (1965) is usually quoted, or a least the 'partial' versions that seem to have become part of education folklore. Implicit in the argument is often a deficit view, that some children use an 'inferior' language in a world where 'superior' forms are required and that they arrive at school with a 'substandard' variety which prevents them from fully participating in school learning (Edwards, 1986).

Although some empirical information was collected to back up versions of the theory, this was often carried out under test conditions or by questionnaire. Little detailed information was obtained about actual language use in home and school (Tizard and Hughes 1984). The argument is also problematic on linguistic grounds too, since there are no good grounds for describing languages or dialects as either superior or inferior (Trudgill, 1975).

But such views seem deeply embedded in teachers' thinking as work by Gordon (1978) and Edwards (1986) shows. Gordon found that Bernstein's theory was often quoted by teachers although it was often poorly understood. Those whose reading on the subject was most superficial were most convinced by it: those who had read more were critical and sceptical. What the theory seemed to provide was an all-too-ready categorization scheme to back up existing attitudes.

In reality, a 'difference' view rather than a 'deficit' one is potentially more appropriate, although even this idea is brought into question by recent research which has directly compared language use by children from different social backgrounds at home and in school. Both Tizard and Hughes (1984) and Wells (1985) show that the experiences of working-class and middle-class children are fairly similar in home contexts. All the children experienced a wide range of language, with middle-class mothers however providing somewhat more. But such differences were not enough to justify the considerable claims made in the earlier studies. For most of the children, language experiences at home were richer and more varied than those at school (or nursery), with children initiating more conversations and asking more questions at home. If we try to link these findings with the information on the achievements of different social classes in the education system, we may have to consider the possibility that it is schools themselves, via teacher categorizations and unfounded assumptions, that may be helping to create and sustain educational disadvantage.

Clearly, the ratio of adults to children in classrooms makes it difficult for teachers and their helpers to deal in a one-to-one way with children. Since this is the case, we should perhaps consider with much greater care the precise nature of the conversations between teachers and children when such possibilities do arise, perhaps the kind of approach adopted by Tough (1977). Contrary to some opinion within the teaching profession, teachers may have a great deal to learn from parents about developing children's language and thinking.

Children Experiencing Difficulties with Language and Communication

It has not been my intention in this chapter to deal directly with the topic of language difficulties. Instead, I have considered the 'normal' course of language development and key issues and principles attached to this, as a means of deriving insights and principles that will enable us to provide more effective analysis and help.

It is no straightforward matter to define a 'language problem', since difficulties arise for many reasons and vary in their severity. Given the wide individual variation in rates and strategies of language learning that we have considered in this chapter, it may be that some children begin late and progress more slowly, while for others the problems are much more fundamental. In this latter case the whole pattern of the developmental sequence may be different.

What is clear is that problems with language and communication may have implications for more general social and emotional development and learning. It has been estimated that approximately 5 per cent of children enter school unable to make themselves understood and that a small proportion of these will have quite severe language problems (Webster and McConnell, 1987). Boys are twice as likely to have problems as girls and children from socially deprived backgrounds are overrepresented.

In the last section, we considered some of the issues in the debate on language and social background and showed that many of the stereotyped views on language 'deficit' have to be reconsidered. But even these researches indicate that there will be some children with impoverished language experiences in the home who will need help on entering school. Cases of extreme deprivation are fortunately rare, but even here, as with the case of Genie, the adolescent girl found in a Los Angeles attic who had been kept in isolation and was unable to talk when found, remedial measures proved effective for most aspects of language.

Language problems occur for other reasons too, of course – anatomical abnormalities, processing problems of various kinds in the brain and hearing difficulties, but simply applying these labels does not solve anything and may in fact act in negative ways. At most they may act as a starting point for the major task which is to describe in detail the child's particular language difficulty, guided by a valid theoretical framework of language development and to plan appropriate teaching strategies on the basis of this. This chapter is structured in a way that should aid this process of analysis, suggesting that all aspects of language should be included yet seeing all aspects in relation to one another.

The child's ability to deal with the sound system, his or her range of vocabulary and understanding of words and the ability to structure sentences, should all be observed and recorded together with comprehension of language in different contexts and all aspects of conversation skills. Beveridge and Conti-Ramsden (1987) provide a more detailed account of such procedures along with suggestions for relevant teaching strategies. They also argue strongly that language development and general cognitive skills go hand in hand, so that aspects of information processing – memory, perceptual discrimination, attentional processes etc. – should be included in intervention plans where appropriate. In this way we may help those children who need it to organize their knowledge better and more fully express their understanding.

If detailed individual analysis is carried out, we should expect to find some varied and idiosyncratic profiles. Beveridge and Conti-Ramsden give an example of Tony, a boy with a good memory, a competent level of 'mechanical' reading and considerable abilities in game playing who had difficulty conversing with others. He found it hard to 'read' the signals from other people in conversation and therefore had problems relating to them. In this case, by using interactional games and role-play this difficulty could be overcome and so permit more productive interaction with others.

Another interesting case-study is provided by Curtiss (1982), who discusses another Anthony, a child of 7 with very low measured intelligence (acknowledging the difficulties of defining and measuring this) but quite considerable language abilities. In particular, he could use complex grammatical structures more or less correctly although his use of some words indicated problems in understanding their meaning. Curtiss comments that such cases were often not referred to them because teachers and parents seemed to equate language ability with general mental ability and make assumptions about future development on this basis. A child's language performance is often taken as an indicator of other abilities in this way, so it is a salutary reminder that the two aspects of functioning may not always be linked in the direct way we sometimes assume.

Conclusions

1   Our view of what skilled language use involves is important, since it directs our attention in either broad or narrower ways when we are appraising children's communicative powers. The work I have summarized in this chapter has hopefully provided a more comprehensive framework for considering communicative development.

2   From time to time, throughout the chapter, I have made specific comments about this appraisal process, stressing the fact that setting and context strongly influence what and how much needs to be said. Labov (1970) many years ago now, drew attention to the fact that it is possible to underestimate the communicative abilities of children and adolescents by not recognizing that it is their definition of the situation and roles that will determine how they choose to communicate. Any appraisal process should take this into account and be as broadly based and naturalistic as possible.

3   Present research suggests that there is no single path towards mature language use and in any case, we frequently cannot define what this is in a detailed way. Individuals vary in rate of progress, strategies used and sometimes in the sequence of learning. Since this is the case, we should beware of setting artificially 'normative' standards when considering any child's progress.

4   As teachers we should reflect carefully on our attitudes towards and expectations of children from different social backgrounds. The evidence reviewed here suggests that the idea of 'language deprivation' is something of a myth, but a myth that still appears to colour teacher

attitudes and behaviour, potentially setting up negative educational outcomes. We should also bear in mind that parents from most social backgrounds seem to be really quite competent developers of children's language and thinking in the pre-school years. Perhaps therefore we should be taking a leaf out of their books when communicating with children in classroom contexts.

Finally, to return to the opening paragraph of this chapter, the term 'miracle' has other connotations too. In the midst of all the important fine-grained observation and recording of children's language that as teachers we need to carry out, we should not lose sight of the slight sense of awe and the sheer pleasure of communicating with children.

References

Aitchison, J. and Chiat, S. (1981), Natural phonology or natural memory: the interaction between phonological processes and recall mechanisms, *Language and Speech*, **24**, 363–72.

Bernstein, B. (1965), A sociolinguistic approach to social learning, in Gould, J. (ed.), *Penguin Survey of the Social Sciences* (Harmondsworth: Penguin).

Beveridge, M. and Conti-Ramsden, G. (1987), *Children with Language Disabilities* (Milton Keynes: Open University Press).

Blewitt, P. (1982), Word meaning acquisition in young children: a review of theory and research in Reese, H. W. (ed.), *Advances in Child Development and Behaviour*, Vol. 17, (New York: Academic Press).

Brown, R. (1958), *Words and Things* (Glencoe: Free Press).

Brown, R. (1977), Introduction in Snow, C. E. and Ferguson, C. A. (eds) *Talking to Children: Language Input and Acquisition* (Cambridge: University Press).

Carey, S. (1982), Semantic development: the state of the art, in Wanner, E. and Gleitman, L. (eds), *Language Acquisition: The State of the Art* (New York: Cambridge University Press).

Chomsky, N. (1957), *Syntactic Structures* (The Hague: Moulton).

Chomsky, N. (1959), Review of 'Verbal Behaviour' by B. F. Skinner, *Language* **35**, 26–58.

Chomsky, N. (1986), *Knowledge of Language: Its Nature, Origin and Use* (New York: Praeger).

Clark, E. V. (1973), What's in a word? On the child's acquisition of semantics in his first language, in Moore, T. E. (ed.) *Cognitive Development and the Acquisition of Language* (New York: Academic Press).

Clark, R. (1982), Theory and method in child language research: are we asking too much?, in Kuczaj, S. A. (ed.), *Language Development: Vol. 1 Syntax and Semantics* (New Jersey: Lawrence Erlbaum Associates).

Cross, T. G. (1977), Mothers' speech adjustments: the contribution of selected child listener variables, in Snow, C. E. and Ferguson, C. A. (eds.) *Talking to Children: Language Input and Acquistion* (Cambridge: University Press).

Cruttenden, A. (1979), *Language in infancy and childhood* (Manchester University Press).

Crystal, D. (1976), *Child Language, learning and linguistics* (London: Edward Arnold).

Curtiss, S. (1982), Developmental dissociations of language and cognition, in Obler, L. K. and Menn, L. (eds.), *Exceptional Language and Linguistics* (Academic Press, New York).

Durkin, K. (ed.) (1986), *Language Development in the School Years* (London: Croom Helm).

Edwards, J. (1986), Language and educational disadvantage: the persistence of linguistic 'deficit' theory, in Durkin, K. (ed.), *Language Development in the School Year* (London: Croom Helm).

Ervin-Tripp, S. (1977), Wait for me, roller-skate, in Ervin-Tripp, S. and Mitchell-Kernan, C. (eds) *Child Discourse* (New York: Academic Press).

Gordon, J. (1978), *The Reception of Bernstein's Sociolinguistic Theory among Primary School Teachers* (University of East Anglia Papers in Linguistics).

Graddol, D., Cheshire, J. and Swann, J. (1987), *Describing Language* (Milton Keynes: University Press).

Grunwell, P. (1981), The development of phonology, *First Language* 2, pt.3, no. 6,161–91.

Grunwell, P. (1986), Aspects of phonological development in later childhood, in Durkin K. (ed.) *Language Development in the School Years* (London: Croom Helm).

Gumperz, J.J. *et al.* (1979), *Crosstalk* (Southall: National Centre for Industrial Language Training).

Hardy-Brown, K. (1983), Universals and individual differences: disentangling two approaches to the study of language acquisition, *Developmental Psychology*, **49**, 4, 610–24.

Horgan, D. (1980), Nouns: love 'em or leave 'em, in Teller, U. and White, S.J. (eds), *Studies in Child Language and Multilingualism* (New York: Annals of the New York Academy of Sciences).

Kuczaj, S. and Lederberg, A. (1977), Height, age and function: differing influences on children's comprehension of 'younger' and 'older', *Jounal of Child Language*, **4**, 395–416.

Kuczaj, S. A. (1986), Discussion: on social interaction as a type of explanation of language development, *British Journal of Developmental Psychology*, **4**, 289–99.

Labov, W. (1970), The logic of non-standard English, in Williams, F. (ed.), *Language and Poverty* (Markham Press, Chicago).

MacWhinney, B. (ed.) (1987), *Mechanisms of Language Acquisition* (New Jersey: Lawrence Erlbaum Associates Hillsdale).

McTear, M. (1985), *Children's Conversations* (Oxford: Blackwell).

Nelson, K. (1973), Structure and Strategy in Learning to Talk, *Monographs of the Society for Research in Child Development*, **39**.

Newsome, J. (1978), Dialogue and development, in Lock, A. (ed.), *Action, Gesture and Symbol* (London: Academic Press).

Ninio, A. and Bruner, J. S. (1978), The achievement and antecedents of labelling, *Journal of Child Language*, **5**, 1–15.

Perera, K. (1984), *Children's Writing and Reading: Analysing Classroom Language* (Oxford: Blackwell).

Peters, A. M. (1983), *The Units of Language Acquisition* (Cambridge: Cambridge University Press).

Rice, M. and Kemper, S. (1984), *Child Language and Cognition* (Baltimore: University Park Press).

Richards, M. P. M. (1977) 'Interaction and the concept of development', in Lewis, M. and Rosenblum, A. (eds) *Interaction, Conversation and the Development of Language* (New York: Wiley).

Robinson, E. J. and Whittaker, S. J. (1986), Learning about verbal referential communication in the early school years *in* Durkin, K. (ed.) *Language Development in the School Years* (London: Croom Helm)

Sachs, J. and Devin, J. (1976), Young children's knowledge of age-appropriate speech styles, *Journal of Child Language*, **3**, 81–98.

Sameroff, A.J. and Chandler, M.J. (1975), Reproductive risk and the continuum of caretaking casualty, in Horowitz, F. D. (ed.), *Review of Child Development Research*, **4** (University of Chicago Press).

Scollon, R. (1979), A real early stage: an unzippered condensation of a dissertation on child language, in Ochs, S. and Schieffelin, B. (eds), *Developmental Pragmatics* (New York: Academic Press).

Shorrocks, D. (1981), An investigation into maternal perception and understanding of the speech of young children (PhD thesis, University of Leeds).

Skinner, B. F. (1957), *Verbal Behaviour* (New York: Appleton).

Snow, C. E. (1972), Mothers' speech to children learning language, *Child Development*, 43, 549–65.

Tizard, B. and Hughes, M. (1984), *Young Children Learning: Talking and Thinking at Home and at School* (London: Fontana).

Tough, J. (1977), *Talking and Learning* (London: Ward Lock Educational).

Trudgill, P. (1975), *Accent, Dialect and the School* (London: Edward Arnold).

Webster, A. and McConnell, C. (1987), *Children with Speech and Language Difficulties* (London: Cassell).

Wells, G. (1985a), *Language Development in the Pre-school Years* (Cambridge University Press).

Wells, G. (1985b) *Language, Learning and Education* (Windsor: NFER and Nelson).

Wells, G. (1986), *The Meaning Makers: Children Learning Language and Using Language to Learn* (London: Hodder and Stoughton).

Chapter 7

Parents as Teachers of Children with Special Educational Needs
Sally Beveridge

Twenty-one years ago, the Plowden report (DES, 1967) gave official recognition to the important role of parents in their children's education. Since then, there has been increasing acceptance of the need for close co-operation between professionals and parents for the educational benefit of all children, but particularly those with special educational needs. The Warnock committee were so convinced of this that they asserted that 'the successful education of children with special educational needs is dependent on the full involvement of their parents', and further, that 'unless the parents are seen as equal partners in the educational process the purpose of our report will be frustrated' (DES, 1978, para. 9.1.).

The wide-ranging implications of a 'full involvement' of parents in all aspects of their children's education are beyond the scope of this chapter. However, a focus on the teaching role of parents of children with special educational needs necessarily involves some appraisal of the concept of partnership espoused by the Warnock committee. It is well-established that much natural teaching takes place at home in the everyday interactions of parents with their children. Moreover, when the children have special educational needs, parents may also be encouraged by professionals to take on more formalized and explicit teaching functions. If parents are to do this, they are likely to need professional reassurance and support, and thus a potential valuable channel is opened up for the development of an active partnership.

Traditionally though, professionals have tended to follow an approach in their work with parents which is more readily associated with a training rather than a partnership model. Indeed, it is notable that a recent review of work which has been undertaken (Topping, 1986) is aptly subtitled 'Training Parents to Teach Their Children'. Research in this area remains dominated by reference to 'programmes of parent-training', which may be characterized by what

Cunningham (1983) has described as the 'transplant', on to parents of selected professional techniques, together with a focus on narrowly-defined teaching objectives for their children.

The training approach, by its very nature, places parents in the role of trainees who lack certain skills and information and are in need of professional direction. Little account may be taken of the unique experience and knowledge of their own children which parents possess. By contrast, the concept of partnership implies a working relationship between parents and professionals in which roles and responsibilities are negotiated on the basis of mutual trust and respect for each others' expertise (Mittler and Mittler, 1982). There is explicit recognition here that parents, as well as professionals, have relevant skills and knowledge. Within a partnership model, therefore, the professional task cannot be viewed as the one-way transmission of information and techniques to parents. What is called for, rather, is a joint problem-solving approach which, drawing on the complementary skills and knowledge of both parties, is informed by mutual learning.

In order to explore the ways in which such a joint problem-solving approach might be developed, it seems necessary to focus attention on the complementary expertise which parents and professionals may possess. In this chapter, therefore, the role of parents as teachers of their own children is considered in some detail. Similarities and differences in parental teaching strategies, and factors associated with individual variation are discussed. The second part of the chapter traces the gradual shift in professional perspectives on the purpose and nature of the work they undertake with parents. Using an example of one particular study which aimed to find ways of matching professional intervention to existing parental teaching strategies and styles of interaction, some implications are drawn for the future development of work with parents as teachers.

Parents as Teachers

Although the role of fathers in their children's development and learning (as well as that of siblings and other family members) has received increased attention in recent years, the majority of research evidence on parents as teachers of their own children is derived from interviews with and observations of mothers.

Several researchers (e.g. Bruner, 1974; Newson, 1977; Schaffer, 1977) have drawn attention to the finely tuned interactions in which mothers typically engage their children from birth. By interpreting their infants' actions as meaningful, they are able to enter into a 'dialogue'. While initially mothers take the major responsibility for maintaining this, very quickly their infants also begin to initiate and sustain communication. The sorts of support that mothers provide to help their infants achieve their intentions, and the techniques they employ to help them acquire social and play skills, are referred to by Bruner as 'scaffolding'.

Hodapp *et al.* (1984) investigated how mothers used 'scaffolding' techniques over a period of time. From when their children were eight months through till sixteen months old, monthly observations were made of mothers playing peek-aboo and rolling a ball with them. The following maternal strategies were recorded. Firstly, mothers used 'stage-setting' procedures, that is, making sure that their children were oriented in the right direction and attending to them, before starting the game. Then, once the game began, mothers channelled their children's approximate responses into more 'ideal' forms by a number of techniques. When children were in the early stages of skill acquisition, they used contextual cues and both verbal and gestural prompts (such as in holding out their hands for the ball). As their children started to show emerging skills however, the use of these cues was faded, and at the same time mothers developed more consistent rules for what constituted an acceptable response in the game, shaping their children's behaviour by the use of praise.

This study highlights some of the similarities which have been observed between the techniques used by mothers to support their children's learning and those which one might expect a trained teacher to use. Such similarities do not imply, however, that mothers necessarily perceive their role as involving explicit teaching of their children. On the contrary, most studies of mothers at home with their pre-school-aged children suggest that little direct instruction takes place. The teaching that does occur is likely to be 'on the fly', initiated as often by the children as by their mothers, and typically linked to the children's activities and interests at the time. Thus it is in a facilitative, rather than in a directly instructional way, that mothers have been described as fostering their children's learning.

There is rather less evidence about the teaching undertaken at home as children grow older. Tizard and Hughes (1984) and Wells (1983) have described the richness of maternal linguistic and cognitive stimulation of children at nursery and infant school age. Others have reported that, during the primary school years, some parents may adopt more explicit teaching aims too, particularly in relation to literacy and numeracy skills (e.g. Farquhar *et al.*, 1986). However, because of the acknowledged importance of the early years in children's development and the central role of mothers in supporting learning during this period, the major focus of research has been on maternal interaction with their pre-school children.

In this research associations have been sought between different patterns of maternal behaviour and their children's cognitive competence. In the search for a pattern of 'optimal maternal care' (Clarke-Stewart, 1973) two main dimensions of variation in maternal interactive style have been identified. The first, on which there is considerable research agreement, is that of maternal responsiveness to their children's behaviour. Clarke-Stewart (1973) argued that it was contingent responsiveness which enabled young children to learn that their behaviour had consequences and that they could control their environment, thus laying the foundations of motivation for later learning. Subsequent studies have tended to endorse this view (e.g. Clarke-Stewart *et al.*, 1979; Bakeman and Brown, 1980; Belsky, 1984).

In many studies, the concept of maternal responsiveness carries with it the implication of warmth, sensitivity and acceptance. Some extend the concept still further, by contrasting responsiveness with intrusiveness, directiveness and control (e.g. Phinney and Feshbach, 1980; Bee *et al.*, 1982). Others, however, argue that these should more appropriately be regarded as a separate dimension of maternal interactive style. They point out that directiveness and control do not preclude sensitivity and responsiveness, and that they need not represent negative aspects of maternal behaviour. Schaffer and Crook (1979), for example, have drawn attention to the responsive timing and adaptiveness to their children's behaviour which characterize many maternal control techniques. Furthermore, some researchers have stressed that maternal guidance and control play an important part in fostering children's learning, and that it is only extreme directiveness or restrictiveness which is likely to have negative consequences. Thus Hess and McDevitt (1984) concluded on the basis of their observations that effective maternal teaching includes directive techniques, through which mothers draw attention to desired behaviour, as well as indirect techniques, which ensure that their children become active participants in their learning.

It would seem then that, while there is general agreement that a pattern of 'optimal maternal care' includes social, emotional and verbal responsiveness, there is far less consensus on what constitutes positive practice in relation to directiveness and control. Certain groups of mothers, notably those whose children have developmental delays and impairments, have been characterized in research studies as directive in their interactions. It is important, therefore, to bear in mind the diversity of opinion about this dimension of interactive style. Before moving on to review the evidence on mothers as teachers of children with special educational needs, however, it is relevant first to consider some of the comparative studies which have been undertaken with mothers of differing socio-economic status.

Parents of Differing Socio-economic Status

It has been acknowledged for some time that children from middle-class backgrounds do better at school that those from lower-working-class backgrounds (e.g. Mortimore and Blackstone, 1983), and that there is an over-representation of lower status families among the children identified by their teachers as showing moderate learning difficulties or emotional and behavioural difficulties (Tomlinson, 1982). Comparative studies of mother–child interactions in families of differing socio-economic status have sought to identify patterns which may be associated with subsequent school performance.

It is important to note that the factors which have been taken into account in order to establish the socio-economic status of the families involved in these studies have not always been clear. The consideration of variables such as the past as well as current occupations of mothers and fathers, ethnicity and years of formal education have often been left implicit. The resulting lack of clarity as to what constitute middle- and working-class family background implies the need for some caution in evaluating their evidence.

Where mothers have been observed in structured teaching contexts with their children, differences have been found both in the type of maternal stimulation and in the degree of maternal directiveness and control. Typically in such studies (e.g. Hess and Shipman, 1965; Bee *et al.*, 1969; Kogan and Wimberger, 1969), middle-class mothers are characterized as more positive, verbal and specific in their teaching and also less directive of their children. Working-class mothers, on the other hand, are described as using more negative and physical teaching strategies, and showing more directiveness and control. Maternal responsiveness has been assessed in this research by the type of feedback provided to the children: middle-class mothers providing more positive and verbal feedback, as contrasted with a greater degree of negative and physical feedback from working-class mothers.

From such studies, then, it might be concluded that, at least as evidenced in formal teaching situations, middle-class mothers approximate more closely to the pattern of 'optimal maternal care' described by Clarke-Stewart (1973), and endorsed by others.

However, some of the assumptions underlying this early research have increasingly been questioned. Mothers were observed in contrived formal teaching situations which may have borne little relation to their usual approach with their children. Furthermore, one group of mothers (middle-class) was used to provide a yardstick against which the interactive and teaching style of other groups was assessed. This led to a focus on differences rather than similarities between groups, and to a value-laden interpretation of those differences. It also detracted attention away from the consideration of within-group variation. One exception to this trend was the home-based study carried out by Tulkin and Kagan (1972). They found few differences in non-verbal behaviour between working-class and middle-class mothers, and interpreted the observed differences in verbal behaviour as being accounted for by a sub-group of highly verbal middle class mothers.

In more recent studies, there has been increased acknowledgement of within-group variability. Phinney and Feshbach (1980), for example, suggested that individual variation is particularly marked among working-class mothers, where they identified both 'positive, non-directive' and 'negative, intrusive' styles of maternal behaviour. More generally, a number of researchers (e.g. Clarke-Stewart *et al.*, 1979; Bradley and Caldwell, 1984) have been led to conclude that there is a significant amount of variation in maternal interaction style that cannot be attributed to social class.

Parents of Children with Special Educational Needs

Given the emphasis in research on the developing mother-child relationship during the pre-school years, it is not surprising that the majority of the evidence on parents as teachers of children with special educational needs derives from the study of mothers whose children have readily identified delays and impairments. Comparisons have been made with the interactions of mothers whose children show no development difficulties. This research shares certain features with the work undertaken to investigate the influence of socio-economic variables, and a similar pattern of changing assumptions over time can be traced.

Historically, the comparative studies tended to follow a 'unidirectional' approach. Working from the assumption that causes of a child's difficulties, or at least contributing factors, might be found in distorted patterns of mother–child interaction, researchers sought and found differences from the yardstick provided by mothers of 'normal' children. Thus Greenberg (1971) reported that mothers of children showing 'atypical' behaviour provided 'insufficient, faulty or extreme' stimulation. Mothers of children with developmental delays and impairments were described as 'overprotective' and 'restrictive' of their children. As Bristol and Schopler (1984) pointed out, if mothers directed and structured their children's play they were regarded as 'intrusive', but if they did not, they might be described as showing 'emotional withdrawal'. Increasingly, however, recognition of the importance of within-group variation has led to an acknowledgement of the many complex factors which may influence mothers in their interactive behaviours. Among these influences, the role of the child him/herself has become so apparent that the interpretation of any observed differences from the interactions of mothers with 'normal' children has become far more tentative.

A brief methodological note about these comparative studies is necessary. First, they have been concerned with a wide range of developmental disabilities, delays and impairments. Some have concentrated on specific conditions, such as Down's syndrome, while others have used broad categories such as 'at risk' or 'mental retardation'. In addition to the more obvious differences between such categories, there is also a wide range of individual variation within them. A further point concerns the basis upon which the comparison groups have been 'matched'. Typically, most studies have used either chronological or mental age measures. Less frequently, children have been matched on specific developmental attributes, such as linguistic competence. Less frequently still, multiple comparison groups have been used. Because of such methodological differences between studies, any attempt to generalize among them is problematic. However, some common themes do emerge from their findings.

Most studies lend support to the view that, by comparison with 'normal' mother–child pairs, mothers of delayed and impaired children are more directive, and their children more passive and less responsive, in their interactions (e.g. Buckhalt *et al.*, 1978; Cunningham *et al.*, 1981; Eheart, 1982; Stoneman *et al.*, 1983). Mothers of children with Down's syndrome have been reported to provide a high level of stimulation which, together with their children's poorly developed social skills, may lead to a higher incidence of interactive 'clashes' (Jones, 1980; Berger and Cunningham, 1983). This does not, however, imply that these mothers lack responsiveness to their children's behaviour. There is no evidence that they show less contingent responsiveness than others. Rather, a normal developmental progression has been reported in maternal responsiveness towards children with Down's syndrome (e.g. Crawley and Spiker, 1983; McConkey and Martin, 1984), with cerebral palsy and with developmental delay (Brooks-Gunn and Lewis 1984).

There has been some suggestion that the high level of stimulation, directiveness and control observed among mothers of developmentally delayed children is itself evidence of their responsiveness, because through such behaviour they are showing a reasonable and adaptive response to their childrens's difficulties. However, Cunningham *et al.* (1981) have argued that directiveness in maternal behaviour cannot be explained by a simple relationship to their children's developmental ability. They observed that developmentally delayed children, like their non-delayed peers, became more interactive, responsive and compliant as they grew in competence, but that their mothers still remained more directive and controlling in their interactions than other mothers.

Why should this be? Some researchers have put forward the view that directiveness and control on the part of mothers may be at least partly associated with teaching activity. There is certainly evidence from a number of studies (e.g. Buckhalt *et al.*, 1978; Jones, 1980; Stoneman *et al.*, 1983) of more explicit teaching activities on the part of mothers of children with Down's syndrome than among comparison groups. Where directiveness and control represent part of positive teaching interactions between mothers and their delayed or impaired children it is possible to conclude, as Bristol and Schopler (1984) did, that mothers are responding to their children's needs by 'providing structure and whatever degree of "intrusiveness" is necessary to elicit a response' (p. 101).

However, not all mothers are likely to respond so positively to their children's particular needs. Some comparative studies have drawn attention to the interactive difficulties which may exist, and of the risks to the developing mother–child relationship if they persist. Such relationships may be characterized by a decreasing level of interaction and maternal involvement with their children (e.g. Wilton and Barbour, 1978; Wasserman and Allen, 1985) and, in extreme cases, by neglect or abuse (Meier and Sloan, 1984).

There is, of course, likely to be as wide a range of individual difference among mothers of children with identified difficulties and needs as among any other group. Where attention has been focused on the nature of this within-group variation, the same dimensions of difference have been reported as were seen in the 'normal' mother–child interaction literature. For example, among mothers of children with Down's syndrome, differences have been observed in the degree of directiveness and responsiveness shown in interaction (Crawley and Spiker, 1983), and in their use of directive and less directive teaching techniques (McConkey and Martin, 1986). Stable individual differences in teaching strategies have also been described among parents of children with a range of developmental delays and impairments (McConachie and Mitchell, 1985). Just as in the case of comparative research based on socio-economic variables, therefore, the study of mother–child interactions where the children have delayed or impaired development has pointed to the need to consider the complex factors which may be associated with the range of individual differences observed.

Influences on Individual Variation

As increased attention has been focused on the wide range of individual variation between parents, three main interacting sources of influence on parent–child interactions have been identified. These may be characterized as: (1) the child him/herself; (2) parental perceptions, attitudes and knowledge; (3) ecological variables.

1 *The child him/herself*

The contribution of the child him/herself to observed differences in parent–child interactions was highlighted by the work of Bell (1968; 1974; 1979) on what he termed 'reciprocal influences'. Reviewing the evidence that approximately half of all mother–child interactions are typically initiated by the children, he suggested that mothers' responses not only shape, but are also shaped by their children's behaviour. Thus, for example, infants who are responsive and active may elicit a high level of maternal stimulation by comparison with those who are inhibited or passive. Greater effort may therefore be required from mothers to maintain interactions with children who are limited in their ability to initiate communication or to signal clear responses.

Where children have sensory impairments, the restrictions on the range of initiating behaviours which are available to them are readily apparent. The resulting interactive difficulties which may be faced by mothers have been well-documented, both in relation to deaf children (e.g. Wood, 1983) and blind children (e.g. Fraiberg, 1974). Other children too may show restricted or delayed ability to initiate and give clear responses in social interactions. For example, children with Down's syndrome have been reported to show delayed development in smiling and laughing (Cichetti and Sroufe, 1976), attachment and fear (Berry *et al.*, 1980; Cichetti and Serafica, 1981) and the use of referential eye contact (Jones, 1980; Berger and Cunningham, 1981). They have also been described as less 'emotionally available' and giving less easily read signals (Sorce and Emde, 1982). Some children with severe mental handicap may be unresponsive, or even averse, to the physical closeness which is so common a feature of early interaction (Blacher, 1984). More generally, it has been suggested that, by comparison with other children, those with developmental delays and impairments may give inconsistent or unclear signals (Eheart, 1982) and provide less positive feedback for their mothers (Kogan, 1980).

Such aspects of their children's behaviour are likely to have implications for the ease with which mothers might establish the type of synchronized and responsive relationship identified in the 'normal' mother–child interaction literature as optimal for their children's development. They may also affect a mother's feelings of confidence in her maternal role. Goldberg (1977), for example, has argued that an infant's 'readability', predictability and responsiveness will all contribute to a mother's perception of her own competence.

While only a minority of children may present such marked interactive difficulties, the notion of reciprocal influences has wider-ranging implications. It stresses that the direction of effects in the relationship between maternal interactive behaviour and children's development cannot be easily identified. Thus, the patterns of maternal behaviour associated with child competence may partly arise from their children's behaviour and abilities, or perhaps more accurately, from their perceptions of these.

The way in which reciprocal influences may operate in mother–child interaction is, of course, likely to be mediated by their past and continuing relationship. The knowledge and expectations of each other that mother and child have, and their interpretations of one another's behaviour, will all affect the nature of their interactions, As the more mature partner in the relationship, with a powerful role as model and 'expert' (Hinde, 1976), the important influence of the mother's knowledge, perceptions and attitudes has long been accepted.

2 *Parental perceptions, attitudes and knowledge*
Parents vary in their views about the nature of the parental role, their beliefs and knowledge about what influences their children's behaviour and development, and their attitudes towards, for example, what constitutes appropriate behaviour in particular situations. Where a child has identified impairments or disabilities, it is well-established that the diagnosis of 'handicap' has a traumatic effect on parents. On the basis of his work with families of children with Down's syndrome, Cunningham (1979) described a model of psychic crisis, in which he

identified phases of initial shock, subsequent emotional reaction, and gradual adaptation and re-orientation. Voysey (1975) has suggested that parental reactions vary along dimensions of responsibility and power. She pointed out that a mother who perceives herself as not responsible for her child's handicap, but having some power in relation to his/her development is likely to adopt a very different interactive approach from that of a mother who feels responsible but powerless. Blacher (1984) has also drawn attention to the differences in mother–child interaction which may result from alternative views of the nature of child development. She argued that mothers who perceive their children's abilities as essentially innate are less likely to make conscious attempts at intervention than are mothers who regard development as being strongly influenced by environmental factors.

It has previously been noted that several researchers have suggested that the directiveness observed among mothers of developmentally delayed children may be explained by a conscious adoption of teaching as part of their maternal role. However, Chazan *et al.*, (1980) found that fewer than half of the mothers of pre-school children with special needs in their survey were trying to help their children's development by specific teaching. Moreover, McConachie (1982) has reported that mothers of developmentally delayed and impaired children show marked differences not only in their perceptions of what constitutes 'teaching', but also in the degree to which they see it as being part of their role. She noted that some mothers, in their concern to treat their child as they would any other, felt that it was inappropriate to undertake any explicit teaching which might emphasize their child's 'differentness'. Not all mothers hold such definite views, though, and indeed some may experience considerable uncertainty as to what their mothering role should be (Rapoport *et al.*, 1977). They may also feel uncertainty about what to expect from their children, and about their own competence to judge what sort of care and stimulation might be appropriate. Both the beliefs held about their children and the uncertainties felt are likely to have considerable impact on mothers' interactions. Their knowledge, perceptions and attitudes are in turn likely to be influenced by wider family, social and environmental variables.

3 Ecological variables

Among the interacting ecological variables which may influence maternal perceptions and attitudes, perhaps most research attention has been given to socio-economic status. Here, as might be predicted from the comparative observational studies previously referred to, between-group differences have been reported, for example in the value which mothers attach to verbal behaviour, and in their attitudes towards control and discipline (e.g. Newson and Newson, 1968). The acknowledgement of within-group variation, however, has led some (e.g. Bee *et al.*, 1982) to argue that a particularly significant influence on individual mothers is the amount of environmental stress or support which they experience. The sources of such stress or support may be both physical and social, and arise within and beyond the family.

The influence of physical stress on mother–child relationships has been acknowledged for some time. The impact of poverty and oppressive or over-crowded housing conditions may be such that interactions are frequently characterized by restrictiveness and control, regardless of a mother's views on child-rearing (e.g. Bradley and Caldwell, 1984). It would seem that, as Newson and Newson (1968) observed, a 'child-centred' approach to child-rearing is made a great deal easier by comfortable material and physical circumstances. Where children have identified special needs, particularly if these include physical impairment, a coherent picture emerges from research of parental stress asssociated with, for example: housing and transport; lack of or unsatisfactory aids and equipment; and the financial as well as the physical strain that can accompany extra or special demands on bedding, clothes and diet (Hewett, 1970; Philp and Duckworth, 1980).

It might reasonably be supposed that the presence of a child with a diagnosed handicap also has a potentially stressful impact on roles, relationships and routines within the family. Indeed, earlier studies tended to portray families in emotional disarray. They were characterized either by marital breakdown and sibling neglect and resentment, or conversely, by an equally problematic 'overcohesiveness'. However, subsequent research (e.g. Hewett, 1970; Philp and Duckworth 1980) has emphasized that not all the stresses observed can be directly associated with the presence of a handicapped child, and has drawn attention to the similarities, as well as the differences, in the range of social and emotional stress and support experienced by all families.

Family, friends and wider social contacts may all influence parental knowledge of and attitudes towards child-rearing. One potentially important source of stress or support beyond the family derives from the involvement of professionals. All parents of young children are likely to have contact with a number of professionals, but this may often be more extensive when their children have identified special needs. Moreover, the importance attached to such contacts and the influence of professional opinion and advice may be stronger. Where this is the case, professionals are likely to have considerable impact on parents' perceptions and understanding of their children's behaviour and development. As Yando and Zigler (1984) have pointed out, it is important therefore to acknowledge that professional involvement may add to as well as alleviate family stress.

The Professional Role

In the preceding discussion it has been emphasized that parents are involved in teaching children in their everyday interactions. Some parents also engage in more formal and explicit teaching of their children without any direct professional encouragement to do so. However, there is considerable evidence that, where their children have identified delays and impairments, most parents wish for practical guidance and support on how they might best promote their children's learning (e.g. Cunningham and Jeffree, 1975; Mittler and Mittler, 1982; Wolfendale, 1983). How far this is true of other parents is less clear, although the picture which emerges from research into parental involvement in the teaching of reading suggest a wide-spread willingness on their part to work together actively with professionals (e.g. Griffiths and Hamilton, 1984; Topping and Wolfendale, 1985). Such parental interest is fortunate from the professional point of view, because it has been recognized for some time now that intervention with children with special educational needs is likely to be more effective where their parents are actively involved.

Bronfenbrenner (1976), in his influential review of early intervention programmes in the US, concluded that the active participation of parents appeared to be crucial to their success. While subsequent follow-up studies of the children involved in these programmes have not pinpointed parental involvement as a single critical factor in the same way (e.g. Lazar and Darlington, 1982), there is much support for Bronfenbrenner's argument that it does act as a catalyst for sustaining and enhancing the effects of any such intervention. Since his findings were published, active parental involvement has been regarded as an essential component of early intervention schemes: indeed, it is interesting to note that in this country, since the 1981 Education Act, Portage (Shearer and Shearer, 1972) has become a predominant form of early provision for children with special educational needs. This home-based service relies on parents as the primary teachers of their own children.

What then, might be the professional role in providing practical guidance and support to parents in their teaching activities? Two complementary perspectives on child development seem particularly relevant to this question. The first, which has been described as an ecological model (Bronfenbrenner, 1977), sets the context in which professional involvement can be seen to operate. The constraints which social and physical environmental factors may place on parental attitudes towards and practice of their parenting role have already been discussed. An acknowledgement of such constraints has clear implications for the way in which professionals might undertake work with parents as teachers of their children. The ecological model, with its emphasis on the immediate and wider environmental influences upon the developing child and his/her family, points to the need for effective interdisciplinary liaison between professionals in any service that they provide.

The second perspective, focusing on individuals rather than systems, derives from the work of Sameroff and Chandler (1975). From their review of research into child development they concluded that, although it is possible to identify both a continuum of 'reproductive risk' and also one of 'caretaking casualty', a wide range of individual variation in developmental outcomes may arise for children born similarly endowed or in similar home circumstances. Their explanation for this incorporates both the notion of reciprocal influences between children and their caretaking environments and also the way in which these affect developing knowledge, perceptions and understanding over time. Sameroff and Chandler use the word 'transaction' to represent the dynamic nature of the process whereby mutual influences operate between child and environment. They argue that, to the extent that a child both elicits and is provided with a reasonably responsive environment, then the transactions will be such that positive developmental outcomes are likely to occur. In extremes of 'reproductive risk' or 'caretaking casualty', however, the transactions between child and environment become more problematic as unproductive cycles of reciprocal influence may be set in motion.

This 'transactional' model holds considerable implications for professional involvement with parents whose children have special needs. As Gaussen and Stratton (1985) have pointed out, such children may both be particularly dependent on, and also make special demands of, their environments. For example, children with severe or complex disabilities may require careful and sensitive adaptation of the environment provided, and parents may need to develop special skills, such as of handling and positioning, or the adaptation of materials. The interactive difficulties which can face parents of children with developmental delays and impairments have already been described. Where such difficulties exist, patterns of parental interaction may necessarily be different from those with 'normal' children (Kaiser and Hayden, 1984). Furthermore, where their children have been identified as 'handicapped' and, by implication 'different' from other children, parents may lack confidence in their ability to provide appropriate learning experiences. Thus it can be seen that parents may need: practical guidance and information about any special strategies required by their children; support in the development of their skills of predicting, interpreting and responding to their children's behaviour; and reassurance about the extra difficulties in teaching their children which can arise when development is slow or impaired. In practice, the way in which professionals have provided such help to parents has traditionally been through some sort of parent education programme.

Parent Education Programmes

Three main models of parent education programme have been identified in the literature. The *experience* model focuses attention on the sorts of activities and stimulation which are developmentally appropriate for the parents' children. It seeks to increase parental 'teaching orientation' (Slaughter, 1983) and the overall level and variety of stimulation which they provide. The *reflective* approach places an emphasis on developing parental awareness and understanding of their own behaviour and that of their children, and of the interacting influences between these (e.g. Sharpley and Poiner, 1980). The *behavioural* model, with its emphasis on the application of learning principles, typically instructs parents in the use of behaviour modification techniques.

All of these approaches share a general goal of supporting parent–child relations, and all have been used with parents, particularly mothers, of children with developmental delays and impairments. However, it is the behavioural training approach, with its more specific aim of effecting changes in children's skills through the modification of parental teaching strategies, which has predominated. Many parent-training programmes have, not surprisingly, reported the need to give time to discussion of attitudes, feelings and perceptions, but the primary emphasis has been on teaching parents about behavioural techniques and how to use them.

A number of reviews of parent-training programmes have been written, ranging from early work which was predominantly reported in case-study form (e.g. Johnson and Katz, 1973; O'Dell, 1974) to more extensive recent accounts including group programmes and training schemes (e.g. Baker, 1984; Topping, 1986). The programmes have varied in their organization and structure and in the training methods used. For example, the relative merits of individual and group training approaches and home- or centre-based interventions have been explored, and a range of methods, from the 'didactic' to the practical (Yule, 1975) have been used. Most parent-training schemes do, however, share certain common characteristics. Typically, parents are provided with information on the behavioural principles underlying methods of observational assessment, task analysis, and the shaping and reinforcement of behaviour. Parental practice of behavioural techniques is usually then focused on the implementation of specific teaching programmes with their children.

Most studies have reported immediate effects on the parents and their children. For example, parents have gained knowledge about behavioural principles and have shown effective use of at least some of the techniques to which they have been introduced. Their children have made progress on the specific behaviours which have been the focus of training, and generally it would seem, both from the attendance figures reported and from anecdotal observation, that parents have been well pleased with their participation.

However, there is less evidence on how far parents have been able or willing to generalize their use of the skills learned in parent-training programmes. Forehand and Atkeson (1977) reviewed the research findings on generalization over time, to other child behaviours, and, where relevant, from one setting to another (e.g. school to home) and to other children in the family. They concluded that the more rigorous were the procedures for evaluating generalization, the less positive was the evidence reported in the research.

Perhaps the most detailed evaluation of a parent-training scheme since Forehand and Atkeson's review is that of Baker and his colleagues (Baker, 1977; Baker *et al.*, 1980). This is of particular interest because of their stated concern, not only with narrowly-defined immediate effects of their group-training programme, but also with whether parents had become 'better able to cope with new problems and to teach new skills as the need arises' (1977, p. 213). They found that socio-economic class, educational status and their assessment of parents' existing skills prior to training were all strongly associated with the immediate results of intervention, but were not predictive of the parents' continuing use of teaching techniques fourteen months later. Rather, this was correlated with the amount of teaching at home that parents had carried out during the training course.

At this follow-up assessment (at which time no further involvement or consultation had taken place with the parents), gains in children's skills that had been made during the course were maintained, as was parental knowledge of behavioural principles. Most parents had continued to carry out some teaching with their children at home, and of these, nearly half were assessed as having undertaken substantial new teaching activities with good use of behavioural techniques. It would seem then, that this project demonstrated training effects which, for at least some of the parents, were generalized over time and to different child behaviours.

Certain issues arose in interview with the parents, which Baker *et al.* felt had implications for enhancing the generalization of effects of training courses. First, they noted that although the emphasis of their programme had been on formal teaching sessions, most of the parents' subsequent teaching was incidental, taking place as and when the opportunity arose. Second, parents reported a number of obstacles to their teaching at home. A major difficulty, not surprisingly, was that of finding time. Further difficulties were associated with the lack of reassurance and encouragement for their teaching, particularly when their children's progress was slow or intangible. Baker *et al.*, argued that, if parent-training schemes were to be effective, such parental concerns should be acknowledged.

They proposed, therefore, that the value of incidental teaching should be explicitly recognized, with particular attention given to the ways in which such teaching could be incorporated into daily routines at home, and that some degree of long-term support and guidance should be offered to parents. Other researchers have reached similar conclusions, and there is little doubt that such modifications to training programmes would facilitate the continued teaching of their children by some parents. However, increasingly concern has been expressed about how far it is possible to individualize parent-training schemes to meet the wide range of variation among children and their families and, indeed, how far a training model is an appropriate one for parent-professional collaboration in children's learning and development.

The Move away from a Training Model

It has long been acknowledged that some parents participate more readily than others in parent-training courses, and that more flexible methods of working may be required if professionals are to meet the full range of parental and children's needs (e.g. Yule, 1975). At the same time though, there has been an understandable reluctance to move too far away from the framework provided by 'tried and tested' schemes of parent-training. The nature of the dilemma posed for professionals is nicely caught in a collection of papers concerned with the use of Portage in this country (Dessent, 1984), in which the attempt to identify essential components of the approach led to considerable debate about the flexibility with which a Portage service could be provided while still retaining its effectiveness.

Such debate is symptomatic of the concerns shared by an increasing number of professionals about the appropriateness of a training model which takes no account of existing parental skills and knowledge. The evidence from mother–child interaction research is that parents are likely to have well-established styles of interacting with and teaching their children. Some will have been more successful than others in overcoming any interactive difficulties presented by their children, and there will also be variation in the effectiveness of their teaching strategies. Moreover, parental teaching styles may well not conform to a conventional behavioural model, for example, in the provision of errorless learning opportunities and consistent reinforcement (e.g. McConachie and Mitchell, 1985). However, several researchers have emphasized that, rather than assuming that parents are in need of redirection, professionals should demonstrate acknowledgement of and respect for existing parental skills.

Yule (1975) pointed out that, if parents are taught that by changing their own behaviour they will alter that of their children, then this may not only undermine parents' confidence in their natural style of interaction, but may also lead to feelings of guilt and self-blame that their previous approach contributed to their children's difficulties. It is unlikely that there is one single 'correct' approach for teaching a particular child. Furthermore, it is as yet unclear how far specific aspects of parental teaching behaviour can be modified, or indeed what effect such modification might have on the parent–child relationship more generally. Kogan (1980), for example, reported that training parents to carry out specific therapy with their children could have negative effects on the quality of their interactions. It may be then that some parents become successful 'therapists' and 'teachers' at the expense of other aspects of their parenting role. A concentration of attention on teaching achievements may put pressure on parents to 'play less and work more' (Wright *et al.*, 1984), and, if their children make little progress, they may feel that they are failing as parents.

These concerns have given impetus to a move away from a training model and towards a more educationally-oriented approach. This changing approach has broader goals than the attainment of narrowly-defined objectives: rather, starting from the parents' own perspectives and priorities, the aim is to help them use and develop further their existing skills in a way which facilitates functional problem-solving and a decreased reliance on professional expertise over time. Such an approach might be better described as 'parent teaching' rather than parent-training. It acknowledges that professionals do have skills to offer to parents to help them foster their children's learning, and it builds on the consensus of research evidence from training schemes that this may be more effectively achieved through a structured focus on specific interactions rather than on diffuse attitudes and behaviours (e.g. Baker, 1984). However, it sets professionals the task of finding methods which, while goal-directed, are not manipulative of parents (Bergan and Duley, 1981), and in which the degree of directiveness is both sensitive to parents' individual needs and abilities, and also informed by mutual learning.

As a first practical step, therefore, it seems necessary to explore the ways in which professional intervention might effectively be tailored to parents' existing skills and strategies. An investigation of the relationship between mothers' interactive styles and the impact of parent teaching work was undertaken in an attempt to address this question (Beveridge, 1986). In this study, repeated observations of mothers in play and teaching activities with their developmentally delayed pre-school children revealed striking and stable differences in their directiveness. Although partly associated with their children's age and developmental status, not all of the variation in mothers' directiveness could be attributed to this. There was no evidence that the degree of directiveness shown was associated with interactive or teaching effectiveness; both directive and less directive mothers were, on the whole, skilled in their interactions with their children. All of the mothers were using at least some of the techniques which would be introduced in a parent teaching course, although they were not necessarily aware of this or consistent in their use. A significant difference which was observed was in the use of particular teaching strategies: directive mothers used more physical, and less directive mothers more verbal, prompting of their children.

The parent teaching course in which the mothers subsequently participated incorporated two discrete, yet complementary, sets of techniques which may be characterized as 'facilitative' and 'manipulative' (e.g. Martin, 1981). The former comprised strategies involved in the setting up of learning situations and the presentation of materials to encourage children's responses, while the latter focused on more direct techniques of active verbal and physical intervention. A different technique was introduced to the mothers each week, and any change in their use of these was monitored throughout the course and reassessed one term later.

The main question of concern in the study was whether maternal directiveness would influence the effects of the course: specifically, would less directive mothers more readily adopt facilitative techniques, and directive mothers manipulative techniques, into their existing style? The results did not demonstrate significant differences between the directive and less directive mothers in their changing use of the two sets of techniques. There was, of course, considerable variation among the mothers both in the way their teaching style developed, and also in their perceptions of the usefulness of particular techniques, but both groups of mothers significantly improved the quality of their use of both sets of techniques. (It should be noted that this effect was achieved without any attempt during the course to 'train' the mothers to some criterion of good use.) However, other more general differences did emerge between the directive and less directive mothers which suggest that directiveness may be a relevant dimension of interactive style for consideration in the development of parent teaching work.

Directive mothers adapted their use of teaching strategies during the course in a way which was closely related to the intervention they received. By contrast, less directive mothers showed generalized changes during each part of the course which were not intervention-specific. This may suggest that participation in the course of itself led to these changes: one possible interpretation is that the formalized approach to teaching which was involved was less familiar to them than to the directive mothers, and therefore required a greater general level of adaptation of their existing strategies. Such an interpretation is necessarily speculative, but there were other indications that less directive mothers may tend towards a less formal view of their teaching role than directive mothers. For example, during the course they were significantly more likely to involve other family members in the teaching at home, and at follow-up a term later, whereas the directive mothers tended to describe a planned approach to their continued teaching, less directive mothers placed greater emphasis on fading out their assistance and encouraging their children to take the initiative.

Three aspects of individual variation are highlighted by this comparison of directive and less directive mothers' approaches to teaching. First, variation in interactive style may be associated with differing use of particular teaching strategies, such as physical and verbal prompting. If methods can be found of building on parents' existing skills and strategies in a way which is compatible with their interactive style, then it is at least arguable that there is less likelihood of undermining confidence in their own abilities.

Second, differing parental perceptions of their teaching role are likely to lead to differing priorities, expectations and routines. It has been suggested that certain risks are associated with an emphasis on formal teaching in the work undertaken with parents, because this may appear to undervalue other aspects of the parenting role. While little empirical evidence of such stressful effects has been reported, it seems probable that courses which focus primarily on highly structured teaching contexts demand a greater degree of adaptation from those parents who naturally adopt a less formal approach in their teaching at home.

Third, the role of all family members in children's development is being increasingly recognized. The way in which fathers, siblings and others perceive their roles and the degree to which they are actively involved in teaching at home will vary from family to family, but it would seem necessary that parent teaching work should take account of this wider family context.

Towards Partnership?

The earlier training approach, with its emphasis on narrowly defined child outcomes, can no longer be regarded as an adequate model for professional involvement with parents as teachers of their own children. There is increasing recognition that there is more to parenting than formalised teaching, and that an 'optimally functioning family is a critical component for a child's development' (Turnbull and Winton, 1984, p. 393). Accordingly, parent teaching schemes have begun to adopt broader aims concerned with the development of parental awareness, confidence and competence in their own role. However, despite the changes which have occurred the concept of parent teaching work still carries with it the assumption that there are skills which parents need to learn and strategies which they may need to change. The partnership model of parent–professional collaboration, therefore, continues to pose some challenges to the way in which such work is undertaken.

The mutual negotiation and clarification of roles and responsibilities appears to be an essential prerequisite for partnership. There may be extreme cases of distortion in the parent–child relationship where professional intervention cannot be regarded as negotiable. However, the partnership model implies that for the majority of parents there should be choice in the level and type of involvement that is offered (Mittler and Mittler, 1982). The evidence suggests that most parents of children with identified difficulties and needs welcome guidance and reassurance on the ways in which they may further their children's learning. They are, therefore, likely to be responsive to any sensitive attempt by professionals to offer practical help. If this is to be undertaken in the spirit of partnership then there is a continuing need for research into the development of flexible methods of working, in which due regard is given not only to existing parental skills, knowledge and priorities, but also to wider family issues and concerns.

References

Bakeman, R. and Brown, J. V. (1980), Early interaction: consequences for social and mental development at three years, *Child Development,* **51**, 437–47.

Baker, B. L. (1977), Support systems for the parent as therapist, in P. Mittler (ed.), *Research to Practice in Mental Retardation Vol 1: Care and Intervention* (Baltimore: University Park Press).

Baker, B. L. (1984), Intervention with families with young severely handicapped children, in J.Blacher (ed.), *Severely Handicapped Young Children and Their Families: Research in Review* (London: Academic Press).

Baker, B. L., Heifetz, L. J. and Murphy, D. M. (1980), Behavioral training for parents of mentally retarded children: one year follow-up, *American Journal of Mental Deficiency,* **85**, 31–8.

Bee, H. L., Barnard, K. E., Eyres, S. J., Gray, C. A., Hammond. M. A., Spietz, A. L., Snyder, C. and Clark, B.(1982), Prediction of IQ and language skills from perinatal status, child performance, family characteristics and mother–infant interaction, *Child Development,* **53**, 1134–56.

Bee, H. L., Van Egeren, L. F., Streissguth, A. P., Nyman, B. A. and Leckie, M. S. (1969), Social class differences in maternal teaching strategies and speech patterns, *Developmental Psychology,*1, 726–34.

Bell, R. Q. (1968), A reinterpretation of the direction of effects in studies of socialization, *Psychological Review,*75, 81–95.

Bell, R. Q. (1974), Contributions of human infants to caregiving and social interaction, in M. Lewis and L. A. Rosenblum (eds), *The Effect of the Infant on its Caregiver* (New York: Wiley and Sons).

Bell, R. Q. (1979), Parent, child and reciprocal influences, *American Pychologist,* **34**, 821–6.

Belsky, J. (1984), The determinants of parenting: a process model, *Child Development,* **55**, 83–96.

Bergan, J. R. and Duley, S. M. (1981), Behavioral consultation with families, in R. W. Henderson (ed.), *Parent-Child Interaction: Theory, Research and Prospects* (New York: Academic Press).

Berger, J. and Cunningham, C. C. (1981), The development of eye contact between mothers and normal versus Down's syndrome infants, *Developmental Psychology,* **17**, 678–89.

Berger, J. and Cunningham, C. C. (1983), Development of early vocal behaviors and interactions in Down's syndrome and non-handicapped infant–mother pairs, *Developmental Psychology,* **19**, 322–31.

Berry, P., Gunn, P. and Andrews, R. (1980), Behavior of Down's syndrome infants in a strange situation, *Americal Journal of Mental Deficiency* ,**85**, 213–18.

Beveridge, S. (1986), *Mothers' interactive styles: their relationship to programmes of parent-teaching* (Unpublished PhD thesis, University of Manchester).

Blacher, J. (1984), A dynamic perspective on the impact of a severely handicapped child on the family, in J. Blacher (ed.), *Severely Handicapped Young Children and Their Families: Research in Review* (London: Academic Press).

Bradley, R. H. and Caldwell, B. M. (1984), The HOME inventory and family demographics, *Developmental Psychology,* **20**, 315–20.

Bristol, M. M. and Schopler, E. (1984), A developmental perspective on stress and coping in families of autistic children, in J. Blacher (ed.), *Severely Handicapped Young Children and Their Families: Research in Review,* (London: Academic Press).

Bronfenbrenner, U. (1976), Is early intervention effective? Facts and principles of early intervention: a summary, in A. M. and A. D. B. Clarke (eds), *Early Experience: Myth and Evidence* (London: Open Books).

Bronfenbrenner, U. (1977), Towards an experimental ecology of human development, *American Psychologist,* **32**, 513–31.

Brooks-Gunn, J. and Lewis, M. (1984), Maternal responsivity in interactions with handicapped infants, *Child Development,* **55**, 782–93.

Bruner, J. S. (1974), The ontogenesis of speech acts, *Journal of Child Language*, **2**, 1–19.

Buckhalt, J. A., Rutherford, R. B. and Goldberg, K. E. (1978), Verbal and nonverbal interaction of mothers with their Downs syndrome and nonretarded infants, *American Journal of Mental Deficiency*, **82**, 337–43.

Chazan, M., Laing, A. F., Shackleton-Bailey, M. and Jones (1980), *Some of Our Children: The Early Education of Children with Special Needs* (London: Open Books).

Cichetti, D. and Serafica, F. C. (1981), Interplay among behavioral systems: illustrations from the study of attachment, affiliation and wariness in young children with Down's syndrome, *Developmental Psychology*, **17**, 36–49.

Cichetti, D. and Sroufe, L. A. (1976), The relationship between affective and cognitive development in Down's syndrome infants, *Child Development*, **47**, 920–9.

Clarke-Stewart, K. A. (1973), Interactions between mothers and their young children: characteristics and consequences, *Monographs of the Society for Research in Child Development*, **38**, 6–7, Serial number 153.

Clarke-Stewart, K. A., Vanderstoep, L. P. and Killian, G. A. (1979), Analysis and replication of mother–child relations at two years of age, *Child Development*, **50**, 777–93.

Crawley, S. B. and Spiker, D. (1983), Mother–child interactions involving two-year-olds with Down's syndrome: a look at individual differences, *Child Development*, **54**, 1312–23.

Cunningham, C. C. (1979), Parent counselling, in M. Craft (ed.), *Tredgold's Mental Retardation*, 12th ed. (London: Ballière Tindall).

Cunningham, C. C. (1983), Early support and intervention: the HARC infant project, in P. Mittler and H. McConachie (eds), *Parents, Professionals and Mentally Handicapped People*, London: Croom Helm.

Cunningham, C. C. and Jeffree, D. M. (1975), The organization and structure of workshops for parents of mentally handicapped children, *Bulletin of the British Psychological Society*, **28**, 405–11.

Cunningham, C. E., Reuler, E., Blackwell, J. and Deck, J. (1981), Behavioral and linguistic developments in the interactions of normal and retarded children with their mothers, *Child Development*, **52**, 62–70.

Department of Education and Science (1967), *Children and Their Primary Schools* (The Plowden Report) (London: HMSO).

Department of Education and Science (1978), *Special Educational Needs* (The Warnock Report) (London: HMSO).

Dessent, T. (ed.) (1984), *What is Important about Portage?* (Windsor: NFER-Nelson).

Eheart, B. K. (1982), Mother–child interactions with nonretarded and mentally retarded preschoolers, *American Journal of Mental Deficiency*, **87**, 20–5.

Farquhar, C., Blatchford, P., Burke, J., Plewis, I. and Tizard, B. (1986), A comparison of the views of parents and reception teachers, *Education 3–13*, **13**, 17–22.

Forehand, R. and Atkeson, B. M. (1977), Generality of treatment effects with parents as therapists: a review of assessment and implementation procedures, *Behavior Therapy*, **8**, 575–93.

Fraiberg, S. (1974), Blind infants and their mothers: an examination of the sign system, in M. Lewis and L. A. Rosenblum (eds), *The Effect of the Infant on its Caregiver* (New York: Wiley and Sons).

Gaussen, T. and Stratton, P. (1985), Beyond the milestone model – a systems framework for alternative infant assessment procedures, *Child: Care, Health and Development*, **11**, 31–50.

Goldberg, S. (1977), Social competence in infancy: a model of parent–infant interactions, *Merrill-Palmer Quarterly*, **23**, 164–77.

Greenberg, N. H. (1971), A comparison of infant–mother interactional behavior in infants with atypical behavior and normal infants, in J. Hellmuth (ed.), *Exceptional Infant*, Vol.2 (New York: Brunner/Mazel).

Griffiths, A. and Hamilton, D. (1984), *Parent, Teacher, Child* (London: Methuen).

Hess, R. D. and McDevitt, T. M. (1984), Some cognitive consequences of maternal intervention techniques: a longitudinal study, *Child Development*, **55**, 2017–30.

Hess, R. D. and Shipman, V. C. (1965), Early experience and the socialisation of cognitive modes in children, *Child Development*, **36**, 869–86.

Hewett, S. (1970), *The Family and the Handicapped Child* (London: George Allen and Unwin).

Hinde, R. A. (1976), On describing relationships, *Journal of Child Psychology and Psychiatry*, **17**, 1–19.

Hodapp, R. M., Goldfield, E. C. and Boyatzis, C. J. (1984), The use and effectiveness of maternal scaffolding in mother–infant games, *Child Development*, **55**, 772–81.

Johnson, C. A. and Katz, R. C. (1973), Using parents as change agents for their children: a review, *Journal of Child Pyschology and Psychiatry*, **14**, 181–200.

Jones, O. H. M. (1980), Prelinguistic communication skills in Down's syndrome and normal infants, in T. M. Field, S. Goldberg, D. Stern and A. M. Sostek (eds), *High-Risk Infants and Children* (New York: Academic Press).

Kaiser, C. E. and Hayden, A. H. (1984), Clinical research and policy issues in parenting severely handicapped infants, in J. Blacher (ed.), *Severely Handicapped Young Children and Their Families: Research in Review* (London: Academic Press).

Kogan, K. L. (1980), Interaction systems between preschool handicapped or developmentally delayed children and their parents, in T. M. Field, S. Goldberg, D. Stern and A. M. Sostek (eds), *High-Risk Infants and Children* (New York: Academic Press).

Kogan, K. L. and Wimberger, H. C. (1969), Interaction patterns in disadvantaged families, *Journal of Clinical Psychology*, **25**, 347–52.

Lazar, I. and Darlington, R. (1982), Lasting effects of early education: a report from the consortium for longitudinal studies, *Monographs of the Society for Research in Child Development*, **47**, 2–3, Serial number 195.

Martin, J. A. (1981), A longitudinal study of the consequences of early mother–infant interaction: a microanalytical approach, *Monographs of the Society for Research in Child Development*, **46**, 3, Serial number 190.

McConachie, H. (1982) The child at home, in S. Beveridge, R. Flanagan, H. McConachie and J. Sebba, *Parental Involvement in Anson House* (Barkingside: Barnardo's).

McConachie, H. and Mitchell, D. R. (1985), Parents teaching their young mentally handicapped children, *Journal of Child Psychology and Psychiatry*, **26**, 389–405.

McConkey, R. and Martin, H. (1984), A longitudinal study of mothers' speech to preverbal Down's syndrome infants, *First Language*, **5**, 4, 1–55.

McConkey, R. and Martin, H. (1986), The development of object and pretend play in Down's syndrome infants: a longitudinal study involving mothers, *Trisomy 21*, **1**, 27–44.

Meier, J. H. and Sloan, M. P. (1984), The severely handicapped and child abuse, in J. Blacher (ed.), *Severely Handicapped Young Children and Their Families: Research in Review* (London: Academic Press).

Mittler, P. and Mittler, H. (1982), *Partnership with Parents* (Stratford-upon-Avon: National Council for Special Education).

Mortimore, J. and Blackstone, T. (1982), *Disadvantage and Education* (London: Heinemann).

Newson, J. (1977), *Intentional Behaviour in the Young Infant*, Paper presented at the conference of the Royal College of Psychiatrists, Child Psychiatry section, London.

Newson, J. and Newson, E. (1968), *Four Years Old in an Urban Community* (London: George Allen and Unwin).

O'Dell, S. (1974), Training parents in behavior modification: a review, *Psychological Bulletin*, **81**, 418–33.

Philp, M. and Duckworth, D. (1982), *Children with disabilities and their families: a review of research* (Windsor: NFER-Nelson).

Phinney, J. S. and Feshbach, N. D. *(1980)*, Non-directive and intrusive styles of middle- and working-class English mothers *British Journal of Educational Psychology*, **50**, 2–9.

Rapoport, R. Rapoport, R. N. and Strelitz, Z. (1977), *Fathers, Mothers and Others* (London: Routledge and Kegan Paul).

Sameroff, A.J. and Chandler, M.J. (1975), Reproductive risk and the continuum of caretaking casualty, in F.D. Horowitz (ed.), *Review of Child Development Research*, Vol. 4 (Chicago: University of Chicago Press).

Schaffer, H.R. (1977), *Mothering* (London: Open Books).

Schaffer, H.R. and Crook, C.K. (1979), Maternal control techniques in a directed play situation, *Child Development*, 50, 989–96.

Sharpley, C.F. and Poiner, A.M. (1980), An exploratory evaluation of the Systematic Training for Effective Parenting (STEP) programme, *Australian Psychologist*, 15, 103–9.

Shearer, M.S. and Shearer, D. (1972), The Portage project: a model for early childhood education, *Exceptional Children*, 36, 210–17.

Slaughter, D.T. (1983), Early intervention and its effects on maternal and child development, *Monographs of the Society for Research in Child Development*, 48, 4, Serial number 202.

Sorce, J.F. and Emde, R.N. (1982), The meaning of infant emotional expressions: regularities in caregiving responses in normal and Down's syndrome infants, *Journal of Child Psychology and Psychiatry*, 23, 145–58.

Stoneman, Z., Brody, G.H. and Abbott, D. (1983), In-home observations of young Down syndrome children with their mothers and fathers, *American Journal of Mental Deficiency*, 87, 591–600.

Tizard, B. and Hughes, M. (1984), *Young Children Learning* (London: Fontana).

Tomlinson, S. (1982), *A Sociology of Special Education* (London: Routledge and Kegan Paul).

Topping, K.J. (1986), *Parents as Educators: Training Parents to Teach their Children* (London: Croom Helm).

Topping, K.J. and Wolfendale, S. (1985), *Parental Involvement in Children's Reading* (London: Croom Helm).

Tulkin, S.R. and Kagan, J. (1972), Mother–child interaction in the first year of life, *Child Development*, 43, 31–41.

Turnbull, A.P. and Winton, P.J. (1984), Parent involvement policy and practice: current research and implications for families of young, severely handicapped children, in J. Blacher (ed.), *Severely Handicapped Young Children and Their Families: Research in Review* (London: Academic Press).

Voysey, M. (1975), *A Constant Burden: The Reconstitution of Family Life* (London: Routledge and Kegan Paul).

Wasserman, G.A. and Allen, R. (1985), Maternal withdrawal from handicapped toddlers, *Journal of Child Psychology and Psychiatry*, 26, 381–7.

Wells, G. (1983), Talking with children: the complementary roles of parents and teachers, in M. Donaldson, R. Grieve and C. Pratt (eds), *Early Childhood Development and Education* (Oxford: Blackwell).

Wilton, K. and Barbour, A. (1978), Mother–child interaction in high-risk and contrast preschoolers of Low socioeconomic status, *Child Development*, 49, 1136–45.

Wolfendale, S. (1983), *Parental Participation in Children's Development and Education* (London: Gordon and Breach).

Wood, D. (1983), Fostering language development in hearing impaired children, in M.M. Clarke (ed.), Special educational needs and children under 5, *Educational Review Occasional Publications*, 2.

Wright, J.S., Granger, R.D. and Sameroff, A.J. (1984), Parental acceptance and developmental handicap, in J. Blacher (ed.), *Severely Handicapped Young Children and Their Families: Research in Review* (London: Academic Press).

Yando, R. and Zigler, E. (1984), Severely handicapped children and their families: a synthesis, in J. Blacher (ed.), *Severely Handicapped Young Children and Their Families: Research in Review* (London: Academic Press).

Yule, W. (1975), Teaching psychological principles to non-psychologists, *Journal of the Association of Educational Psychology*, 10, 1–12.

Chapter 8

Behaviour Problems and Cognitive Processes
Peter Galvin

Introduction

For many years as a teacher in special education of children with behaviour problems it appeared to me, and doubtless to those pupils who came within my care, that the term special education was something of a misnomer, although doubtless the pupils would have put it another way. Ten years later, despite isolated 'pockets' of progress my view remains substantially the same. In the case of children with behaviour problems the strategies used to bring about behavioural change have tended, on the whole, tò be rather simplistic, often restrictive in nature and applied in an ill-conceived and inconsistent manner. Admittedly, for children with behaviour problems in special education, groups tend to be smaller, responses to problems may be more sympathetic and curricular adaptations sometimes more individually oriented, but beyond this, I would argue, very little happened or happens to children that could in any way be described as special.

As a teacher in the early 1970's the predominant, although perhaps inconsistent, psychoanalytic or humanistic (it was often difficult to tell which) persuasion of schools for maladjusted children seemed to offer little to the teacher other than the understanding that psychiatrists did the real work and teachers were expected to accommodate children who needed to 'act out' or 'regress' within the parameters of 'accepting or unconditional regard'.

Education, either academic or behavioural, was little in evidence. We were told we were expected to improve something called the self-image and provide a warm and secure environment but we were not told how. Little in the way of guidelines nationally, locally or within the school iteslf gave us any clear view of our task. Unsurprisingly then, when behavioural methods came to our notice many of us incorporated them eagerly into our working practices. Behavourism offered an alternative (as yet, in the opinion of the author, a still under-used one in special education), one which gave back the control to teachers and yet which systematically and successfully helped children to develop new skills. It is the view of the author that workers in special education owe a great debt to behavioural practices. As a working educational psychologist this psychological paradigm underpins the majority of my work. When consistently and thoughtfully applied behaviourism goes a long way to supporting special education's efforts to become special.

In some instances, however, the behavioural paradigm has seemed limited. It is appropriate (in the author's opinion) as the basis for action with many children, but as the s–r (stimulus–response) connection, proposed by behavioural psychologists as the basis for an explanation of human behaviour, did not take into account the effect of how the organism or human-being perceived, interpreted or felt about what behavioural psychologists would have to describe as, the objective 'reality' of that stimulus, it seemed at times, not to encompass the real complexity of the behaviour problems of some children. With many of the children I taught, no matter how clearly I constructed to them that 'reality', they consistently, almost obstinately, it appeared, continued to misrepresent it. Within the confines of psychoanalytic theory it is unlikely that I would have been able to pursue the implications of this misrepresentation very much further. The child's personal construction of 'reality' would probably have remained an introspective mystery.

This chapter argues that the strengths of cognitive psychology in combination with the strengths of behavioural psychology, have made it possible for the teacher of children with behaviour problems to have 'his/her cake and eat it'. The bringing together of paradigms enables the worker to acknowledge the importance of the child's personal interpretation of events and yet lose none of the structure and clarity inherent in behavioural psychology when planning a programme of behavioural change. Cognitive psychology enables us to understand more clearly how children actually misrepresent 'reality', how often this misrepresentation itself causes behaviour problems and how we can devise clear and precise methods of bringing about a change in that misrepresentation. The cognitive contribution, far from remaining an 'introspective mystery', could be described, understood and ultimately, where and when appropriate, these cognitive processes could be modified to bring about behavioural change. When combined with the strengths of applied behavioural psychology, specifying precisely the target behaviour/s, the small steps towards this target, the careful monitoring of progress, the contingent rewarding of desired behaviours and discouraging of inappropriate behaviours, the options for behavioural change are greatly increased. This combination of strengths has led to the formation of a psychological paradigm which has been given the title, amongst others, of cognitive-behaviourism.

The cognitive-behavioural paradigm proposed that the relationship between the environment and human behaviour could be better represented in terms of the s–o–r (stimulus–organism–response) connection. This connection suggested that what children (and adults) thought about the events which happened to them was as important as the events themselves. So in the case of behavioural problems, it is suggested that these can result from an unhealthy view of a healthy environment as well as an unhealthy environment *per se*. Epicuteus put it succinctly when he said: 'Man is disturbed not by things but the view he takes of them.' Or as Alfred Adler said: 'It is very obvious that we are influenced not by ''facts'' but by our interpretation of facts' (both from Meichenbaum, 1977).

Psychologists and others were not, therefore, limited in the cognitive-behavioural paradigm to a so-called objective reality of the situation, but were able to consider the cognitive view children took of this reality. For example, children will have their own views of the setting in which they 'behave', the targets we ask them to achieve, the rewards we offer them and this view may differ from ours. The contribution of cognitive psychology to our understanding of how behaviour problems arise and how they may be 'modified', has, in the author's view, offered an advance in our ways of working with these problems such that they may genuinely deserve the title 'special'.

The exact nature of the contribution of cognitive psychology forms the basis for the rest of this chapter. But briefly the contribution is as follows. Ledwigge (1978) said that cognitive therapy could be defined as that which aimed to change behaviour by changing the pattern of thought which accompanied the behaviour. The core of any advance made by cognitive-behaviourism has been seen in the area of helping children (and adults) to examine and change, either through discussion or through 'teaching' programmes, the manner in which they think. Moreover, this chapter proposes that patterns of thought are changed through changing self-talk or what we say to ourselves. In fact, as Ellis and Bernard (1983) state, cognitive behavioural practices have become almost synonymous with verbal self-instruction.

The importance of self-instruction is based upon the assumption that effective self-talk is an important aspect of a healthy life style. Those of us whose development patterns have followed 'normal' paths do this automatically and effectively. We are particularly inclined to need to talk to ourselves when the going gets tough. Watson and Tharp (1986) say, we probably talk to ourselves 'in precisely those situations you find most fearful, most depressing or most difficult to cope with' (p.94). Many of us reduce our stress levels through self-talk; for example, we tell ourselves to stay calm in a traffic jam. We make the environment more understandable through self-talk, for example when we say out loud the words of a particularly difficult recipe. In other stressful or threatening situations we use self-talk to moderate the effect of these situations and if we do it effectively we feel better for it.

Some children, it appears, do not use self-talk or do not use it effectively to guide their behaviour. They do not use self-talk to help self-control their behaviour. This chapter proposes that children who do not use self-talk to facilitate self-control are particularly prone to demonstrate problematic behaviour. In fact a lack of self-control is almost a definition rather than a characteristic of children with behaviour problems. DiGiuseppe (1983) says that children with behaviour problems are frequently characterized by behavioural and cognitive impulsivity:

> they often respond to a situation quickly with inappropriate behavior without first assessing the consequences of their behavior (p.112).

In addition, the concern expressed by many professionals about the long-term maintenance and generalization of behaviour learned during the course of a behavioural programme, can be addressed through encouraging self-control to take over from experimental or external control. In summary, the chapter argues that the development of self-control skills through use of effective self-talk should be, for some children at least, a fundamental aspect of programmes of behavioural change.

The optimism generated by this view of the cognitive contribution must be tempered with a certain amount of realism. Cognitive methods have much to discover about the most consistently efficacious ways of helping children with behaviour problems. Readers will have noted that I said 'some' children. As we shall see later in this chapter, cognitive change or restructuring may be concerned with the replacement of existing unhelpful cognitions, or alternatively, with the filling of what might be described as a cognitive void. There is some suggestion in the literature that children who 'won't behave' – those with what have been described as conduct disorders – would benefit from programmes more concerned with the construction of new, rational cognitions. On the other hand, children with emotional problems, who it is sometimes assumed 'can't behave', need to have their existing cognitions restructured (DiGiuseppe, 1983). This matching of strategy to type of behaviour problem or speculated root of problem is not, however, clearly established at this time so further work will need to be carried out in this area.

Perhaps more importantly, we are unclear about which children and for which type of behaviour problem 'straight' behavioural methods are most appropriate, and when these need to be supplemented with or replaced by cognitive strategies. In theory this dilemma is a significant one in that it is usual for behavioural psychology to argue that attitudinal or cognitive change follows behaviour change, whereas cognitive-behavioural psychology may, on occasions, argue for quite the opposite – change attitudes or thinking and behaviour change will result (this is a simplification of existing practice, but it is not an unreasonable one). Certainly this is a dilemma for some philosophy-bound professionals. Skinner (1985), for example, remains unequivocal that 'states of mind' are the products of behaviour rather than the causes of it. It may be, however, that for workers in the field the dilemma is less problematic than it at first appears.

First, it has a simple resolution, if we accept that behaviourist approaches tend, on the whole, to be less time-consuming, less organizationally demanding and therefore 'simpler' to implement whereas cognitive-behavioural approaches tend, on the whole, to be more complex and more time-consuming. If we accept this premise then perhaps the resolution is to try the 'simpler' behavioural methods first and move on to more 'sophisticated' cognitive approaches if these tactics are partially or entirely unsuccessful.

Second, common sense and research would suggest that behavioural approaches are appropriate and efficacious in working with many children while with others (for instance, those who are impulsive, quick to anger or those whose cognitive patterns are clearly jumbled) a cognitive-based strategy will be a more appropriate approach. So there is room for the philosophically uncommitted to try both approaches.

Third, and perhaps most importantly, as the comparative efficacy of the two approaches remains largely unproven, the trend, since Ledwigge (1978) made this observation, has been to combine therapies and strategies rather than compare their efficacy. This is an important point: while the chapter describes the cognitive aspects of programmes and strategies, clearly, as the term cognitive-behavioural implies, these approaches have in their practical application been combined with behavioural and other approaches.

A point recently restated by Vingoe (1984) suggested there was little evidence to support the view that cognitive methods in isolation were effective in bringing about behavioural change, but when combined with other approaches programme results are encouraging. It seems then that workers and children will benefit if we remain open-minded about when to use which strategy or perhaps more accurately which combination of strategies.

The aims of this chapter are to consider why it is that some children come to be the 'victim' of their faulty cognitions, to describe the nature of those cognitions which contribute to behaviour problems and to identify the nature of assessment procedures and programmes of action which are designed to bring about cognitive change. Here again optimism must be tempered with caution. This is an ambitious project for such a short chapter when whole text books address the area. Particularly as Bernard and Joyce (1984) note that no common theory of cognitive psychology underpins the various approaches to working with children with behaviour problems (in fact Dryden and Golden (1986) describe ten different forms of cognitive therapy in their recent book).

I have chosen to confine the explanations and strategies described in this chapter to two compatible although different paradigms, those emanating from

Cognitive Behavioural Therapy (CBT) based originally on the work of Aaron Beck and those from Rational Emotive Therapy (RET) based upon the work of Albert Ellis. It is the commonalities that concern us in this chapter rather than the differences. However, I should make brief reference to those differences not considered in depth in this chapter before passing on.

The chapter does not consider, in detail, whether approaches/programmes/strategies could better be described as education or therapy. I have used the terms programmes and strategies, workers or professionals, rather than teacher or therapist unless quoting directly from the writings of others. Similarly I have used 'child' rather than client, adolescent or youngster unless quoting from others. I have used the singular form in most cases but this should not lead the reader to the opinion that the great majority of techniques cannot be used with groups of children because I believe that they can.

Finally, I have used the term behaviour problems to include emotional problems, psychological disturbance or maladjustment. While distinctions are made in the literature (and briefly in this chapter) between emotional disturbance and conduct disorders, for example, they are not discussed in depth here.

Nor does the chapter consider differences between paradigms in terms of the emotional, affective or feeling processes and their relationship to cognitive and behavioural processes. RET is generally more concerned with the affective component of behaviour usually in the form that 'bad' thoughts lead to 'bad' feelings which lead to 'bad' behaviour. There is reference in the last section of the chapter to programmes with an affective component, but there is not scope here for exact analysis. In addition Ellis and Beck see differences in the nature of those cognitive structures underlying behaviour problems – these are referred to in the section of faulty cognitions – but the chapter does not cover this area in detail.

Similarly, differences exist in the emphasis each approach puts on learned as opposed to the biological or genetic tendency of human beings to think and act rationally or irrationally. Some differences are discussed but again, it is not the intention of the chapter to consider these in great depth; readers interested in this area must look elsewhere (Dryden, 1984, ch. 3; Dryden and Golden, 1986; Bernard and Joyce, 1984; and Ellis and Bernard, 1983, ch. 1 are all excellent sources of further information for the readers looking to expand their knowledge in the area).

Despite these difficulties and qualifications it is not unreasonable or unrealistic to finish this introduction on a note of optimism. Ellis and Bernard (1983) say

cognitive restructuring approaches strongly endorse the position that not only can (1) emotional disturbance and behavioral maladjustment be understood from an analysis of the cognitive-mediational repertoire of the individual but furthermore, (2) emotional and behavioral change can be brought about by modification of the mediational competence of the individual (p. 15).

One result of this view is that

> University and other professional training programs have increasingly incorporated the cognitive restructuring approach, and it would seem that the cognitive school is one of the most important in its field and will play a major role in the shaping of mental health practice and beyond (Ellis and Bernard, 1983, p.6).

The rest of this chapter will attempt to describe the characteristics of this major role.

Regulating Behaviour through the Use of Language

The concept that behaviour problems or emotional disturbance emanate from a lack of self-talk has its basis in the work of the Soviet psychologists Luria and Vygotsky. Luria (1961) and Vygotsky (1962) suggested that verbal mediation has an inhibitory function in behaviour. American psychologists Camp and Bash (1981), calling on the work of their Soviet counterparts, describe the process thus

> from an early age language has an activating, social and instrumental function, but at first, no inhibitory function. In the second year of life, most children begin to respond to parental inhibitory commands but do not respond to their own overt inhibitory statements. Later in the pre-school years, children become able to inhibit or regulate their behaviour through their own covert commands, but covert commands, even in the form of whispers, are not effective. Some time between 5 and 7 years, most children develop the capacity to inhibit or regulate their behaviour through covert verbal activity (pp. 3–4).

This process of cognitive change, such that verbal mediation or self-talk comes eventually to 'control' behaviour, 'appears to be a major feature of the great shift in thinking that occurs between 5 and 7 years of age' (Camp and Bash, 1981, p.3). Watson and Tharp (1985) describe the example of the father who tells his son not to kick the wastepaper basket; the next day the son approaches the wastepaper basket, but this time having drawn back his foot to kick it, stops in mid-stride and says out loud 'don't kick the wastepaper basket'. For some time after this, Watson and Tharp suggest, the sight of the wastepaper basket may cause the child to mutter the instruction aloud, thereafter the child may move his lips in 'silent self-instruction'. Eventually all traces of speech disappear and behaviour becomes 'automatic'. In the words of Vygotsky, the self-controlling speech 'goes underground' and in effect thinking based upon language begins. Watson and Tharp suggest that in the process of transferring from adult control to self-control, very young children 'imitate and incorporate adult speech'. The child repeats often, with the very same inflection, the language used by the father. In the case of so-called normal development by imitating adult language, inhibition or control of behaviour is learned by children from adults.

For some children the development of these inhibitory processes does not take place or takes place only partially. Some children do not learn how to control their own behaviour effectively through self-talk and as a result may frequently come to exhibit behaviour which is problematic (both to themselves and to others).

We are not sure why some children fail to develop, only partially develop or develop inappropriate cognitively-mediated, self-control skills. We can, however, begin to describe a number of factors which seem relevant.

As with explanations based on other psychological paradigms, the process or processes seem part 'environmental' (some children simply learn how to behave badly) and part 'within-child' (some children are temperamentally inclined to be badly behaved). CBT and RET literature places a somewhat different emphasis upon learned behaviour as opposed to temperamental predisposition. CBT workers have tended to stress the learned nature or environmental view of mal-adaptive behaviour. Hence (as in the behavioural paradigm) children who do not experience good models of behaviour, positive reinforcement for appropriate behaviour and punishment contingently and consistently for inappropriate behaviour, do not develop appropriate behavioural and/or cognitive skills. RET workers have given more emphasis to 'within-child' factors, for example the biological predisposition of humans to think irrationally. Here again, however, the importance of learning is indicated when they state that this tendency is usually 'corrected' by environmental influences. Dryden and Golden (1986) summarize the RET viewpoint thus: people respond to (and seek out) events either in a rational or irrational manner because 'a) of their biological or genetic predisposition, b) their constitutional history, c) their prior interpersonal and social learning and d) their innately predisposed and acquired habit patterns' (p.135).

A more detailed examination of the cognitive-mediation literature, shows agreement that the process involves an interaction of a number of factors within the two broad areas of environment and temperament. It appears to be this interaction of factors which 'generates' behaviour problems. I shall return to the nature of this interaction in a moment.

In order to elaborate on the differences and pull together the similarities between the 'environmental' and 'temperamental' viewpoints Jaremko (1986) proposes two dimensions of 'psychopathology' which are helpful when analysing and understanding emotional and behavioural problems. These two dimensions relate to the two groups of children already described – those who don't appear to use cognitive mediation and those who use it inappropriately. Jaremko calls these dimensions cognitive undercontrol and cognitive overcontrol.

In the case of the former, Jaremko suggests that children (and adults) experience a lack of cognitive activity which leads to a hypersensitivity to environmental factors. It might be said that some children do not mediate the effects of the environment by thinking and considering what is happening to them. They therefore tend, like straws in the wind, to be blown hither and thither. These children are less likely to delay or consider the implications of their actions or to wait for long-term reinforcement; they think and act impulsively. Such children are often labelled agressive, hyperactive or inconsequential.

In the case, however, of cognitive overcontrol we have the different situation where individuals do use cognitive processes to mediate behaviour, but in this case they employ inappropriate cognitive mediation. Such individuals think (or believe) in a rigid and therefore irrational manner. As a result they have a predisposition to behave in an irrational manner. The nature of these irrational beliefs is discussed further in the next section.

If we consider Jaremko's first category in a little more detail then a number of factors seem to predispose children to this 'lack' of cognitive activity. Knaus (1983) with reference to children with low tolerance of frustration, suggests seven reasons why children fail to develop appropriate cognitive control mechanisms:

1 *Expressive language* The child may have limited overt expressive language skills in the manner of Bernstein's (1961) restricted code. Consequently, the child has no adequate vocabulary to express desires or discontents. In the absence of overt language usage an equal lack of covert language usage may result.

2 *Poor modelling* If the child has been exposed to models – adults or children – who display low frustration tolerance and inconsequential behaviour then the child will often imitate these behaviours.

3 *Social conditioning* In some cases the prevailing culture encourages children to believe that achievement should be tension free and that frustration should never arise and if it does then the child has a right to get mad. Under such circumstances the child would feel that there is simply no reason to consider the appropriateness or otherwise of this reaction.

4 *Poor coping skills* When children lack the behavioural skills of organization of their efforts – one example might be time management – they are more likely to experience frustration which will increase the likelihood of behaviour problems occurring.

5 *Reward for delay* Some children quickly discover that if they put things

off, avoid undesirable events through lying or excuse making or through using other more aggressive behaviours, quite often they will get away with it. When avoidance is successfully achieved in this way this may lead to a lack of or reduction of the child's inclination to generate alternative cognitive strategies for tackling the problem.

6 *Misreading the signal* Instead of using the feelings generated by frustration as a positive signal to slow down and work out what the best response would be, some children use the feelings as an indication to avoid the unpleasant event or stimulus. Consequently they never learn how to develop cognitive skills to cope with frustration appropriately.

7 *Constitutional predisposition* While some children are genetically disposed to be great athletes or musicians and have the 'ability' to remain calm under pressure other children seem predisposed towards 'low frustration, tolerance, perpetual distortions, anxiety or depression'. Knaus is at pains to emphasize that this does not mean that the inevitable result of such predisposition is that the prophecy shall be fulfilled for good or bad.

The second group of children – those who overcontrol their behaviour – do mediate their behaviour through cognitive processes but this group of children think in an unhelpful, inappropriate manner. Such children tend to come more within the remit of RET and unsurprisingly the explanation for what Ellis and Bernard (1983) call childhood maladjustment comes from the RET literature. Ellis and Bernard also formulate their explanation of childhood behaviour problems in terms of the interaction between 'person' and 'environment'. Bernard and Joyce (1984) describe the interaction in more detail:

> People demonstrate characteristic ways of thinking about and relating to their environment which exert an influence on their environment. Similarly, situations themselves modify the behaviour and attitudes of people by both providing (or not providing) appropriate learning experiences and enrichment opportunities as well as rewarding and punishing consequences for behaviour within certain contexts. We believe that there is an almost inexorable reciprocal relationship between abnormal behaviour and a deviant environment such that abnormalities in either the person or the environment of the person tend to bring out abnormalities in the other. It would seem, therefore, necessary to determine how persons and environments interact and covary together in analyzing psychopathology (Ellis and Bernard, 1983, p.19).

Ellis and Bernard (1983) suggest that further understanding of this interactive process may lie in a consideration of three major and interacting dimensions of what they call, psychopathology. The three dimensions are:

1   The cognitive-affective developmental status of the child.
2   Psychological conditions affecting the child.
3   Environmental conditions affecting the child.

1 Cognitive-affective Developmental Status

The first again relates directly to language usage. Ellis and Bernard (1983) suggest that the emotional experiences of early childhood are limited by the cognitive level or vocabulary that children are able to bring to these emotional experiences. These cognitive limitations can lead to children acquiring beliefs about themselves and their surroundings which are untrue and irrational.

Such ideas and beliefs have a profound effect upon the behaviour of children. Children with behaviour problems are often characterized by their usage of cognitive schema or logical reasoning processes that would be appropriate only as Ellis and Bernard say 'to more immature levels of thinking and primitive belief systems'. Under so-called normal developmental conditions we would expect parents and others to correct these false assumptions as the child grew older. With some children, however, this does not occur; indeed the beliefs and ideas may become even more firmly fixed by the unsatisfactory nature of early childhood experiences. For example, children who see that their parents are predisposed to violence to get what they want come to hold the same belief and see no reason in what they see around them to change this held belief.

2 Psychological Conditions

I have taken four examples from the writings of Bernard and Joyce (1984) of psychological functioning which may be relevant in trying to understand more clearly the exact nature of the contribution of cognitive variables to the production of behaviour. It is suggested that the skills of the child in these four cognitive/psychological areas will increase or decrease the likelihood of the child experiencing problems of behaviour. They are summarised here:

(a)   *Attention processes* are those cognitive processes that determine which aspects of both their 'external and internal worlds' children pay attention to or ignore. Children cannot learn from what they do not pay attention to. While these selection processes are not fully understood – we do not know, for example, why a child chooses or subconsciously attends to certain stimuli but not others – we do know that what is observed will be important in determining how children subsequently behave.

(b)   The *mediational processes* which children employ (these are frequently but not always verbal) to interpret those external or internal events include the store of concepts that the child has available for 'representing and understanding experiences'. In other words, what children say to themselves about those experiences has a great effect on how successfully children regulate their world. This aspect of psychological processing is fundamental to the RET paradigm. The beliefs and values, understandings and assumptions, whether healthy or unhealthy, that children hold will influence the manner in which experiences are received, interpreted and stored.

(c) Similarly the *logical reasoning processes* or the way in which 'children interpret and draw generalizations and conclusions from personal observation – employ premises, assumptions and beliefs deductively to arrive at conclusions' (Ellis and Bernard, 1983, p.22), are another aspect of cognitive funtioning.

(d) Finally the ability of children to employ *cognitive strategies* such as the capacity to generate plans and solutions to any new difficulties–personal and interpersonal – they encounter, will also be influential in determining the success or failure children encounter in their daily lives.

3 Environmental Conditions

Again as with CBT-based explanations, the role of the environment can be a significant one in 'causing' behaviour problems. Children need appropriate environmental conditions for healthy cognitive-affective development to take place. For example, children who genuinely find school a frustrating experience, who believe that school and the learning process is something over which they have no control and which does not meet their needs, are operating within those environmental conditions which generate inappropriate cognitive-affective development. If children are not rewarded for effort, for example, as well as achievement, then they inevitably come to understand that effort is not a desirable behaviour.

Children, in order to learn appropriate situation-specific behaviour, require feedback or input from the environment after a behaviour has been 'performed' to facilitate, through this feedback, the development of cognitive mediation of emotions and behaviour. They need to be told when they are thinking, feeling and behaving in an OK fashion and when they are not, in order that they may repeat or avoid, as appropriate, the process/es. Some children in school and at home do not have access to appropriate feedback.

RET has been particularly concerned to explore those 'environmental conditions' generated by parental child management styles. More specifically, the irrational beliefs that parents may hold about how children should be brought up and also the beliefs that teachers and other adults have about how children should behave. These beliefs are likely to affect the nature of the feedback we give to children which in turn will have influence over cognitive-affective development of the child. If these reactions or expectations are unhealthy or unrealistic they may lead to a form of cognitive development on the part of the child which is equally unhealthy and unrealistic. Expecting too much of children or having unreasonable inappropriate expectations and irrational beliefs 'often create inappropriate levels of emotionality that manifests themselves in maladaptive parent-child interaction' (Ellis and Bernard, 1983, p.23).

In summary, CBT/RET workers look to environmental, physiological and psychological factors in their explanation of the process wherein behaviour problems develop. They suggest that factors from these areas are interactive or reciprocal. It often remains unclear with a given child as to whether unhealthy environmental experiences/learning experiences predominate in causing children to think maladaptively or whether maladaptive thinking generates an unhealthy view of the environment which then goes on to become self-fulfilling.

In practice, it is usually both the 'reality' of the environment, or the nature of the experiences a child has and how the child actually interprets or reacts to that 'reality', or those experiences, that combine to produce an understanding, on the part of the professional, as to how problems occur and how they may be tackled. As I have suggested before, assessment and treatment phases quite often combine working at the level of changing the child's circumstances, the behaviour and his/her thinking. The professional involved will clearly not adhere to the view that cognitive change was required if, in fact, the child appeared to hold a perfectly reasonable view of what was happening to him/her. It is important to keep this in mind when reading the final sections of this chapter.

Types of Cognitions

The discussion in the last section on the role of faulty cognitions or irrational beliefs which, in combination with other factors, may contribute to behaviour problems, leads on quite naturally to a fuller consideration of the nature of these cognitions. As these cognitive processes underlie so much of treatment techniques it is important that they be described in some detail. Futhermore, it is the author's view that the advances made in cognitive restructuring procedures are based primarily, and perhaps unsurprisingly, upon the greater understanding practitioners have developed of specific cognitive processes which underlie both so-called normal and maladaptive behaviour. It is this increased understanding that is the cornerstone upon which the credibility of the strategies of remediation have been founded. The fact that workers are able to specifically identify the nature of cognitions which lead to behaviour problems has given weight to the view that these cognitions can be retaught or changed.

Perhaps the greatest emphasis regarding the exact nature of faulty cognitive processes in behaviour problems has come from workers in the field of RET. It is this paradigm that has tended to be more concerned with the precise nature of cognitive dysfunctions – particularly the difference between rational and irrational beliefs – than workers in the CBT field, although as will be seen later CBT has also made an important contribution to our understanding of cognitive processes and behaviour problems. It is with the rational and irrational beliefs of the RET field that we begin this section. Dryden and Ellis (1986) describe the manner in which these irrational beliefs contribute to behaviour problems in terms of their own ABC framework, not to be confused with the behavioural ABC framework.

Because of limitations of space only the simplest description of the ABC format is given here: the reader is advised to look to the writings of Ellis for more detailed descriptions. Dryden and Ellis suggest that in pursuit of life goals human-beings encounter (or actively seek out, as not all events just happen to us) some activating event or experience (A), the event or experience activates or produces a belief (B) about this event or experience which may be rational or irrational. If it is rational it leads to a rational consequence (C) which may be cognitive, emotional or behavioural; if it is an irrational belief then an irrational consequence ensues.

Dryden and Ellis (1986) describe rational beliefs as being non-absolute in nature, they are preferences, desires, wishes, likes and dislikes. When a person has these preferences etc. fulfilled they feel pleased and satisfied, when a person does not get what they want they feel displeasure and dissatisfaction. Irrational beliefs on the other hand are absolute and expressed in the form of musts, shoulds, oughts and have tos and they lead to feelings such as depression, anxiety, guilt and anger. Feelings generated by rational beliefs do not significantly interfere with getting what a person wants. Indeed a degree of dissatisfaction or discomfort may well be goal-enhancing, a degree of discomfort encourages us to try harder.

However, feelings generated by irrational beliefs tend to interfere with getting what we want. They negatively affect our judgement, fix us like rabbits in a car's headlights, reduce us to inaction, or generate what Dweck and Reppucci (1973) refer to as 'learned helplessness', the feeling that the 'victim' has no power to influence events for the better and that if something good does happen it was good luck or fate and nothing to do with the individual's efforts to bring it about. Irrational beliefs generate the feeling that the person is, in absolute terms, no good. Failure (or even success) in an exercise is usually attributed to lack of ability rather than lack of effort or to good or bad luck. The child with strong irrational beliefs is left with the opinion that there is very little that they can do to influence their lives for the better.

Bernard and Joyce (1984) summarize three clusters of irrational beliefs:

1 'I must do well and be approved of.'
2 'I must get what I want.'
3 'I must be comfortable and life should be fun.'

Virginia Waters (1982) elaborated upon these beliefs for younger children in the following manner:

1 'It's awful if others don't like me.'
2 'I'm bad if I make a mistake.'
3 'Everything should go my way; I should always get what I want.'
4 'Things should come easy to me.'
5 'The world should be fair and bad people must be punished.'
6 'I shouldn't show my feelings.'
7 'Adults should be perfect.'
8 'There's only one right answer.'
9 'I must win.'
10 'I shouldn't have to wait for anything.' (p.572).

Waters (1981) itemizes a slightly different list for adolescents:

1 'It would be awful if peers didn't like me. It would be awful to be a social loser.'
2 'I shouldn't make mistakes, especially social mistakes.'
3 'It's my parents' fault I'm so miserable.'
4 'I can't help, that's the way I am and I guess I'll always be this way.'
5 'The world should be fair and just.'
6 'It's awful when things do not go my way.'
7 'It's better to avoid challenges than to risk failure.'
8 'I must conform to my peers.'
9 'I can't stand to be criticized.'
10 'Others should always be responsible.' (p.6).

Children who hold absolute beliefs of this nature consistently, frequently, for a long time and in many different situations, come to behave in a fashion commensurate with these beliefs; that is they behave in a maladaptive unreasonable absolute fashion. It follows quite naturally that teachers are rubbish, parents know nothing, all coppers never had parents, and it is therefore logical that such children behave in a disruptive fashion in school, ignore the advice of their parents and break the law.

The cognitive-behavioural paradigm also provides an insight into specific, unhealthy cognitive processes. Weishaar and Beck (1986) call upon the work of Beck (1967) and Burns (1980) in describing types of cognitive distortions:

1 Arbitrary inferences – drawing a particular conclusion even though there

is no supporting evidence for this conclusion or even when the evidence is to the contrary.

2 Selective abstraction – filtering out the positive part of an event and dwelling on the negative aspects.

3 Overgeneralization – taking a single event as evidence of complete personal incompetence or adopting a complete view of somebody in highly emotional terms when in fact it is only one part of the person's behaviour that is objected to.

4 Magnification (or catastrophizing) or minimization – exaggerating the significance of an event or alternatively refusing to accept the importance of an event.

5 Personalization – taking an event that while not directly aimed at the person assumes the importance of a personal attack.

6 Dichotomous or all-or-nothing thinking – an overly simplified and rigid perception of events as good or bad, right or wrong.

7 Cognitive deficiency – a disregard for an important aspect of a life situation.

These types of thinking and those described initially in this section will be familiar to workers with children with behaviour problems. They lead, for example, to children stating that nobody likes them because they take part in and lose a fight, that a teacher hates them because of one telling-off, that anybody who tells them off is an enemy, that getting one sum wrong means that they are no good at maths, that when a teacher says 'I know you were provoked, next time try to keep calm' the child does not hear the qualification but only hears the telling off.

If we consider particularly those children who have difficulties in their social relationships with their peers, adults, teachers and parents, they are frequently characterized as lacking in interpersonal skills. In these instances there is an apparent absence of the following cognitive skills identified by Spivack and Shure (1974).

1 Sensitivity or perspective taking: the understanding that people inevitably have difficulties at some time or other in their efforts to relate to others and that others may have a different perspective or view of that problem from the one assumed by the individual.

2 Alternative solution thinking: refers to the processes used to generate a number of possible solutions to a problem. While many children would probably only pause to consider one or two viable alternatives, the skill of generating a number of options – the more the better – would, it is argued, lead to the best possible chance of arriving at an appropriate solution.

3 Means–end thinking: this skill is concerned with the thinking processes

that a child would use to break down a target goal into a series of more easily achievable objectives. In other words being able to work out the means of achieving a particular end.

4   Consequential thinking: a number of the possible solutions might on deeper consideration turn out to hold certain undesirable consequences for the child and/or for others. Children need to be able to see the advantages and disadvantages of a behaviour once thought of.

5   Causal thinking: the skill of linking cause and effect; children need to be able to understand that connections exist between behaviours and their consequences and also in RET terms to be able to understand that there may be a connection between events, emotional states and cognitions.

Teaching children how to employ these thinking strategies or cognitive processes forms the basis of a number of the cognitive-behavioural programmes described in the final section of this chapter.

Assessment Procedures

As I have suggested earlier, it is difficult to be unequivocal about which children are prone to the cognitive deficiencies described in the last section and who, therefore, would benefit from intervention based upon some form of cognitive restructuring.

The initial meeting with the child will be important as the worker will seek to determine which, if any, of the faulty cognitive processes (or absence of) already described affects the child you are working with. Is it in fact the case that the child's current behavioural reaction is a perfectly reasonable reaction to an unsatisfactory environmental setting? It may take more than one meeting to determine the suitability of the child for a cognitive-based approach. In consequence, while the main focus of assessment will obviously be the thinking styles of the child, it will not be exclusively so.

Young (1983) suggests that the aim of assessment and problem-definition in RET terms is to 'obtain a diagnostic assessment of the client's reality-based and psychologically induced complaints' (p.92).

In CBT terms the assessment process may not be as involved and may be simply concerned with identifying a child who has difficulties moderating their behaviour and who is, for example, impulsive or prone to angry outbursts. Not all programmes will, therefore, begin with the same form of assessment, it will depend upon the age of the child, the type of problem and the circumstances under which the programme will proceed.

As a generalization the use of questioning in assessment procedures is the primary method of eliciting information about the problem, particularly in terms of the behaviour itself and the values, beliefs, expectations, attitudes, interpretations which seem to facilitate the behaviour. The process would usually take the form: what is the behaviour, what is the thinking behind this behaviour or what cognitive errors lead to this behaviour? The assessment particularly in RET terms, attempts to determine the idiosyncratic styles of thought of the child. Questions of the 'What if———' type are frequently used to allow the worker to have access to the child's styles of thought.

Sometimes when direct questioning fails, if the child refuses to accept that s/he has a problem or finds it difficult to express their thoughts on the problems or if the child is quite young, then more oblique routes must be followed. In practice, finding out about the child's cognitive style may be supported by any number of activities or techniques. Dryden (1984), for example, recommends the use of personal photos or mementoes, paintings, poems or records to evoke a dialogue with the child and initiate an understanding of how the child thinks.

Alternatively we may set up some kind of artificial problem situation to give us an idea of how the child might typically react to difficulties and to help us understand the child's thinking styles better. Within this context, Elkin (1983) describes those questions which he feels will support the worker at the point where s/he attempts to identify the cognitive style of the child within this 'artificial' setting. Elkin relates the questions initially to the manner in which the child deals with a posed problem (examples of which will be described shortly). In this case the questions are, of course, not posed to the child but serve as guidelines for the worker.

1   How does the child go about solving the problem?
2   How does the child deal with frustration?
3   How does the child deal with success or failure?
4   What kind of self-talk is involved?
5   What can be said about the child's cognitive style?
6   What are the child's underlying belief systems?
7   What are the child's more common affective responses?
8   What are the child's defensive behaviours?

As Ellis and Bernard (1983) suggest, the worker at a slightly more sophisticated level is attempting to answer the questions:

1   Is the child distorting reality?
2   Is the child evaluating situations in a self-defeating way?
3   Does the child lack appropriate cognitions?
4   Does the child lack practical problem-solving skills?

This method of assessment, as I have suggested, involves setting the child some kind of problem to solve. This may be quite simple – completing a jigsaw puzzle or a math's puzzle, or it may involve a problematic social situation – 'What would you do if you moved into a new school and nobody wanted to talk to you?' This approach to assessment is based on a method pioneered by Spivack and Shure (1974) called the Pre-school Problem Solving Test. The child is presented with a problem and this allows the worker to assess what Spivack and Shure refer to (also described elsewhere in this chapter) as means–end thinking, the ability to generate a number of ways to solve a particular problem or their alternative thinking skills.

Similar to this is the 'What Happens Next Game' also devised by Spivack and Shure which measures the child's ability to anticipate consequences. Elkin gives the example of the little boy who takes his neighbour's dog for a walk without asking permission. The child is asked what might happen next in the story.

Perhaps the most common assessment instrument, and one which can be used with groups of children as well as individuals, uses the sentence-completion technique. The technique can be used with children giving their answers out-loud or in written form.

1   When I do poorly in a test I think ——
2   I think school is —
3   The thing I like best is ——

A similar technique has led to the development by Knaus (1974) of two surveys of irrational beliefs. The first has 18 questions and is for 7–10 year olds and contains questions such as:

When somebody calls your friend or mother a bad name
1   You have to fight.
2   You have to tell him off.
3   You can think before you act.

The second survey with 37 questions intended for 10–13 year olds starts with the question:

A person who feels angry toward another person thinks:
1   He can't stand the other person's behaviour.
2   The other person has no right to act the way he does.
3   Nobody is perfect and this person is no different.
4   All the above answers are correct.

Another somewhat similar instrument was developed by Kassinove, Crisci and Tiegerman (1977). This inventory contains 33 ideas which children between the ages of 10 and 18 are expected to rate in terms of agree, disagree or uncertain. For example:

People need the love or approval of almost everyone they consider important. Do you agree, disagree or are uncertain about this idea?

None of these instruments have been standardized in terms of validity or reliability to the point where an assessment might say this child has scored at this percentile of irrational beliefs and therefore required 'treatment'. Nor is it likely we would wish any assessment tool to perform this function. These instruments should, however, prove valuable in giving the worker an area of focus and may prove useful in determining the progress made by the client if pre- and post-intervention measures are required.

An extension of the techniques described above is the Storytelling Technique. Pictures taken from magazines or from tests such as the Children's Apperception Test (CAT) can be used to stimulate the child to tell a story about what they think is happening in the picture. The worker can use questions such as: 'What do you think is going to happen next?' Or with a specific cognitive-behavioural slant, Elkin suggests:

1 'How is the girl feeling?'
2 'How will the little girl get out of this situation?'
3 'What do you think she was thinking?'

Alternatively the worker can begin a story and the child/ren can finish it off or fill in the missing thoughts, feelings and actions. Elkin suggests that a useful way to categorize the information obtained from this type of exercise and one which brings together the cognitive-emotive-behavioural aspects of the child's perception of the event or situation is in the format:

1 What is the event or situation described?
2 What cognitions does the child have about the event?
3 What behaviour does the child describe (of the child in the story) as a way of dealing with or responding to the story?

A thoughts-feelings and actions diary operates on a similar basis but allows the worker (if the child is able or willing) to gather information from outside of the 'therapeutic setting' about episodes which have occurred which were upsetting or anger provoking. This takes the form:

1 What happened.
2 What I thought.
3 What I felt.
4 What I did.

The think-aloud and thought-sampling approaches again suggested by Elkin are similar to those already described with the child given a puzzle or a problem to solve. They are asked either to think aloud as they attempt to carry out the task or they are asked what they are thinking at a particular point in the exercise. This gives the worker information about the child's cognitive processes.

Finally, role-play, if the worker is comfortable with this approach, can be a useful assessment technique. The role-play can be constructed to recreate situations from the child's life that are causing distress to the child (this approach may be particularly effective with groups of children as the opportunities for realistic role-play are increased). The worker asks the child/ren to imagine that this is their first day in school and that when they approach a group of children to play with they are rejected. The child/ren are asked what they might do and say, how they might feel and what they might think. This information, as with all the other assessment techniques, will give the worker an idea of current skills and the progress that the children are making as the progamme proceeds.

Strategies for Bringing about Cognitive Change

This final section describes a number of programme or strategy options which are available to workers with children showing behaviour problems when the primary focus of intervention is the change, improvement, and development of cognitive processes to guide appropriate behaviour more effectively. It is important to point out again that the strategies and programmes described here have, in their practical application, often been combined with strategies from other areas to form an eclectic programme of remediation. This marriage of strategies has typically led to an increased efficacy of treatment results.

These other programmes have included behavioural methods-contracts, self-monitoring, contingent reward and punishment, relaxation training, systematic desensitization, assertiveness training, stress management and so on. While space does not permit an examination of these techniques, nevertheless the part played in the treatment process by these additional techniques should be acknowledged. The section begins by looking at general approaches or strategies used in CBT or RET. It concludes by describing the characteristics of a number of CBT and RET programmes.

The strategies/programmes described in this section have in common the fact that they use various forms of language development and/or regulation through talking to ourselves to modify the thinking processes and behavioural actions of the child.

The intention of the professional is to encourage the child to be able to use self-talk effectively and particularly when 'the going gets tough'. At times when school life becomes stressful, tempting, and unstructured, some children become badly behaved; they do not consider the consequences of their actions, they become impulsive, they make poor cognitive decisions. The aim of cognitive-based programmes is to teach such children how to talk to themselves in a positive and productive manner and in a manner which produces appropriate rather than inappropriate behaviour.

I have suggested before in this chapter that two broad approaches to teaching children to talk to themselves exist. Described in simplest terms one involves teaching children what to think and the other how to think; in crude terms to think differently or to think more. As the strategies and programmes described are based upon work carried out in the CBT and RET fields this tends to influence whether the programmes are designed to teach children how to think or what to think. In practice the edges between these two bases for action tend to blur. Indeed, sometimes, as Bernard and Joyce (1984) say

> We simply have to tell the client how best to handle the situation without going into what he should be thinking and saying (p.248).

Nevertheless, one of the first decisions faced by the worker is that of trying to decide which format is appropriate for the child/ren in question. As a generalization, it might be said that with younger, less able children and those less committed to the programme, the evidence suggests that the simpler and more situation specific the verbal cue or self-talk is, the more likely it is that behaviour will be guided by it. In other words the child is taught a specific covert verbal phrase which is appropriate and perhaps specific to the situation in which behaviour problems occur, they are encouraged to repeat the phrase learned during the session in the real-life setting.

In cognitive-behavioural methods there exists a by-now-well-accepted sequence of teaching the child how to talk effectively to him/herself. This particular model from Goldstein and Glick (1987) is based upon the work of Meichenbaum and Goodman (1971):

1   The therapist models the task performance and self-instructs out loud while the child observes.
2   The child performs the task, instructing himself out loud as he does so.
3   The therapist models task performance and whispers self-instructions while the child observes.
4   The child performs the task instructing himself in a whisper as he does so.
5   The therapist performs the task using covert self-instructions with pauses and behavioural signs of thinking such as raising her eyes toward the ceiling or stroking her chin.
6   The child performs the task using covert self-instructions (p. 69).

With more able, more sophisticated or older children the worker may be more inclined to teach the child a general problem-solving process which can be applied in any problematic situation. Again the above format can be utilized but the modelled instructions will be less situation specific and will follow a more general problem-solving format:

1   What is my problem – what am I supposed to do?

2   How can I deal with this problem – what are my options, which of these options will be my plan?

3   Did I use my plan?

4   How did my plan work – what do I need to change?

We should not, however, necessarily assume that young children cannot benefit from the problem-solving approach. Waters (1982) describes a problem-solving format which can be used even with very young children.

1   Define the problem in concrete, behavioural terms.

2   Generate as many alternative solutions as you can without evaluating them. Remember, quantity is more important than quality; the more solutions the better.

3   Go back and evaluate each alternative solution, giving both positive and negative consequences and eliminating absurd solutions.

4   Choose one or two of the best solutions and plan your procedures step by step.

5   Put your plan into action and evaluate the results (p. 576).

Clearly all approaches have their advantages; one might be more immediately effective but lacks generalizability and vice versa. It would seem that practitioners should be prepared to use variations on either approach as and when the circumstances determine.

The options available to the worker when attempting to teach children 'what-to-think' are extremely broad. One option may involve nothing more than the worker sitting down with the child and giving, or better still working out together, a phrase or a motto which will influence their behaviour in a specific setting. At a somewhat more sophisticated level the teacher may ask the child to visualize the setting in which problems frequently occur and to repeat, usually covertly or by whispering, a statement such as 'Relax, I'm mature enough to deal with this.'

RET makes particular use of Rational Emotive Imagery (REI) to help children visualize a threatening scene whilst the worker may talk the child through the scene and discuss the difficult bits or alternatively the worker can role-play the child and demonstrate how the child might use self-talk to help themselves through the situation when it next occurs. For younger children teaching self-talk may involve giving the child a simpler and more catchy statement: 'Sit in my seat and make my work neat.' For other children one word, even a nonsense word, may serve as a reminder to produce appropriate behaviour. Getting this word 'right' can make a difference to the efficacy of this form of behaviour control.

John Maclean, the Llanelli rugby coach, originally used the word 'push' to try to exhort his scrum to greater efforts. When he began using the word 'drive' instead, the response amazed him. So it is worth considering which particular word works best with a particular child or group of children. RET therapists suggest that self-talk phrases or words should be catchy, forceful and passionate, the covert equivalent of 'stop being so —— stupid and get on with it! This is particularly the case when the objective is to stop negative or inappropriate thoughts (sometimes called thought-stopping).

RET strategies tend to fall more often into the 'how-to-think' category. The intention here is to cause the child to dispute those irrational beliefs that the worker believes generate behaviour problems. Dryden and Ellis (1986) call it detecting irrational thoughts or beliefs, debating these thoughts or beliefs as a way of giving them up, discriminating between appropriate and inappropriate thoughts and beliefs, and helping the child in defining the language used when describing these thoughts and beliefs.

So strategies for change involve teaching the child how to monitor their current or automatic thoughts, how to identify deep-seated irrational beliefs, to understand how they construe the world and to recognize the connection between these thoughts or beliefs, the way they subsequently feel and the behaviour this produces. The aim is to get the child to see the consequence of this thinking style, to push the child through the process of understanding where these beliefs will lead.

To understand how events that have happened to the child in the past may have been 'caused' or 'precipitated' by their thinking style, the worker aims to summarize and feedback so that the child understands their thoughts; to 'recruit and amplify' in RET jargon. For example to ask the child 'Have you ever felt like this before?' or to point out that when the situation, thought or feelings recur they don't have to feel, think or act the same way. By using questions based on 'inference chaining' – what happens if, what happens then, what next, what do you think others would think, what does this mean to you, what do you think about yourself – the child is led or encouraged to develop a better, that is more rational, way of thinking.

The worker aims to enable the children to understand the positives and negatives of their thinking, to recognize their cognitive errors – where they are personalizing innocuous events, thinking in absolute or black and white terms – by standing back or depersonalizing the thoughts. Through a process of collaboration worker and child aim to generate alternative ideas which lead to both an understanding and change in the child's thinking.

As with CBT approaches, a number of strategies are available to bring about this change, first in the artificial setting and ultimately *in vivo*. As a very general rule these tend to be more discursive and less didactic than CBT strategies but again this is a generalization as RET approaches may contain an element of teaching about the nature of irrational beliefs and thoughts.

As suggested in the last section on assessment, children can be encouraged to examine their irrational beliefs, emotions and behaviours by keeping a diary. In fact self-recording is one of the most used techniques in CBT/RET practice and it is frequently used as a homework task which supports the generalization of techniques learned in the programme to home or school situations. A common format for such an exercise/diary is based upon particular incidents which occur throughout the week and which are tackled by the child:

1   What happened?
2   How did I feel?
3   What were my automatic thoughts?
4   What behaviour resulted from these thoughts in the past?
5   What were my alternative (more rational) thoughts in this instance?
6   What behaviour resulted from these thoughts?
7   How did I feel afterwards?

It can be seen that an examination of the cognitive antecedents and consequences plays an important part in helping the child understand the processes involved in the production of inappropriate behaviour.

Other strategies employed by RET workers include formulating analogies of what the child is doing and what you wish them to do and relating these analogies to their hobbies, interests or heroes. For example a child who was particularly interested in football might respond well to the idea that just because you miss (or because Brian Robson misses) one tackle or goal, you do not rush off the field and refuse to play any more but you keep trying. Missing one tackle does not make you a bad footballer just as having one fight does not make you a bad person, not being able to tackle does not make you a bad striker if you are good at scoring goals and so on. Relating the analogy to an interest makes the comparison much more powerful.

Working through the worst possible scenario, a child may find his/her behaviour is affected because a class mate won't speak to them. The worker might ask the child 'Suppose they never spoke to you again is that so bad, couldn't you cope with it, wouldn't you just get on with things even if this happened?' The message to the child is that the worry is out of proportion to the possible consequences, even at their worst.

Disputing occurs when a child says, for example, that they will only be popular if they can fight well; the worker can dispute this by saying 'Do you only like children who can fight?'

When a child says s/he is stupid because s/he does stupid things RET describes the technique whereby the worker starts to bark like a dog and asks the child 'Does that make me a dog because I bark like one or, if I were to pour a glass of water over my head, while that would be a stupid act, would it necessarily make me a stupid person?'

Rational role reversal involves the worker playing the child and the child the worker: the worker describes the problem saying stupid or irrational things about the problem and the child must help the worker to be rational. By forcing the child to help the worker deal with his/her problems the child develops a keener understanding of the irrationality involved.

I have said before in this chapter that methods of cognitive change are many and various; sometimes the worker may help the child by describing what to think and at other times by describing how to think. I have also suggested that the edges between approaches quite often tend to blur. RET describes a process called practical problem-solving which combines both approaches. For example, a child may have difficulty completing homework, s/he may feel hopeless and depressed. The worker can do a number of things: s/he can help the child to develop more rational self-statements – 'I can do it, it's just a matter of getting organized.' S/he may also help the child develop general cognition strategies. Two possible examples are consequential thinking (if I complete this homework I'm going to do better in my exams) and means–end thinking (devising as many strategies as possible to get the homework done – 'I can do it when I come in; I can get my mother to ask how its going every now and again', etc.). Finally, the child can be encouraged to produce behavioural skills – working through the homework in a given order, keeping a homework book and so on – which may help the child to get the work done.

In addition to these general principles of change, a number of programmes have been formulated by CBT/RET workers which may be used with individuals or groups. Some of these are commercially available while others are described in sufficient detail in their original sources to enable those workers with limited experience in this field to set them up reasonably easily. One such commercially available programme is called *Think Aloud* (Camp and Bash, 1981). These materials aim to teach children who apparently do not automatically use language, or whose language is self-stimulatory, immature or otherwise inappropriate, how to effectively use language to guide their behaviour. The *Think Aloud* materials enable the worker to teach general problem-solving skills to children. Originally intended to teach self-verbalizations to aggressive boys the programme of 23 lessons has been applied to a wider range of problems including children who are

> impulsive, who tend to respond without adequately thinking through
> the consequences of their actions, who lack a sense of cause and effect,
> or lack a repertoire of alternative ways of thinking about problems,
> solutions or consequences (p.16).

Think Aloud, the authors state, may be used either in a therapeutic way or as a preventative educational programme. The programme is intended for children aged 6–8 although there is some suggestion that these materials might be most effective with somewhat older children whose thinking is less content- or situation-specific-bound and who are more able to comprehend the need to generalize the principles involved. In order to teach children 'how to think' they are taught, as they think aloud during a difficult task, to ask and answer four questions:

1   What is my problem? or What am I supposed to do?
2   How can I do it? or What is my plan?
3   Am I using my plan?
4   How did I do?

The materials are organized in such a way that children can begin to practice these skills with simple academic-type tasks – for example, colouring inside a circle where the child might say to him/herself:

1   'What am I supposed to do?'
2   'I know, I'm supposed to colour in the circle neatly.'
3   'If I keep reminding myself by saying up to the line but not over it, this might help.'
4   'Am I doing what I'm supposed to do?'
5   'Yes I'm not colouring over the line?'
6   'Well done, that plan worked pretty well.'

These same principles can be applied to increasingly more difficult and socially oriented situations such that the child comes to develop those cognitive processes, for example, consequential behaviour, means–end thinking and so on, described earlier in the chapter.

British material in this area is limited, but one example is John Thacker's *Steps to Success* (1982). This package uses a similar format to the *Think Aloud* programme to 'help children to help themselves'. Based upon the work of D'Zurilla and Goldfried (1971) and Spivack *et al.* (1976) it aims to teach social problem-solving skills to groups of children aged 11–13. A section on working with individual children is also included. *Steps to Success* uses video materials which the teacher makes using the provided scripts, of 'real-life' problem-situations (for example, starting a new school) to promote discussion on the areas described below. At key points the video is stopped and discussion takes place around the particular teaching point of the programme. For example, is it normal for all children to experience problems at some time or other? A cartoon is used to reinforce the 'message' and to give the children an easily remembered image to support their future efforts.

The programme has five units:

1   Problem-solving orientation
2   Problem identification and goal setting
3   Generation of alternative solutions
4   Consideration of consequences and decision making
5   Making plans and checking for success

1 Problem-solving Orientation

Thacker suggests that if children are to benefit from the programme they must first accept that 'problematic situations are a part of normal life' and that these events are often a result of the child's actions. This optimistic view of difficulties suggests to the child that they are not simply victims of their environment but that they possess a degree of personal control over their lives. As I have already suggested, it is common for children with behaviour problems to blame everybody else but themselves, so this initial view of what is happening to them is an important one.

Second, it is important that children come to recognize cues such as feelings, emotions or physical reactions (feeling upset, sad, unhappy, angry, tense, sweaty, hot etc.) and use these cues to bring into action the problem-solving techniques employed in the programme. Finally, children are encouraged to adopt a 'stop and think then act' orientation to problems rather than acting either impulsively or of doing nothing at all.

2 Problem Identification

In this unit children are taught to:

1 separate the relevant from the irrelevant elements of the problem
2 avoid vagueness in defining the problem
3 consider external events but also their own thoughts and feelings
4 distinguish between short and long term goals

3 Generation of Alternative Solutions

The third unit concentrates on the skill of generating alternative solutions to the problem other than the one the child might ordinarily have chosen. This includes brainstorming possible solutions and is more concerned with coming up with as many possible ideas than at this stage evaluating them.

4 Consideration of Consequences and Decision-making

Unit four helps children develop a criterion for deciding which of the proposed alternatives are most suitable. The suitability of the solution will depend upon whether it stands a good chance of success and whether it would meet the long-term goal set earlier. With the aid of a 'reminder' cartoon showing a child thinking of possible solutions to a problem the child considers:

What would happen if you tried these out? Would they work? Are there any snags? Imagine ahead to see snags and if none, then decide whether a solution makes you happy, other people happy or whether a solution makes you sad, other people sad (p. 19).

5 Making Plans and Checking for Success

Unit five examines how children who having thought of good solutions to their problems can then go on to make a 'concrete step-by-step plan to make it work'. By using role-play children are able to explore the advantages and disadvantages of a particular approach and refine a plan a bit at a time, paying attention to what Thacker calls 'the fine detail of social skills' required to implement the solution.

Both the *Think Aloud* and *Steps to Success* materials are now 7- and 6-years-old respectively and perhaps they lack the breadth of approach to behaviour problems that more recently published materials can offer. Anger or impulse control has proved a fertile ground for those concerned with cognitive-behavioural methods and it is interesting to note the eclectic nature of strategies used in the newer materials concerned with this area.

Feindler and Acton (1986), for example, present a variety of programmes in the form of lesson plans for working with adolescents both in groups and individually. Feindler and Acton bring together techniques from behavioural psychology, relaxation training, assertiveness training and, as would be expected from the title of their book (*Adolescent Anger Control: Cognitive-Behavioural Techniques*), their programmes include a clear cognitive component. This cognitive component is evident in a number of proposed strategies.

One such strategy is the use of 'visual imagery'. Here the adolescent is asked to delay an immediate impulse and to relax by evoking a pleasant visual image which is calming – for example, sitting by a quiet stream or thinking in terms of sports analogies such as 'float like a butterfly', or employing cooling-down images such as 'deep freeze'. Similarly, in order to aid understanding of the process which 'automatically' takes over, adolescents who have poor impulse control and quick tempers are asked to visualize a stick of dynamite with a lighted match. It is explained to them that each of us have a particular match which 'lights our fuse', which might be a particular person or situation and so on. Feindler and Ecton say:

> Picture your mind and your body as if they were a firecracker. The match that lights your fuse is the trigger. The fuse is your mind and your body is the contents of the firecracker. The longer you let the fuse burn, the more you risk blowing up and losing control of your anger. How quickly you put the fuse out depends upon how well and how

quickly you can stop and control your negative thoughts and feelings (pp. 92–3).

The concept of triggers or covert antecedent events which set off inappropriate behaviour is explored at some length in the text. Indirect triggers are described as misperceptions or misattributions of events such as feeling blamed or feeling that someone doesn't like them even when no evidence supports this view. The teacher models and emphasizes how these internal dialogues 'can increase anger out of proportion'.

The importance of helping adolescents develop self-reminders to break the chain of antecedent events is a key aspect of the programme. Indeed the recognition of the role of cognitive antecedents in inappropriate behaviour and the manner in which these may be changed to generate acceptable behaviour forms an important part of any programme of cognitive change. Feindler and Acton suggest how these self-reminders may be used by asking the group to think of ways in which they remind themselves, for example, to bring certain things to class, to give examples of how talking to oneself can be used in a sporting context and in keeping calm when under pressure. The group (in this case) are asked to generate a list of self-reminders: 'slow down, take it easy, take a deep breath'.

A similar technique described in the programme is 'thought-stopping' based upon the work of the behavioural psychotherapist Wolpe (1958). It is explained by the teacher that thought-stopping is a technique that the adolescent can use to stop inappropriate/negative thoughts. The adolescent is instructed to close his/her eyes and think a negative or disturbing thought. After a short while the teacher will shout loudly 'Stop!' If the negative thoughts cease then the adolescent is instructed to substitute a positive thought. The adolescent can eventually come to control his or her own thoughts by inwardly shouting 'Stop' as shouting out loud would clearly be inappropriate in many social situations. This form of cognitive restructuring can be explained by the teacher who might employ the following dialogue:

> Like a carpenter who is hired to make repairs or rebuild something, we too, when we find something faulty or weak with the way we think about the trigger, must restructure or rebuild that thought into something more positive . . . By doing a self-assessment of our intense if faulty negative thoughts we will have the opportunity to rebuild and restructure these thoughts into something more positive (p. 102).

Helping children to self-evaluate their behaviour has already been mentioned and is a key aspect of behaviour change programmes. In this programme self-evaluation is a method by which the adolescent can provide him/herself with feedback as to how he/she behaved or felt during a conflict situation. Just as a consideration of cognitive antecedents is a vital part of cognitive restructuring programmes so too is the role of cognitive consequences. For example, is what the adolescent says after-the-event reinforcing the undesirable behaviour – 'that showed him he won't call me names again'. Instead adolescents are encouraged to commend themselves when they have behaved appropriately and covertly berate themselves when they have behaved inappropriately. Feindler and Acton recommend the use of a 'hassle log' in which the adolescent writes down the kind of self-evaluative statements they have made, asking themselves whether they were reinforcing or punishing and thereby build up a picture of their 'current repertoire' of self-statements. The teacher is asked to provide examples of positive and negative self-evaluations which they may use to reinforce or punish their own behaviour.

Thinking ahead is a strategy which utilizes both problem-solving and self-instructions to estimate or anticipate future negative consequences for current aggressive behaviour. If I misbehave now, such and such will happen, so I must not get involved now. Problem-solving techniques previously outlined are also described and these techniques and a number of others combine to form a programme of cognitive behavioural restructuring which might take the following form:

Session 1 Explaining the rationale for the programme, defining the rules of the programme, explaining the activities that will be used – homework, use of video, group discussion, introducing relaxation techniques, explaining rewards.

Session 2 Introducing the 'hassle' log, discussing how participants had handled problems in the past, using self-assessment, introducing the idea of ABC's.

Session 3 Collecting and reviewing homework, introducing the idea of 'triggers', practising progressive relaxation.

Session 4 Reviewing 'triggers' and 'hassle logs', discussing the rights of adolescents with regard to rules/laws and authority figures in family, school, community and current setting, introducing assertiveness training techniques, using video tapes to show appropriate and inappropriate assertion techniques.

Session 5 Reviewing assertion techniques.

Session 6 Reviewing techniques and materials used so far, introducing self-instruction training.

Session 7 Using self-instruction training to guide behaviour, to remember to do things, to guide behaviour during conflict or anger-producing situations.

Session 8 Reviewing anger control techniques, introducing the 'think ahead' procedure to self-control behaviour, showing appropriate and inappropriate thinking ahead.

Session 9 Reviewing 'thinking ahead' procedures.

Session 10 Reviewing techniques used so far, developing self-evaluation as to how a situation was handled, focusing on coping statements used by participants before, during and after conflict situations.

Session 11 Reviewing relaxation training, assertion techniques, reminders and 'thinking ahead', using problem-solving techniques.

Session 12 Reviewing whole programme, ABC's, triggers, relaxation techniques, assertion techniques, reminders, 'thinking ahead', self-evaluation statements and problem-solving.

Finally, this section concludes with an example of a similar programme of cognitive change but this time based upon RET principles. It emphasizes the view that RET is not exclusively an individually oriented, therapy-based paradigm but can be used with groups of children in an educational context. As I suggested in the introduction to this chapter the reader will see the added emphasis put upon the role of feelings in this programme. This example is from the writings of Bernard and Joyce (1984) and is in fact one of three programmes described by them for children of 5–7, 8–12 and 13–17. I have chosen the programme for the youngest age group to demonstrate that RET is not only intended for older, more articulate children.

Session 1: Getting to know you This involves playing the name game, that is, adding your name to that of the children who have gone before and repeating, for as long as possible, the list of names. This session also asks the children to tell the group leader and other children something about themselves in terms of their favourite and disliked activities. Finally, it asks the children to learn a concrete way of expressing the intensity of a feeling by holding their arms wide apart for a strong feeling and close together for a mild one.

Session 2: We all have feelings This session aims to increase the children's knowledge of feeling words, by learning new words to describe feelings and then to connect feeling words with facial and bodily expressions in pictures. The session uses games and discussion about a story to reinforce the ideas.

Session 3: More about feelings The aims of this session are to enable the group to identify what a group member might be feeling and then to decide whether that feeling is a pleasant or unpleasant feeling.

Session 4: Sharing our feelings and self-talk Children are invited to talk, in this session, about past situations in which they can remember experiencing particular feelings. With the use of the 'feel wheel' children spin the wheel and where the pointer lands they are asked to share a time when they have had that feeling. The feelings are happy, worried, sad, angry and scared.

Session 5: Mistakes in our thinking In this session by using a story format to illustrate how one friend hated another friend because of what she thought the friend said about her (mistakenly), the children learn that people can make mistakes in their thinking about other people. They learn that assumptions are often made without evidence, that they can feel unpleasant because of what they may be thinking and that this thinking can be changed.

Session 6: The link between thinking and feeling This session looks at why 'sensible' thoughts lead to more pleasant feelings whilst 'not sensible thoughts' lead to less pleasant feelings. 'Not sensible thoughts' are those based on demandingness of others – 'Mummy must let me—', exaggerations –'It will be awful if I'm not invited to this party,' overgeneralizations – 'nobody likes me.' These thoughts lead to feeling bad. 'Sensible' thoughts express realistic expectations and preferences and help us appraise events in a way that helps tolerate frustration and think clearly to solve problems. The session uses games and discussions about stories to put over these ideas.

Session 7: Name calling This session introduces the idea that no one person is only one thing, that they are made up of many different characteristics so if a person calls another person a name this does not make them that name. It intends to increase toleration of name-calling by showing children how to make rational self-statements when they are called names. It discusses the idea that all people have good and bad characteristics and that people only upset themselves when they are called names by what they say to themselves about the name-calling. The group take each child in turn and name several of his/her characteristics. The child identifies positive and negative characteristics of themselves so that they realize they are many other things than the name called.

Session 8: Mistake making This session introduces the idea that all people make mistakes at some time and that just because they make a mistake does not mean they will always make mistakes. The group discuss what it feels like when a mistake is made and make up some 'sensible' thoughts to have when a mistake is made – 'I made a mistake this time but now I know how to do it.'

Session 9: Sensible self-talk This session uses poster-making to support the idea that the children can and should use sensible thoughts. The individual child choses a 'sensible thought' from a list or box – 'Mistakes are not bad,' 'Things aren't always fair' – and then each child draws a poster called 'Sensible me', showing them in an appropriate situation where that thought might be used and using that thought depicted in the form of a thought bubble.

Session 10: Behaving well This session establishes the thought-behaviour link. It uses 'real-life' examples to support the notion that 'sensible thoughts' lead to 'sensible' ways of behaving and that 'not sensible' thoughts lead to 'not sensible' ways of behaving. For example the children might discuss whether it is sensible to tear up your work if it gets too hard. Is this based upon the idea that things should always go your way and that work should never be hard?

Session 11: Awfulizing The focus in this last session is on exaggeration as a form of irrational self-talk. Group leader and participants discuss the notion of exaggerations and are asked whether things are usually as bad as they seem at the time? Is it helpful to exaggerate things? What can be done to keep from exaggerating about these situations?

Sessions for older children lay greater emphasis on the nature of thinking and the differences between rational and irrational thoughts are explored in more detail. The sessions also consider in greater depth how these irrational thoughts can be disputed or challenged. The thoughts–feelings link and the idea that we are all complex – neither all good nor all bad – is further considered. The notion that events may occasion a feeling but not cause them, in that the same event can occasion different feelings in different individuals, leads older children to the view that when events are interpreted in an irrational manner this leads to bad feelings about the event and hence bad behaviour. Ways of changing the view that the participants take of events are examined through games, role-play, discussion, exercises and activities.

This type of programme lays greater emphasis upon the cognitive-emotive link with behaviour than CBT methods. It also emphasizes the role of specific cognitive processes in feeling and behaving badly. As with the CBT programmes, a wide range of activities and techniques are employed in the programme to bring about appropriate cognitive change.

It is this latter emphasis which unites the efforts of workers to help children with problems to change their behaviour. While it has sometimes proved extremely difficult to unite CBT and RET methods within this one chapter, it is hoped that the commonalities of techniques and programmes have been evident where and when they exist and that the differences between approaches serve to enrich the options available rather than confuse the reader. As I have said elsewhere in this chapter, when strategies from different paradigms are thoughtfully married together the result has been increased efficacy of programme results. I trust this chapter has made this possible union seem more rather than less likely.

Conclusion

Somebody once said that the world is a tragedy to the man who feels and a comedy to the man who thinks. Perhaps we might also suggest that life can be a tragedy to many children who remain victim to their own irrational or ill-formed thoughts. I have attempted, in this chapter, to set down the manner in which some children can have more control of their cognitive processes such that they may feel happier and behave better. Yet despite having written several thousand words I feel I have done no more than scratch the surface of the field of cognitive-restructuring. Much more could be said about the philosophy, or more correctly philosophies, that underpin this approach to behaviour problems and the programmes and strategies that have emanated from these philosophies. I have sometimes crudely lumped together cognitive paradigms without complete regard for their differences and I have similarly omitted to describe many strategies which a more complete summary would, doubtless, have included.

Despite these shortcomings I hope I have succeeded in my main ambition of presenting to the reader a flavour of those options which are available to the worker interested in bringing about behavioural change through the use of cognitive restructuring techniques. I also hope that I have given some indication as to why workers with children with behaviour problems should take these techniques seriously. This chapter argues that these techniques can be clearly articulated and are pragmatically achievable. It is the view of the author that the inclusion of cognitive processes does not, as Skinner suggested in 1974, cast the 'problem in insoluble form'. Rather, as Lieberman suggested, I would prefer to think that the time has come when we are able to reap the fruits of introspection without getting entangled in its thorns. If workers can add the options available in the cognitive paradigm to the best of what exists in other areas of behaviour change then we may all feel that the techniques, strategies and approaches we offer to children under the guise of special education will be unequivocally special.

References

Beck, A. T. (1967), *Depression: Clinical, Experimental and Theoretical Aspects* (New York: Hoeber).

Bernard, M. E. and Joyce, M. R. (1984), *Rational Emotive Therapy with Children and Adolescents: Theory, Treatment Strategies, Preventative Measures* (New York: John Wiley and Sons).

Bernstein, B. (1961), Social structure, language and learning, *Educational Research*, 3, 163–76.

Burns, D. D. (1980), *Feeling Good: The New Mood Therapy* (New York: New American Library).

Camp, B. and Bash, M. A. S. (1981), *Think Aloud. Increasing Social and Cognitive Skills: A Problem-Solving Program for Children* (Champaign, Illinois: Research Press).

DiGiuseppe, R. A. (1983), Rational emotive therapy and conduct disorders, in A. Ellis and M. E. Bernard (eds), *Rational Emotive Approaches to the Problems of Childhood* (New York: Plenum Press).

Dryden, W. (1984), *Rational Emotive Therapy: Fundamentals and Innovations* (London: Croom Helm).

Dryden, W. and Ellis, A. (1986), Rational-emotive therapy, in W. Dryden and W. Golden (eds) *Cognitive-behavioural Approaches to Psychotherapy* (London: Harper and Row).

Dryden, W. and Golden, W. (eds) (1986), *Cognitive-Behavioural Approaches to Psychotherapy* (London: Harper and Row).

Dweck, C. and Reppucci, N. (1973), Learned helplessness and reinforcement responsibility in children, *Journal of Personality and Social Psychology*, 25, 109–16.

D'Zurilla, T. J. and Goldfried, M. R. (1971), Problem-solving and behaviour modification, *Journal of Abnormal Psychology*, 78, 107–20.

Elkin, A. (1983), Working with children in groups, in A. Ellis and M. E. Bernard (eds), *Rational Emotive Approaches to the Problems of Childhood* (New York: Plenum Press).

Ellis, A. and Bernard, M. E. (eds) (1983), *Rational Emotive Approaches to the Problems of Childhood* (New York: Plenum Press).

Feindler, E. L. and Ecton, R. B. (1986), *Adolescent Anger Control* (New York: Pergamon Press).

Goldstein, A. P. and Glick, B. (1987), *Aggression Replacement Training: A Comprehensive Intervention for Aggressive Youth* (Champaign, Illinois: Research Press).

Jaremko, M. E. (1986), Cognitive-behaviour modification: the shaping of rule-governed behaviour, in W. Dryden and W. Golden (eds) *Cognitive-behavioural Approaches to Psychotherapy* (London: Harper and Row).

Kassinove, H. Crisci, R. and Tiegerman, S. (1977), Developmental trends in rational thinking: implications for rational-emotive school mental health programs *Journal of Community Psychology*, 5, 266–74.

Knaus, W. J. (1974), *Rational Emotive Education: A Manual for Elementary School Teachers* (New York: Institute for Rational Living).

Knaus, W. J. (1983), Children and low frustration tolerance, in A. Ellis and M. E. Bernard (eds), *Rational Emotive Approaches to the Problems of Childhood* (New York: Plenum Press).

Ledwigge, B. (1978), Cognitive Behavior Modification: A Step in the Wrong Direction? *Psychological Bulletin*, 85, 2, 353–75.

Luria, A. (1961), *The Role of Speech in the Regulation of Normal and Abnormal Behaviors* (New York: Liveright).

Meichenbaum, D. (1977), *Cognitive Behavior Modification: An Integrative Approach* (New York: Plenum Press).

Meichenbaum, D. H. and Goodman, J. (1971), Training impulsive children to talk to themselves: a means of developing self-control, *Journal of Abnormal Psychology*, 77, 115–26.

Skinner, B. F. (1974), Why I am not a cognitive psychologist, *Behaviorism*, 5(2), 1–10.

Skinner, B. F. (1985), Cognitive science and behaviourism, *British Journal of Psychology*, 76, 291–301.

Spivak, G, and Shure, M. B. (1974), *Social Adjustment of Young Children: A Cognitive Approach to Solving Real-Life Problems,* (San Francisco: Jossey-Bass).

Spivack, G., Platt, J. J. and Shure, M. B. (1976), *The Problem-Solving Approach to Adjustment* (London: Jossey Bass).

Thacker, J. (1982), *Steps to Success: An Interpersonal Problem-Solving Approach for Children* (Windsor: NFER, Nelson).

Vingoe, F. (1984), Cognitive behaviourism: a synthesis for the future?, in D. Fontana (ed.), Behaviourism and Learning Theory in Education, *British Journal of Educational Psychology*, monograph 1 (Edinburgh: Scottish Academic Press).

Vygotsky, L. S. (1962), *Thought and Language* (New York: Wiley).

Waters, V. (1981), *The Living School* RETwork: 1, 1.

Waters, V. (1982), Therapies for children: rational emotive therapy, in C. R. Reynolds and T. B. Gutkin (eds), *Handbook of School Psychology* (New York: John Wiley and Sons).

Weishaar, M. E. and Beck, A. T. (1986), Cognitive therapy, in W. Dryden and W. Golden (eds), *Cognitive-behavioural Approaches to Psychotherapy* (London: Harper and Row).

Watson, D. L. and Tharp, R. G. (1985), *Self-Directed Behavior: Self Modification for Personal Adjustment* (Monterey, California: Brooks/Cole).

Wolpe, J. (1958), *Psychotherapy by Reciprocal Inhibition* (Stanford: Stanford University Press).

Young, H. S. (1983), Working with children in groups, in A. Ellis and M. E. Bernard (eds), *Rational Emotive Approaches to the Problems of Childhood* (New York: Plenum Press).

Chapter 9

Computers and Cognitive Gain for Special Educational Need Pupils
Alan Dobbins

Stated simplistically the thesis of this chapter is that at this time computers, *per se*, cannot create understanding and insight or, for that matter, affective change in SEN pupils. That is, *computer based learning* (CBL) is ineffective with SEN pupils; rather computers, when their use is carefully orchestrated by a class teacher, might help support a teaching strategy which is aimed at creating understanding and insight: in other words *computer assisted learning* (CAL) can be effective. Conventional wisdom is that simulation type software can promote cognitive gain when presented in a CBL mode. For SEN pupils it is argued that this is not the case but that all types of software, namely drill and practice, data base, word processing as well as simulation software can promote cognitive gains when used as part of an organized and innovative teaching approach via a CAL mode.

The first section of this chapter overviews the development of hardware and languages and suggests that computers of the type now found in schools have only recently become (1) sufficiently powerful and sophisticated to support the presentation of complex simulations and (2) languages, which drive these computers have also only recently become powerful and flexible enough to allow the ease of expression necessarily required for the programming of complex simulations designed to promote cognitive gain. While recognizing that hardware and software are nowadays sufficiently powerful, it is, nevertheless, argued that CBL is not an efficient strategy to promote cognitive gain in SEN pupils. Furthermore, even though software based on a behavioural model does not demand the degree of sophisitication in either hardware or language that is required for simulation software, the notion of programmed learning presented via a computer in CBL mode is also seen as inefficient.

The second section of this chapter focuses on the computer as a teaching aid, i.e. its use in CAL mode. Initially, the different types of software which are available are overviewed and some examples of each type are given. In this section it is argued that when the computer is used as an aid or tool by teachers to support a teaching strategy then cognitive gain can accrue. The chapter ends with examples of good practice of computer use in promoting gains in the teaching situation.

Computer Based Learning

Development of the Hardware

The mainframe computers which serviced six or eight schools in a network or time-sharing basis in the 1960s and early 1970s were direct descendants of the thinking which resulted in Colossus, a massive computer developed in Britain, to help decipher German communication codes during the Second World War. ENIAC, the shortened version of Electronic Numerical Integrator and Calculator, was developed in America at about the same time to determine missile trajectories and to predict the weather. The invention of the transistor in 1948 and later, the development of the integrated circuit, resulted in an increase in power and a reducion in size which made the stand-alone computers currently found in schools possible. ENIAC, thirty years ago, occupied 3000 cu.ft. of space, requiring 140,000 watts of power, weighed 30 tons, had 18,000 vacuum tubes, 70,000 resistors and 10,000 capacitors. Current micro computers cost about 10,000 times less than did ENIAC, weigh a fraction of it and are more powerful and faster acting.

As is suggested by the name ENIAC the original conception for the computer was to provide a 'right' answer to a problem of numerical base; in short to function as a powerful and sophisticated programmable calculator. Colossus's 'right' answer was the identification of a code structure; ENIAC's 'right' answer being the identification of the parameters of missile trajectories. Initially the reduction in size and the increase in power did nothing to change the 'sophisticated calculator' notion for computers. The first mini computers such as Digital Equipment Corporation's PDP series focused on business use, e.g. haulage companies used minis to identify the best route structures, banks used minis to update customer accounts etc. Computers were seen and used primarily as tools to enhance business efficiency by calculating quickly and accurately before displaying, via VDU or printer, the 'right' answer.

The introduction of a computer on a chip in 1971 when the Intel Corporation produced the 4004, created the era of the microcomputer and enhanced the possibility of computer use in teaching situations. Nowadays the considerable reduction in size and cost afforded by the use of 'chips', in conjunction with the development of peripheral devices, e.g. sound out, concept keyboards, joysticks,

.ouch-sensitive screens, each helping to minimize problems at the operator – machine interface, to produce easier, if not easy communication between operator and machine, has produced a corresponding change in the type of people who use computers as well as the range of uses to which they are put.

The first computers used in education were large expensive mainframe computers which were often located in customized buildings which were not part of a school campus. Schools were connected to these computers by telephone link; messages to and from the computer were transmitted and received via VDU or printer. Besides being big and expensive to operate, the early computers were difficult to use; programming or even operating a computer required extensive training, sometimes to the level of the bachelors degree in computer science. Moreover, these early computers were not very reliable, and maintenance and repair costs were very high. Within schools the mathematics department typically assumed responsibility for computer use which was most often of the 'programmable calculator' type resulting in convergence to the 'right' answer.

Where once a comprehensive knowledge of the functioning of a computer was required to gain access to its operation, nowadays the power and flexibility of desktop, stand-alone hardware, in conjunction with the many different peripheral devices which are available, has resulted in a level of sophistication beyond that required for successful operating, even by the severely retarded.

Development of the Software

In order to be activated, any computer must receive a set of instructions. These instructions are called programs or software. In the early days of computing the instructions or software were written in a fashion which was easy for computers to understand but not so easy for people to comprehend. Then, programing was a specialized task which required sophisticated training. Just as people use many different languages to communicate to one another, there are a number of different languages for computers. Computer languages can be categorized into three levels (1) machine (2) assembly, and (3) higher level languages. Machine language, which is the only language computers understand directly, is very complex and specific and is difficult to learn; even the simplest of programs, such as the addition of two numbers, requires the writing of many commands. To facilitate efficiency in programming, assembly languages were developed.

Most computers can be programmed in assembly language, and because the vocabulary is made up of wordlike codes rather than numbers, assembly languages are easier to use than machine language. Higher level languages are the easiest in which to program because they use English or English-like words and indeed have a syntax structure that is not unlike that of English grammar. Computers do not understand higher level languages directly, but this problem is solved by using an interpreter, i.e. a program that translates the vocabulary the programmer understands into machine language.

In 1963 a simple high-level language called BASIC (Beginners All-purpose Symbolic Instruction Code) was developed by John Kemeny and Thomas Kurtz at Dartmouth College in the United States. Since that time BASIC has been revised and expanded many times. There are other high level languages, some of which have advantages over BASIC in some situations, e.g. COBOL, COMAL, but, at this time most educational software is written in BASIC. Even though the latest versions of BASIC are very powerful and are also user-friendly and make the writing of advanced and complex programs possible, higher level, more powerful languages, termed author languages e.g. ILS, PILOT, MICROTEXT, are continuing to be developed which make program writing that much easier again, to the extent that complex presentations involving sound, colour and perceived movement are now possible.

For a machine to promote cognitive gain, screen presentations in the form of simulations need to be sophisticated, complex and comprehensive. These requirements can only be achieved when the hardware and languages available are both powerful and flexible. Microcomputers of the type typically found in schools have only recently reached minimum required levels in each of these parameters of use.

Computer Based Learning (CBL) Based on a Cognitive Philosophy

There has been one serious and important attempt at involving computers in teaching pupils understanding and meaning rather than facts, or the application of rules. Seymour Papert and his colleagues at the Massachusetts Institute of Technology developed LOGO, a language so simple to use that it reverses the usual relationship between computer and pupil found in conventional computer based instruction. There the 'clever' program teaches the 'dumb' student: in LOGO the pupil teaches the machine, and by so doing, through a process of hypothesizing and debugging, gains understanding and insight.

More than a decade has passed since Papert and his colleagues constructed LOGO as the logical computer-based end-product of the combination of cybernetic and Piagetian principles; also, it is seven years since Papert extolled the virtues of LOGO in his book *Mindstorms* (Papert, 1980) where he argued that pupils who experienced LOGO learned more than a computer language, but powerful ideas, skills and heuristics as well. *Mindstorms*, in conjunction with the user-friendliness of LOGO and its capacity to bring ideas to life via the reality of the moving turtle, presented a prescient collage of education in the future which involved the joining of computers and pupils to result in the mastery of a powerful technology, with the resultant recognition of powerful ideas. Not unnaturally, Papert excluded the use of computers for the type of computer-based instruction which emanates from a behavioural base; in their place pupils would program and learn in 'mind boggling leaps'.

The innovativeness of the concept, housed solidly in its Piagetian base, ensured the immediate interest of those in mainstream and special education, where the use of LOGO with the learning disabled, emotionally disturbed, gifted as well as the delinquent has been reported (Watt, 1982). LOGO fits easily into a child-centred philosophy of teaching and has been enthusiastically embraced by many in the profession; the following would be a typical response.

> I really do feel that I have been using that extra potential of the computer. LOGO enables the children themselves to have control over their own learning. It is flexible and so well structured in itself that the children build on their own knowledge as they progress. They experience the 'joy of discovery', and become totally absorbed. They have the freedom to work at their own level and to be in control of the speed and depth of learning. They also begin to get ideas about programming computers through meaningful activity. LOGO has not alienated the children and after nearly six months of continuous use I have not yet been asked, 'Do I have to go on the computer today?... They experience 'real problem solving', with practice in identifying and analysing their problems. They need to find strategies and can consider a variety of approaches. Using the computer in a second-rate role, mimicking other forms of teaching and offering old diets in a novel setting is not for me! (Maxwell, 1984).

Does pupil interaction with a computer through a language such as LOGO promote cognitive gain? In short does it work? This most fundamental of questions needs to be answered at two levels.

First, Papert argues that LOGO is not only a programming language but is a philosophy of education based on the premise that procedural thinking is a powerful intellectual skill and that LOGO makes this skill accessible to pupils in differing situations. Examples of everyday activities which involve procedural thinking include any task which requires sequencing, e.g. (1) giving someone directions to get to the village or a particular house or (2) writing down a recipe for a favourite dish. Papert suggests that in the day-to-day environment 'procedures' are used but they are not reflected upon, or for that matter, recognised as an approach to thinking which can result in the development of an appropriate answer to any problem. He argues that when pupils program in LOGO they are provided with an opportunity to define, discuss, analyze and manipulate procedures and, in so doing, they come to recognize the characteristics of procedural thinking.

The general 'problem-solving' effectiveness of LOGO has yet to be demonstrated in the regular classroom, though some encouraging results have been reported by Noss (1984) and Howe, O'Shea and Plane (1979). There is, though, substantial evidence of a descriptive nature which suggests that experience with LOGO does improve a subject's reasoning and problem solving skills (Milner, 1973; Seidman, 1981; Albeson *et al.*, 1976; Watt, 1979; 1982; Solomon and Papert, 1976, Weir, 1979; Papert, Watt, Disessa and Weir, 1979). Alternately, there are a few studies which suggest that Papert's view of LOGO as a 'structure' from which logical thinking can develop may be over optimistic (Michayluk and Yackulic, 1984; Michayluk and Saklofske (in press).

Second, research into the effects of LOGO on the development of precise skills in, and the acceptance of concepts of mathematics has been disappointing. Many researchers have used a case-study approach (Lawler, 1980; Solomon and Papert, 1976) rather than an experimental methodology. Krassnor and Mitterer (1984) have been critical of this; but, methodology aside there is little evidence which suggests that LOGO can influence mathematical skills. For example Milner (1973) found LOGO did nothing to change Grade 5 mathematical skills or concepts. Howe, O'Shea and Plane (1979) in a very elaborate study found that although the LOGO group scored higher on a test of general mathematics, the control group scored higher on a mathematics attainment test. Siann and Macleod (1986) showed no differences between control and experimental (LOGO) groups on a number of tests. Hughes *et al.* (1984) are exceptions; they used pupils from primary schools located in a severely disadvantaged area of Scotland and via a pre – post design showed improvements on basic number skills after exposure to a LOGO based programme over a period of 5 months.

Given its philosophic base, for LOGO to make its maximum impact the ideal classroom should be of 15–20 pupils, and there should be 5–10 computers which pupils use frequently. In this classroom pupils would work at the computer on a regular basis, either individually or in small groups. As they discover ways of creating interesting things, resultant programs or procedures would be shared with other pupils to modify or enhance or adapt to their own use. As this is happening the teacher is in the background, observing progress, offering guidance whenever required and planning experiences for the future. The Chiltern MEP project (Noss, 1984) has shown that the introduction of LOGO into schools will not be a trivial undertaking.

LOGO and Special Educational Need Pupils

The child-centred approach can be problematic for special-need pupils. Even though Papert has argued that LOGO is usable by the very young the experience of some in special needs is that it can often be extremely dull, as it takes a fairly intellectual pupil to be fascinated by drawing mathematical shapes ad infinitum, or painstakingly to draw a face which would take five minutes to do on paper. The full repertoire of LOGO potentials will certainly not be utilized by the very great majority of those with special needs. Some believe (Michayluck and Yackulic, 1984) that only pupils who have reached the stage of formal operations are capable of fully utilizing the potentials of LOGO. Others point out that those at the level of concrete operations would find it difficult to manipulate symbols and to grasp such concepts as recursion, multiple inputs and permutation.

The kernel of these criticisms is the ease, or more precisely the lack of it, with which special-need pupils can communicate via LOGO with a computer. Even though LOGO is relatively simple to learn, there can be no doubt that many with special needs find it difficult to cope with, and given this, find difficulty in gaining control of the computer. This concern has been recognized and there have been attempts e.g. LOGOTRON to make easier the 'driving' of the computer, as well as the use of peripheral devices, particularly the concept keyboard, to present LOGO in pre-programmed chunks.

Computer Based Learning (CBL) Based on a Behavioural Philosophy

In the early 1960s about the time that mainframe computers first appeared in schools, the psychologist B. F. Skinner developed the teaching machine. The first teaching machines were mechanically operated devices which presented a student with a question or statement and invited a response. If the student's response was correct the machine organized the presentation of the next question or response. Teaching machines are interesting for many reasons, perhaps the most fundamental of these reasons is that the notion of programmed instruction, as it is presented by teaching machines, is the natural end product of a behavioural approach to learning. In programmed instruction material is broken down into small steps which are called frames. That which is presented in a frame can be thought of as the *stimulus*, the action or choice of a student, the *response*, and the recognition of a correct response by the presentation of the next stimulus as *reinforcement*. While programmed instruction, as an instructional technique, was first presented through machines it can also be presented via texts. Nowadays, teaching machines of the clunk-click type hold historical interest only, but there are thousands of programmed texts available today which cover topics from pre-reading skills to college-level mathematics.

Programmed instruction comes in two basic types, linear and branched. Linear programmes demand the reading of text sequentially from the first frame to the last. The learner proceeds through a learning sequence which has been pre-determined by the person who designed the program. Authors of linear programs try to write frames that can be understood by the great majority of students who use the text, since errors are not easy to handle in linear programs. The result is often a program written for the lowest common denominator rather than for the average or above average student. With the exception of allowing students to learn at their own speed, programmed instruction, particularly linear programmes, are difficult to adapt to learning needs.

The other type of programmed instruction, branching, does try to deal with different learning patterns. Instead of breaking material into hundreds of thousands of frames, branching programmes teach large chunks of information before testing the student. Then, if a student makes an error on one test he or she is branched to other material that deals with the particular mistake. Thus a student who answers most test questions correctly may never read most of a branching programme since much of the material is read only by students who do not understand the initial presentation. Branching texts are extremely difficult to write because the writer must anticipate all types of errors a student is likely to make and provide appropriate instructional assistance.

Programmed instruction was the organizational base supporting the first programs which attempted to use the computer to teach pupils in CBL mode some 10–15 years ago. That this was the case is not surprising as about this time (1) the hardware was relatively unsophisticated in comparison with that of today, and (2) it was difficult to write programs then because higher-level languages were not as powerful as those of today. Both (1) and (2) mitigated against the development of complex and accurate simulations. Also, the behavioural approach to the teaching of special-need pupils was enjoying popular acceptance as the most efficient approach. It was not surprising then that the concepts behind the notion of a machine actually teaching, i.e. creating gain in attainment without teacher involvement, was quickly applied to the more flexible and powerful medium of computers.

Teachers tended to be sympathetic to computer use of this type (Siann and Macleod, 1986). To be successful, behavioural based software needs to be pedagogically sound and capable of providing opportunities for learning which are not available through traditional methods of instruction, i.e. individualized teaching, individualized work cards etc. Siann and Macleod (1986) report on a recent survey of 600 behavioural type software packages with only 5 per cent as 'first rate' and the rest 'simply depressing'. They also report that those which were acceptable lacked flexibility and failed to provide important insights into the subject material which might be obtained when a teacher works with a pupil and investigates the reasons which are given when a pupil makes a particular choice. These disadvantages are very apparent when a pupil presents with a special educational need.

Computer-based Learning and Special Educational Need Pupils

It didn't take the teaching profession long to realize that computers do not think, they process, they are lightning fast and totally infallible but they are mindless. It is for these reasons that CBI, which has a logical appeal based (1) to a large extent on the ability of simulation software to be comprehensive, dynamic and accurate and (2) for behavioural based software to be precise within a programmed instruction model, has been seen as less than successful. A computer is not a good substitute for a teacher. Computers can do some things better than teachers, e.g. give information in a precise and ordered way, provide exercises, and test pupils in a standard fashion and perhaps above all provide marks, but they cannot deal with the unexpected questions or unprogrammed misunderstandings. Teachers, particularly those with a special education background, can do this rather well. Intuition cannot by definition be programmed.

Clarke (1985) in her keynote address to the Concerned Technology in Education Conference in Edinburgh identified 10 characteristics of pupils with moderate learning difficulties and estimated that these pupils comprise between 70 and 80 per cent of those with SENs.

1   difficulty in making and extending associations
2   restricted ability to make abstractions
3   lack of intellectual curiosity
4   inability to generalize effectively
5   short attention span
6   poor STM and LTM
7   limited ability to transfer
8   early experience of failure
9   limited ability in basic skills
10   difficulty in communicating needs about feelings.

Even given the sophistication and flexibility of current hardware and the power of present-day languages the first nine of Clarke's list mitigate against the successful use of a computer *as a teacher* for those pupils with any one or a combination of these characteristics.

Computer Assisted Learning

Among teachers there is a well known saying, 'It's not what you teach but the way in which you teach it.' In other words it is possible to optimize a learning or teaching process by selecting an appropriate instructional technology with which to implement it. Here the term instructional technology refers to a wide range of aids, devices and machines which can be used by teachers in the presentation of content or the rehearsal of skills. 'Aids, devices and machines' include slide projectors, videotape recorders, educational TV and radio, tape recorders, training devices and simulators, as well as computers. This concept recognizes the computer, as an 'aid' or 'tool' to be used by teachers, rather than as a 'teacher' as it is used in CBL mode. It equates the computer, conceptually at least, with blackboard and chalk, and sees the computer as a tool which a teacher can use where, when and how s/he wishes in order to make his/her teaching more effective.

That this notion of computer use has a label 'CAL' might be seen as strange given that the teacher who uses a videotape is not involved in video-assisted learning ('VAL') or one who uses a slide-projector involved in 'SAL'; but it might be explained by the computer being a dynamic learning aid, i.e. one which can interact with a pupil, rather than a passive aid as are all other aids available for use in the classroom.

CAL use has been classified a number of different ways. The following four categories are discussed here:

1   drill and practice
2   simulation
3   word processing
4   information handling.

Drill and Practice

There can be little doubt that 'drill and practice' is the easiest form of CAL to develop and use. In 'drill and practice' it is assumed that the pupil arrives at the computer with some prior training. 'Drill and practice' type software is available in many, if not all subject areas. While pupils may practise diagramming sentences, computing square roots, or solving algebraic equations, they will have learned the mechanics of the task most probably through teacher-centred instruction. 'Drill and practice' programs get mixed reviews from both computer educators and others. To some this type of approach is seen as a throwback to the concept of mental exercises; others argue that the rote-learning of pedagogical practices is useless, and argue that pupils must develop cognitive understanding and discover things for themselves, if true learning is to take place. The perspective of Gagne (1965) incorporates both behavioural and cognitive theories into a workable description of learning.

Many who teach those with SENs would argue that 'drill and practice' opportunities are required, more so for them than for other pupils. Traditional 'drill and practice' methods such as mimeographed sheets of exercises, flashcards and memorization rituals demand substantial preparation time, can be boring for the pupil and inefficient as a teaching strategy, as it is difficult to tailor for precisely the amount of practice needs to each pupil. When 'drill and practice' is organized and presented via a computer the potential for increased efficiency exists (1) through identifying, via pre-test, areas in which a student needs practice and (2) by keeping a running record of performance. Moreover, the computer can do these things in an innovative and self-motivating fashion. The good drill and practice program will be (1) easy to use, (2) adaptable to a variety of uses, (3) interesting to the learner and, of course, (4) educationally valid.

For SEN pupils drill and practice programs are probably best used in subject or skill areas where mastery requires a significant amount of practice. Good examples include letter and shape recognition and manipulation of arithmetic rules. The better 'drill and practice' programs provide practice over a range of skills, utilize the pupil's performance to determine how much and what type of practice to provide, as well as giving some form of feedback to the teacher on the performance of individual students, and even class patterns.

Presently there are hundreds if not thousands of 'drill and practice' type programs available to teachers over all subject areas. Acornsoft markets 'Number Balance' which gives practice in adding or subtracting two numbers, and/or in multiplying or dividing. They also market 'Missing Signs' which provides practice opportunities in some or all of the rules of arithmetic; 'Word Sequencing' presents a series of jumbled proverbs, nursery rhymes or simple sentences which have to be re-arranged correctly; 'Sentence Sequencing' presents six lines of text out of order, and requires pupils to provide the correct order; Chalksoft market 'Angle' which gives practice in the use of protractors and in measuring angles; DR Daines market 'Counting' which is a practice program for counting shapes up to nine. CET Information Sheet (No. 5) provides a useful summary of 'drill and practice' programs available up to 1983; the brochures of publishing houses and software companies provide up-to-date summaries on that which is available.

Simulations

When 50 pence is dropped into an arcade game and control is taken of an inter-stellar fighter with laser guns and force field shields, money is being spent on a computer simulation. Simulations are dynamic models or descriptions, often of complex events or conditions. They are the naturally occurring end-product of a model of learning which is more complex than that from which individual 'drill and practice' emanates. Simulations provide opportunities for the pupil to explore and gain understanding rather than learn in accord with a stimulus–response approach.

There are several advantages to simulations. Simulations are attractive and interesting to pupils, probably more so than any other form of instruction presented by computer. They are cheaper than allowing pupils to learn in the 'real world' and often the capacity of the computer to manipulate more than one variable simultaneously, and project the simulation in living colour with associated sound out, allows for a simulation which could not be presented by traditional teaching methods. Also, they are safe in as much as students can gain experience in areas which might, in the 'real world', be dangerous. Skills and understanding gained from participation in a simulation transfer easily to other situations.

The power and flexibility of current hardware in combination with the flexibility of languages make complex simulations nowadays easier to prepare. Simulation type software is increasing in complexity, realism and scope, over many subject areas, at a speed not matched by any other type of software. The following are a few of the many programs available. Concepts of geography can be taught by simulating an airline flight from London to Los Angeles or to Adelaide, or, by having those who survived an aeroplane crash trek out of an uninhabited area and by so doing understand the logic of contour lines. Pupils studying environmental science or biology can assume the role, and be presented with the problems of a fox living in a city. A pupil can become a Viking and travel from Scandinavia across the North Sea to raid selected parts of the East Coast of England, or be part of an archaeological dig in Ancient Egypt. The increase in the ease of programming, as a consequence of the use of more powerful languages in conjunction with the increasing memory space of desktop computers, is seen in the production of simulations which are much more realistic, colourful, and meaningful even than those developed only a few years ago, e.g. Mary Rose, Saqquara.

Simulations provide the pupil with an opportunity to explore their own answers and even explore the logic or method utilized to arrive at those answers, rather than having to accept teacher dictate. Simulations can also be effective in teaching simple facts.

Word Processing

The ease with which pupils, even very young pupils, have taken to word processing in schools has completely destroyed the notion that the computer is only a sophisticated programmable calculator. Word processing software, such as Prompt or Writer, provides a basis for the development of written text to a level of sophistication beyond that achievable via any other approach because of the ease with which it can be changed or extended. A pupil's perceived ownership of the developing text is a motivating factor which can be used by teachers, not only to improve aspects of language use such as spelling or increased knowledge of syntactic rules, but also to enhance understanding of the concepts or relationships expressed between them. The use of peripheral devices, particularly the concept keyboard, but also sound out, has made word processing available to everyone. Those who have word processed with pupils, even pupils with substantial special needs, recognize the power of a pupil presented printed text as a basis for learning via behavioural or cognitive approaches.

Information Storage and Retrieval

Information storage and retrieval packages allow pupils to handle substantial amounts of information, and to retrieve from an information base in a fashion which is meaningful, accurate and comprehensive so as to allow the development of conclusions and generalizations, resulting in understanding and a gain in knowledge. Furthermore, retrieval can be achieved at a speed which defies the conventional logic of pre-computer times. Currently, numerous data handling packages are available which are being used in schools, e.g. Factfile, Query, Quest, Scan. Each one of these packages is a skeleton of rules and constraints within which data can be stored and selectively retrieved. Also 'new' information can be generated from transformations or manipulations of the input data base.

A frequent and meaningful use of an information storage and retrieval package is as a base of information describing aspects of the community within which a school is located. Small Area Census returns provide a rich source of information which can be supplemented by direct methods of measurement such as observation and/or interview/questionnaire. Interrogation of a data base to establish 'new' information uses the computer as an aid in a 'discovery' approach to learning; pupils can present information, hypothesize and test assumptions, before arriving at conclusions relevant to the content of the data base and, by so doing, gain insights into the nuances and relationships held therein.

Examples of Computer Use to Promote Cognitive Gain in SEN Pupils

Here follow examples of how each of the four types of software overviewed earlier are currently being used in one special school for pupils with learning difficulties. In each example the computer is used to support a teaching approach, i.e. in CAL mode. In this school it has long been recognized that the computer does not function *as a teacher*, i.e. CBL mode, anywhere near as well as does the human version.

Drill and Practice

It might seem strange to argue that drill and practice opportunities presented via computer can enhance understanding. Some might see 'drill and practice' as creating a 'change in behaviour' without any increase in 'understanding'. Those who work with SEN pupils quickly become aware of the requirement to 'go over', 'go over', and 'go over' that which is being taught and to provide opportunities for 'practice', 'practice', and 'practice'. Also there is a ready acceptance by those in special needs of Gagne's (1965) pyramidal description of learning. When 'drill and practice' is offered with tutorial type support, understanding can follow. Consider the following example.

A pupil has difficulty in understanding the concept of subtraction and operating the subtraction rule. Initially the teacher might spend time presenting numbers of objects, e.g. balls, bottles etc, and by a process of positive counting identify that when 'two' are taken from 'five', 'three' remain. When a pupil is comfortable with the concept of positive counting a computer can help by providing examples that are both stimulating and motivating. Initially the teacher might work with the pupil on the machine which would present (say) five stars in a box from which two are removed.

As a response, a pupil might need to press any key on the keyboard when the correct answer appears or might be required to press the correct number on the keyboard. The software package would present many different number combinations of objects for subtraction in different shapes from stars to ships or balloons to bottles. Also, it would record the number of correct and incorrect responses. More work with the teacher would link the number of objects to the numerical representation and, ultimately, subtraction of numbers rather than objects. Back to the computer for practice at subtracting numbers, rather than counting objects.

Even though the example here might be seen as low-level given that it focuses on a simple rule of arithmetic, it is, nevertheless, a good example for a number of reasons. First, it demonstrates the relationship of teacher to machine; here the machine is used to support the teacher's strategy in a very precise way. It is not used to create new knowledge but is used as an important aid in the teacher's attempt to stimulate learning. Second, it shows how a computer can be closely linked with a teaching approach. Third, the type of software highlighted in the example is easily found, not only for arithmetic problems but also for 'rule' type problems in other subject areas. In the above example the chronology would be as follows (1) teacher explanation, (2) teacher demonstration with balls, bottles (3) pupil practice, (4) teacher and pupil on computer, (5) pupil on computer, (6) teacher reviews pupil progress on computer, (7) teacher links numerical equivalent to numbers of objects, (8) pupil with teacher practices subtraction of numbers, (9) pupil practices number subtraction on computer, (10) teacher explores and generalizes the concept of subtraction.

The final step could justifiably be claimed to be that which creates a catholic perspective of the concept of subtraction and by so doing promotes cognitive gain. The in-depth understanding of the concept of subtraction would not be possible without the capacity to generate a right answer to a subtraction problem.

Simulation, Word Processing and Information Handling

Each of these three software types are best used by teachers whose teaching strategy to promote increased understanding is through project work. Given this, the example here is collective in as much as it reflects the same style of computer use irrespective of the type of software utilized. Project work, which has as its central tenet the notion of pupils learning through exploration and discovery within the frame of reference set by the teacher, is a teaching strategy which is receiving increased use in special need settings. The teacher's task in project work is to create and manage an environment within which information, opportunities, and support are readily available to pupils who 'find out' or research. In a 'project' approach the classroom and the resources held within, in some cases the school and all which is held within, is seen as a potential resource from which information can be gained. Good use of the computer as a resource would see a pupil using it as and when it would aid development of the project, but not at the expense of other classroom or school resources, such as the book corner or library, which might for a particular task be a better resource to enhance development of the project.

The first major software package created to support a project work approach was the 'Mary Rose' developed through the initiative of the MEP. The 'Mary Rose' package provided opportunities to discover historical, geographical and mathematical information. It was, and still is, an excellent simulation package. Perhaps because it was the first major simulation package, the 'Mary Rose' was sometimes badly used by teachers who operated as though it were the learning resource rather than one source of information and experience among many which could be available to pupils. In short, sometimes project work around the Mary Rose was computer-led rather than teacher-led.

Consider a project entitled 'Countries of the World' with the general aims of establishing the concepts of size and distance, and the recognition of differences between the peoples of different countries. Included in the specific objectives would be the identification of continents and some countries within those continents. The teacher sets the frame of reference, including a time frame for completion of the project. Traditional classroom resources are available including texts, encyclopaedias and other resource books, as well as video tapes and hired films. The innovative teacher might even arrange for students from the nearby university, who are from the targeted countries, to visit the school. The computer can also help.

Simulation programs similar to the airplane example given earlier can aid the establishment of distance and size concepts, they will also help identify cities to countries, to continents. Information storage and retrieval programs could provide classification information on different peoples from skin colur to predominant language(s) spoken. Environmental type information, e.g. altitude of cities, rainfall distribution, and temperature information would be easily available from a storage and retrieval package. A word-processing package, with a picture capability, provides an easily created and readily changeable hard copy of any write-up(s) required. If the project is a whole-class project it might well be that a pupil working on one aspect of the project need not use the computer at all over the period of the project, as other resources provide a richer seam of information, though some pupils may make considerable use of the computer.

Two points need to be made here. The first is that in this example the computer assumes its rightful place as a resource to be used by pupils when and where greatest gains can accrue. It is only one of a number of resources or aids available to teachers and pupils. Second, a project approach to learning, supported by each of the three types of software discussed here is not something which might be a good idea to consider for the future. The approach as described here is the current approach to project work in a day school, located within the Swansea area, for special-need pupils with learning difficulties.

References

Albeson, H., Bamberger, J., Goldstein, I. and Papert, S. (1976), *LOGO progress report 1973-1975 Washington, DC: National Sciences Foundation.*

Clarke, M. (1985), *Computers and Special Educational Need Children* Keynote address, Concerned Technology in Education Conference, Edinburgh.

Gagne, R. M. (1965), *The Conditions of Learning* (New York: Holt, Rheinhart and Wilson).

Howe, J. A. M., O'Shea, T. and Plane, F. (1979), *Teaching mathematics through LOGO: an evaluation study*, DAI Research Paper No 115.

Hughes, M., Macleod, H. and Potts, C. (1984), *The Development of LOGO for Infant School Children*, (Edinburgh: University of Edinburgh).

Krassnor, L. and Mitterer, J. (1984), LOGO and the development of general problem solving skills, *The Alberta Journal of Educational Research*, **30**, 133–44.

Lawler, R. (1980), *The Progressive Construction of Mind (One Child's Learning: Addition).* LOGO Memo 57, (Massachusetts: Massachusetts Institute of Technology).

Maxwell, B. (1984), 'Problem structuring and solving skills 1: Turtle mathematics, in R. Jones (ed.), *Micros in the Primary Classroom* (London: Edward Arnold).

The Mary Rose Project. (1984) from Ginn, Prebendal House, Parson's Fee, Aylesbury, Buckingham.

Michayluk, J. and Yackulic, R. (1984), Impact of a LOGO program on native adults. *Canadian Journal of Educational Communications*, **3**, 4–6.

Michayluk, J. and Saklofske, D. (in press), Some effects of the LOGO computer program with emotionally disturbed children, *Canadian Journal of Educational Communications*.

Milner, S. (1973), The effects of computer programming on performance in mathematics, paper presented at the *Annual Meeting of the American Education Research Association*, New Orleans, Louisiana.

Noss, R. (1984), MEP Chiltern Project Children in control, *Times Educational Supplement*, 3531–47, 2 March.

Papert, S. (1980), *Mindstorms: Children, Computers, and Powerful Ideas* (New York: Basic Books).

Papert, S., Watt, D., Disessa, A. and Weir, S. (1979), *Final Report of the Brookline LOGO Project. Part II: Project Summary and Data Analysis* (Massachusetts: Massachusetts Institute of Technology).

Seidman, R. H. (1981), The effects of learning a computer programming language on the logical reasoning of school children, paper presented at the *Annual Meeting of the American Education Research Association*, Los Angeles, California.

Siann, G. and Macleod, H. (1986), Computers and children of primary school age, *British Journal of Educational Technology*, **17** (2), 133–44.

Solomon, C.J. and Papert, S. (1976), *A Case Study of a Young Child doing Turtle Graphics in LOGO*, LOGO Working Paper 44, (Massachusetts Institute of Technology, Massachusetts).

Watt, D. (1979), *Final Report of the Brookline LOGO Project: Profiles of Individual Student Work*, LOGO Memo 54. (Massachusetts Institute of Technology, Massachusetts).

Watt, S. (1982), LOGO in the schools, *Byte*, **71**, 116–34.

Weir, S. (1979), LOGO as an information prosthetic for communication and control, *Seventh International Joint Conference on Artificial Intelligence*, 970–4.

Chapter 10

Cognitive Processes and Motor Behaviour
Rosemary Connell

Observe any playground, classroom or gymnasium and the rich and diverse nature of skilled motor behaviours will be apparent: children controlling their own bodies while running and jumping, manipulating implements like pencils or scissors, or responding to objects like balls moving in the environment. While a few children will show exceptional precision in the control of such actions, others will be found mistiming, misjudging, fumbling and erring in their performance. Some will exhibit an intelligent and creative selection of actions, others make inappropriate choices or shy away from decisions altogether.

Children who show difficulties in the execution and learning of motor skills are easy to see, but it is often less easy to understand the cause of their inadequacy. It is possible to describe these children in very broad terms as those with a physical disability such as spasticity, loss of limb or poor muscle tone; those with a mental handicap; those with specific or general learning difficulties; those with impoverished previous experience, and those with an inappropriate affective disposition. The last two are greatly influenced by the child's sociocultural background which determines the degree of encouragement and the range of opportunities made available for the development of physical skills. The interest shown by parents influences the attitudes children develop and the degree to which they value physical expertise.

Even if high levels of motivation are present and the child is adequately endowed with physical and psychomotor abilities such as strength, stamina, speed, co-ordination and fast reactions, his or her performance, and even more, his/her learning of motor skills will depend on his/her cognitive skills.

The focus in this chapter will be to uncover how inefficient cognitive activity can give rise to poor movement performance and difficulties in learning motor skills. While teachers are generally knowledgeable about difficulties in reading or number, many admit to their lack of understanding of normal and abnormal motor development (Henderson and Hall, 1982).

Cognitive psychology as an area has received considerable research interest since the 1950s, but it has been in the past fifteen years only, that motor skills researchers have paid it much attention. Adams (1976) was one of the first to do so commenting that:

> motor behaviour is draped with more cognitive activity than most are willing to admit (p.89).

The relationship between motor and mental ability as determined by IQ tests is typically reported to be positive but low within the normal range of IQ, eg. Singer (1968). However, the lower the intelligence the greater the decrease in motor proficiency. Rarick, Dobbins and Broadhead (1976) reported 6–13-year-old children with an IQ ranging between 50 and 75 exhibiting inferior performance on 39 motor performance tasks such as sit-ups, balance and agility skills and tracking tasks when compared to 6–9-year-old children of normal intelligence. While developmental delay has been suggested as one reason for poor performance (Francis and Rarick, 1959), deficiencies in the perceptual-cognitive domain have also been isolated as likely mediators (Kelso *et al*, 1979; Kephart, 1960; Sugden and Gray, 1981).

While below average intelligence is likely to be accompanied by difficulties in learning across the curriculum some children of average or above average IQ do experience specific learning difficulties, eg. reading or number difficulty. Poor movement skills have also been reported as characteristic of such children. For example Das (1986) reported the work of Taylor (1982) who found that reading-disabled children of above average intelligence showed significantly poorer performance on 11 out of 15 simple motor tasks such as throwing and catching, aiming at a target, balancing on one leg etc. An analysis of their errors during performance showed: a lack of motor control; an inability to follow a pattern; an inability to recognize errors and an inability to use advice on strategy usage. The latter three deficiencies could clearly give rise to difficulties in reading.

A deeper understanding of the cognitive involvement during the performance and learning of motor skills has been made possible with the evolution of information processing models of behaviour. This has enabled a change from a product approach where attention is given to the motor performance itself, to a process approach, where the antecedents of the response outcome are considered. Recent definitions of motor skills reflect this change, e.g. Whiting (1975) defined motor skills as:

> complex, intentional actions involving a whole chain of sensory, central and motor mechanisms which through the process of learning have come to be organised and coordinated in such a way as to achieve pre-determined obectives with maximum certainty (p.6).

The information processing model views the child as a complex machine which controls the flow of information from input to response. Information is sensed, briefly stored and that which is selected for further processing, perceived or interpreted. Responses are selected and planned and finally implemented. The processes of perception and response selection are heavily dependent on memory (both memory of the immediate situation and of previous experiences). See Figure 10.1.

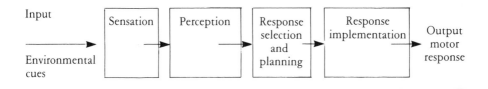

Figure 10.1 A simple information processing model applied to motor performance

For the beginner, each stage requires attention while the more advanced performer is able to curtail or bypass some stages altogther, thus releasing attention for other things. For example, experts recognize familiar situations or cues in the environment more quickly and have a bank of movement responses ready to perform when particular cues occur. This means that their decision-making time is considerably reduced, and would account for the expert appearing to have 'all the time in the world'. It is also important to realize that processing of information can occur at more than one stage at once, e.g. a cricketer may be planning his/her movement to catch the ball while s/he is monitoring its flight, and also be making a decision about his/her return delivery to the wicket.

The task of skipping illustrates the large amount of information which needs to be processed if performance is to be successful. Imagine the child faced with a rope being turned by two others. His/her goal is to enter the rope while it is turning and skip for twenty skips (see Figure 10.2).

The task clearly involves considerable attention to cues, prediction and decision-making, and deficiencies in any of these processes will lead to poor performance. Morris and Whiting (1971) and more recently Brown (1987) have advocated the use of the information processing model as a diagnostic tool for teachers of children with poor movement skills.

Most attempts to model the way in which man processes information have incorporated the concepts of structural and functional capacity (e.g. Atkinson and Shiffrin 1969; Pascual-Leone, 1970). Practically these are not easy to separate but theoretically, structural capacity refers to the absolute capacity of the nervous system to process information, i.e. how much can be attended to at any one time. Pascual Leone called this a person's mental space (Ms space). Functional capacity (Mf space) refers to the indiviual's ability to use his attention capacity in the most

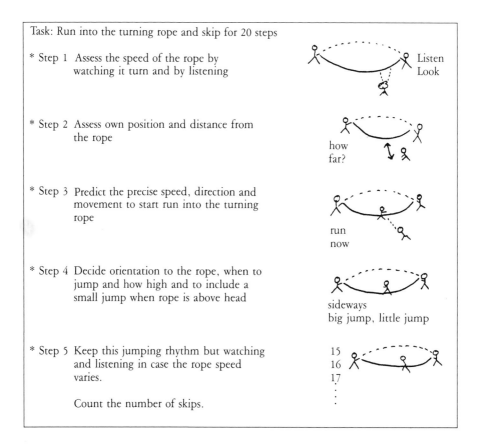

Task: Run into the turning rope and skip for 20 steps

* Step 1 Assess the speed of the rope by
           watching it turn and by listening

* Step 2 Assess own position and distance from
           the rope

* Step 3 Predict the precise speed, direction and
           movement to start run into the turning
           rope

* Step 4 Decide orientation to the rope, when to
           jump and how high and to include a
           small jump when rope is above head

* Step 5 Keep this jumping rhythm but watching
           and listening in case the rope speed
           varies.

           Count the number of skips.

Figure 10.2 Cognitive involvement in a skipping task

efficient way. For example, the child skipping must keep in mind the number of skips made, adding successive ones while watching and listening to the rope. If the child finds that counting or skipping when performed alone demand his whole attention (Ms space), s/he will be unable to perform the two together.

Recognizing that the task is difficult and working out a way to deal with the overload, like using the fingers of the hands to reduce memory load or asking the rope turners to count, is illustrative of the efficient deployment of capacity (functional capacity). The teacher needs to be aware of the information load that a task imposes on each child and when necessary, either reduce it or teach strategies which the performer can use to cope with the demand.

Pascual-Leone devised a method of quantifying the attentional demand of tasks. He distinguished between three sources of information which would take up mental space: the executive scheme, the operative scheme and the figurative scheme. The executive scheme directs the implementation of the operational schemes which process the task-relevant information or figurative schemes. In culinary terms, the executive is the recipe, the operative schemes are the processes like chopping or mixing used to transform the ingredients (figurative schemes) into a new form. In the skipping example, the executive scheme lists the steps involved in attaining the goal, the operational schemes refer to the perceptual, memory and decision-making operations, and the figurative schemes refer to knowledge of the changing position of the performer and the rope, and the changing score.

The attentional capacity which a child has available is considered by Pascual-Leone to increase with age, and has been used to account for the progression through Piaget's stages of cognitive development. Because of the difficulty in assessing an individual's Ms space this is not a particularly helpful construct for the teacher trying to uncover reasons for poor performance or learning. However, observation of the manner in which the attentional capacity is deployed is more promising. Maccoby (1969) favoured this approach. She considered that

> it is not especially useful to think of a deficit in terms of the child having a more limited information processing capacity or memory storage capacity in the usual meaning of these terms. Rather, the problem would seem to be that the capacity that the young child does have is not effectively engaged (p.88).

Atkinson and Shiffrin (1968) used the term control processes to describe the ways in which the individual deploys his attention. They are controlled by an 'executive' and may be thought of as the goal-directed tactics of cognition. Examples would be selective attention, labelling, organization and rehearsal. The use of control processes within a motor task is not difficult to visualize. Take, for example, the child in a small-sided game of football. S/He needs to maintain a state of attentive readiness and then to selectively attend to relevant cues such as who has the ball, where team mates and opponents are, where the goal is. S/He needs to distribute his/her attention optimally in a situation of numerous demands. S/He must be able to search and retrieve quickly from his/her memory the best response in the situation. S/He must be able to put himself in other people's shoes and sequence his/her thinking. For example, when a team mate has the ball, s/he should inhibit the natural response to chase the ball but say to him/herself 'if I had the ball, I might look for a team mate to pass to, therefore, I should move into a space'.

There is no shortage of evidence to show that mildly mentally retarded children show an impoverished use of control processes. Sugden (1978 and 1980) for example, examined the development of rehearsal in the visual-motor and motor memory of normal and mentally retarded boys. The latter showed behaviour similar to younger normal boys, i.e. a lack of spontaneous use of memory strategies such as rehearsal. Wade, Newell and Wallace (1978) found significantly poorer performance of mentally handicapped versus non-handicapped individuals on a motor task requiring rapid decisions. Anwar (1981) reported poor performance on aiming and discrimination tasks and Wade (1980) found impulsive behaviour shown by mentally handicapped children during a coincidence-anticipation task.

It is possible to teach children to use control processes, e.g. Reid (1980) found that in teaching mentally handicapped children a mnemonic strategy was a successful way of improving performance. The problem is to make the child aware that strategies are needed. Alderson (1972) suggested that part of the reason why young children fail to catch a ball is that they have not yet realized that the problem lies within themselves and that they need to examine their own approach to the ball-catching situation.

Campione, Brown and Ferrara (1982) also considered that strategies are only beneficial to the extent that learners can anticipate their need, select from among them, oversee their operation and understand their significance. The poor learner is likely not to transfer a strategy learnt in one situation to another. Poor transfer of strategies has been reported by Belmont and Butterfield (1971) as characteristic of mentally retarded children, and Shif (1969) concluded from his research, that the mildly retarded acquire information which is 'welded' to the form in which it is learned (Campione and Brown, 1974). A stereotype of response is also characteristic of young learners with whom older children with learning difficulties seem to have so much in common. Paris and Cross (1983) have written:

> The trademark of poor learning is not so much bewilderment about what to do as it is pursuit of inappropriate goals and the persistent application of inefficient strategies.... The incorrigibility of young learners is due partly to the tenacity with which they cling to their beliefs about how to engage tasks (p.152).

A willingness to monitor and evaluate task performance is therefore presumed to be central to effective learning. Bernstein (1967) acknowledged this fact when he described motor learning as finding solutions to motor problems:

> practice when properly undertaken does not consist in repeating the means of solution of a motor problem time after time, but in the process of solving this problem again and again by techniques which are arranged and perfected from repetition to repetition (p.134).

The cognitive involvement in learning motor tasks was also emphasized by Fitts and Posner (1967). They suggested that the first phase a learner passes through should be called the cognitive phase. This is the period when an individual develops an understanding of what the task involves and the goal s/he is aiming to achieve, and in which s/he retrieves previous experiences to assist in solving the new problem. The second phase – the associative phase – is also heavily

Initial skill aquisition

1	2	3	4	5	6	7	8	Skill refinement
Understand the purpose of the task	Discover which stimuli are relevant	Attend to relevant cues and ignore distracting	Plan response	Execute response	Examine feedback received during and after the response: did I succeed? Did I do what I intended?	Plan next response in light of (6)	Excute response	Fixation repeat correct response or Diversification adapt response to meet varying situational needs

Figure 10.3 An IP model of skill aquisition (adapted from Gentile, 1972)

dependent on mental activity as it is then that the learner develops new responses which more closely fit with task requirements, e.g. by combining and modifying previously learned subroutines.

A third writer to focus on the cognitive involvement in motor skill learning, Gentile (1972), proposed that the learner passes through a stage of initial skill acquisition followed by skill refinement. As Figure 10.3 shows, she saw initial skill acquisition as involving eight steps. Having understood what the task involves and deciding which stimuli are relevant, the learner plans a response. Once the response has been executed, the learner makes two evaluations. First, s/he evaluates his/her response on the basis of its success in achieving the desired result, and secondly, on its match or mismatch with his/her intention. There are occasions when an action is not performed quite as intended yet success results, e.g. miskicking a successful shot at goal. The learner then has to make decisions about his/her next attempt. Does s/he repeat the movement pattern, modify it, change his/her goal or give-up? This sort of decision-making takes time, effort and logical thought processes. It is questionable whether young children go through this sort of decision-making efficiently. For example, Barclay and Newell (1980) gave 8-, 10-, and 14-year-olds the chance to establish their own post-know-ledge of results time, i.e. the time between KR of one trial and the commence-ment of the next, in a positioning task. The younger chidlren always responded in less than five seconds. This would suggest that it is important for the teacher to teach the child how to process knowledge of results effectively.

Connell (1984) drew up a hypothetical decision tree which could reflect the decision-making during the post KR interval between trials on an underarm aiming task (see Figure 10.4). While this sort of theoretical modelling may be useful as a starting point, the teacher must carefully observe successive attempts and discuss with each child how s/he is tackling the task rather than make inferences from models.

While successful learning will require interpreting and acting on feedback, the learner may also be required to decide upon his/her own method of plan of practice, e.g. in swimming, should s/he practise fifteen widths of the full front crawl stroke or five legs only, five legs and breathing, and then five full stroke? While teaching children with learning difficulties has tended to be highly directive, a more participative style of teaching may have much to offer.

Connell (1984) investigated the practice plan selection of 9- and 13-year-olds and adults in an aiming task. Learners could select from four throwing distances where they wished to take 32 practice throws. The object of the practice period was to prepare for a test which would involve throwing from each of the four lines and from a 'mystery' distance (see Figure 10.5). The 9-year-olds used a wider range of strategies than the older subjects, including some which could be considered im-mature and unhelpful, e.g. throwing all balls from a single distance. Questioning after the task revealed that almost half of the 9-year-olds had no preconceived

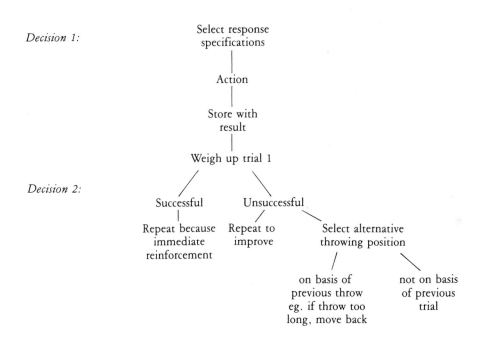

Figure 10.4 Trial by trial decision tree in an underarm aiming task

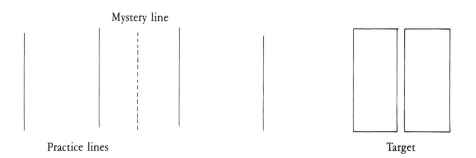

Figure 10.5 Underarm throwing task for assessing practice strategy

plan. There is no guarantee that a plan would have resulted in improved performance, but the interesting fact is that the process of planning was not apparent.

This raises the question of whether teachers should be more concerned with teaching the process of learning rather than focus on specific skill learning. Typically motor skills teaching emphasizes the learning of specific responses to particular cues, especially when children with learning difficulties are the learners. Less evident are problem-solving approaches, when the emphasis is on analysis of the problem and selection and evaluation of solutions, skills which are not context-bound.

The movement education approach to teaching gymnastics and dance, and more recently, the 'teaching for understanding' approach to games teaching are methods which are exceptions. In the former the teacher sets a task which can be answered in a number of ways. The learners experiment with a variety of solutions, with the teacher reinforcing good exemplars and encouraging the development of a wide vocabulary of movements which answer the task. The learning process involves each learner generating his/her own solutions and evaluating those produced by his/her peers.

The teaching for understanding approach to games teaching was developed specifically because of a dissatisfaction with traditional technique-orientated instruction. Bunker and Thorpe (1983) state that such an orientation has led to:

a) a large percentage of children achieving little success due to the emphasis on performance i.e. 'doing'
b) the majority of school leavers knowing very little about games
c) the production of supposedly 'skilful' players who in fact possess inflexible techniques and poor decision making capacity
d) the development of teacher/coach dependent performers (p.5).

The approach starts with a game and its rules, leading to the development of tactical awareness and decision-making. Rather than beginning with skills, the perfection of techniques comes later when the learner sees the relevance of each skill. Teachers of children who have difficulty learning may find these approaches particularly useful as they focus on the process of learning rather than simply the development of a restricted range of stereotyped movement responses. The advantages to be gained from these teaching methods are threefold: the opportunity for the child to be actively involved in the learning and thereby develop learning skills; second, the chance for each child to work at a task at his own level, thereby reducing the sense of failure, and third, the opportunity for creative responding. In open skills in particular, e.g. games, where environmental unpredictability is high, diversity of response is essential, so the learning process must emphasize the generation of new responses rather than the repetition of existing ones.

Whereas Fitts and Posner (1967) and Gentile (1972) have described the cognitive activity involved during the learning of motor skills Adams (1971) and Schmidt (1975) have produced testable theories directed specifically at motor learning. Schmidt's schema theory is particularly attractive for several reasons. First, unlike Adams's theory which proposes that repetition of the correct movement is needed for effective learning, Schmidt sees errors equally as useful as long as the learner is aware of the mismatch between his/her goal and his/her performance. The main thrust of the theory is that variable practice including errorful performance assists in the building and strengthening of two rules or schema which allow the production and recognition of accurate motor responses. This is especially useful in the generation of novel actions, a requirement already recognized as necessary in open skill situations like games playing. Movement education teaching approaches work on the basis that variable practice will result in effective learning. There is considerable experimental support for the benefits of variable practice with children although those with learning difficulties have not been used as subjects. It is suggested that variable practice may be highly desirable for children with learning difficulties because it avoids problems arising from boredom. Furthermore, acceptance of errors, as long as knowledge of results is available, should result in the teacher putting less pressure on the child who does not produce perfect performance.

The significant involvement of cognition in both the performance and learning of motor skills should by now be clear. This clearly implies that children

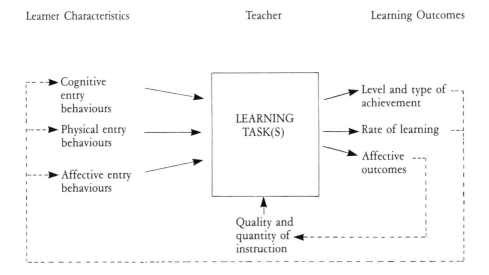

Figure 10.6 Interactions in the teaching-learning process

with learning difficulties are likely to find motor-skill learning problematic. If the teacher is to facilitate learning he must recognize the inter-relationships between the learner, the teacher, the task and the outcome. A model of these inter-relationships is presented in Figure 10.6.

The teacher must be aware of the way each child thinks, the ease with which s/he moves, and the way s/he feels about the task presented to him/her for learning. An awareness of these characteristics should then enable the teacher to design his/her teaching method and adjust the task so as to match the learner's needs. For example, a consideration of cognitive entry behaviours would including the following :

- *Establishing the child's level of understanding of language*   If this is poor, the teacher may use visual demonstrations more frequently.

- *Assessing the child's ability to concentrate*   Frequent changes of task will be needed for those with short attention spans.

- *Establishing the child's ability to attend selectively*   Where this is poor the teacher may reduce the cues in the environment to relevant ones only and then slowly introduce other cues. An alternative approach would be to concentrate on the discrimination of relevant from irrelevant cues in order to develop the child's powers of selective attention.

- *Establishing the child's ability to remember instructions and demonstrations*   The teacher can assist the child to remember the sequence of movements in a complex skill, or a sequence of actions as might be found in gymnastics or dance, by breaking down the task into parts and gradually building up the whole, or encouraging the child to use memory strategies such as labelling, chunking or rhyming.

  An example of the use of labelling in teaching the back crawl in swimming would be to ask the child to imagine the face of a clock and to say what time it is when s/he places his hands into the water.

  Learning a serving action in tennis can be helped by chunking if the learner is told to open his arms like a pair of scissors, scratch his/her back with the racket and then throw it at the ball. Developing a rhyme of the critical points in a sequence also reduces memory load. For example, the elements of putting the shot can be remembered easily as 'Chin, knee, toe. Make a bow. See it go'.

- *Establishing the child's ability to plan his/her response*   The teacher can inhibit impulsive responding by encouraging the learner to stop and think out his/her plan of action. S/he may be advised to verbalize it aloud. Obviously, this is only useful in self-paced tasks when the performer is not time-constrained by external events.

● *Establishing how the child evaluates his/her performance*   The teacher can help the child who appears not to alter his/her performance on successive attempts by providing him/her with a checklist of questions such as 'Did I succeed?', 'Did I perform the action as I intended?', 'Why did the action fail?', 'How could I make it better?'

With regard to physical and affective entry behaviour the teacher must be able to:

● adjust the task goals so that they can be achieved by each child
● fully extend each child; this is most easily achieved by setting open tasks which can be solved in a number of ways through problem solving
● provide continued support for those that need it but aim to reduce assistance gradually so that each child increasingly takes control of his own learning
● utilize competition in a manner which is motivating to all children, e.g. by including competition against oneself ('beat your own record' activities).

Clearly the outcomes from the teaching-learning process are critical in future planning by the teacher as the rate and level of achievement, and the child's feelings about these outcomes will modify the learner's entry behaviour to subsequent learning tasks. They will also provide feedback to the teacher about the effectiveness of his chosen teaching method.

An awareness of the cognitive processes involved in the performance and learning of motor skills should enhance the teacher's understanding of some of the reasons for poor motor behaviour. The chapter has suggested that children will show differences in the rapidity and efficiency of basic information processing (control processes), differences in their patterning (strategies) and differences in strategy selection and evaluation skills.

The teaching guidelines generated from the research and theories outlined in the early part of the chapter and brought together in the model presented here are by no means exhaustive, nor are they limited to the teaching of motor skills. They are not guidelines specifically for use with children with learning difficulties but are considered to be especially valuable in facilitating learning in this group of children.

References

Adams, J. A. (1971), A closed loop theory of motor learning. *J. Motor Behavior*, **3**, 111–50.
Adams, J. A. (1976), Issues for a closed loop theory of motor learning, in G. E. Stelmach (ed.), *Motor Control: Issues and Trends* (New York: Academic Press).
Alderson, G. J. K. (1972), The perception of velocity, in H. T. A. Whiting (ed.), *Readings in Sport Psychology*, (London: Kimpton),
Anwar, F. (1981), 'Visual-motor localizations in normal and subnormal development' *British Journal of Psychology*, **72**, 43–57.

Atkinson, R C. and Shiffrin, R. M. (1968), Human memory: a proposed system and its control processes, in K. W. Spence and J. T. Spence (eds.), *The Psychology of Learning and Motivation*, vol. **2**, (New York: Academic Press).

Barclay, C. R. and Newell, K. M. (1980), Children's processing of information in motor skill acquisition, *Journal of Experimental Child Psychology*, **30**, 98–108.

Belmont, J. M. and Butterfield, E. C. (1971), Learning strategies as determinants of memory deficiencies, *Cognitive Psychology*, **2**, 411–20.

Bernstein, N. (1967), *The Coordination and Regulation of Movements*, (New York: Pergamon).

Brown, A. (1987), *Active Games for Children with Movement Problems* (London: Harper & Row).

Bunker, D. and Thorpe, R. (1983), A model for the teaching of games in secondary schools, *Bulletin of Physical Education*, **19**, 1, 5–8.

Campione, J. C. and Brown, A. L. (1974), The effects of contextual changes and degrees of component mastery on transfer training, in H. W. Reese (ed.), *Advances in Child Development and Behaviour*, **4**, (New York: Academic Press).

Campione, J. C., Brown, A. L. and Ferrara, R. A. (1982), Mental retardation and intelligence, in R. J. Sternberg (ed.), Handbook of Human Intelligence (Cambridge: Cambridge University Press).

Connell, R. A. (1984), Cognitive explanations of chldren's motor behaviour (Unpublished doctoral dissertation: University of Leeds).

Das, J. P. (1986), Information processing and motivation as determinants of performance in children with learning disabilities, in M. G. Wade and H. T. A. Whiting (eds.), *Motor Development in Children: Aspects of Coordination and Control* (Amsterdam: Martinus Nijhoff).

Fitts, P. M. and Posner, M. I. (1967) *Human Performance* (California: Brooks/Cole).

Francis, R. J. and Rarick, G. L. (1959), Motor characteristics of the mentally retarded, *American Journal of Mental Deficiency*, **63**, 792–811.

Gentile, A. M. (1972), A working model of skill acquisition with application to teaching, *Quest*, **17**, 3–23.

Henderson, S. E. and Hall, D. (1982), Concomitants of clumsiness in young children, *Developmental Medicine and Child Neurology*, **24**, 448–60.

Kelso, J. A. S., Goodman, D., Stamm, C. L. and Hayes, C. (1979), Movement coding and memory in retarded children, *American Journal of Mental Deficiency*, **83**, 792–811.

Kephart, N. C. (1960), *The Slow Learner in the Classroom*, (Ohio: Merrill).

Maccoby, E. E. (1969), The development of stimulus selection, in J. P. Hill (ed.), *Minnesota Symposium on Child Development*, **3**, 68–98.

Morris, P. R. and Whiting, H. T. A. (1971), *Motor Impairment and Compensatory Education* (Philadelphia: Lea & Febiger).

Paris, S. G. and Cross, D. R. (1983), Ordinary learning: pragmatic connections among children's beliefs, motives and actions; in J. Bisanz and R. Kail (eds.), *Learning in Children: Progress in Cognitive Developmental Research*, (New York: Springer-Verlag).

Pascual-Leone, J. (1970), A mathematical model for the transition rule in Piaget's developmental stages, *Acta Psychologica*, **32**, 301–45.

Rarick, G., Dobbins, D. A. and Broadhead, G. (1976), *The Motor Domain and Its Correlates in Educationally Handicapped Children* (New Jersey: Prentice Hall).

Reid, G. (1980), The effects of memory strategy instruction in the short term motor memory of the mentally retarded, *Journal of Motor Behaviour*, **12**, 221–7.

Schmidt, R. A. (1975), A schema theory of discrete motor learning. *Psychological Review*, **82**, 225–60.

Shif, Z. L. (1969), Development of children in schools for mentally retarded, in M. Cole and I. Maltzman (eds), *A handbook of Contemporary Soviet Psychology* (New York: Basic Books).

Singer, R. N. (1968), Interrelationship of physical, perceptual-motor and academic achievement variables in elementary school children, *Perceptual and Motor Skills*, **27**, 1323–32.

Sugden, D. A. (1978), Visual motor short term memory in educationally subnormal boys, *British Journal of Educational Psychology*, **48**, 330–9.

Sugden, D. A. (1980), Developmental strategies in motor and visual motor short term memory, *Perceptual and Motor Skills*, **51**, 146.

Sugden, D. A. and Gray, S. M. (1981), Capacity and strategies of ESN boys on serial and discrete tasks involving movement speed, *British Journal of Educational Psychology*, **51**, 77–82.

Taylor, K. J. (1982), *Physical Awkwardness of Reading Disability: A descriptive study*. MSc. dissertation, University of Alberta.

Wade, M. G. (1980) Coincidence anticipation of young normal and handicapped children, *Journal of Motor Behavior*, **12**, 103–12.

Wade, M. G., Newell, K. M. and Wallace, S. A. (1978), Decision time and movement time as a function of response complexity in retarded persons, *American Journal of Mental Deficiency*, **83**, 135–44.

Whiting, H. T. A. (1975), *Concepts in Skill Learning* (London: Lepus).

Notes on Contributors

Sally Beveridge Lecturer in Education, University of Leeds. Formerly Director of the Anson House Preschool Project, Hester Adrian Research Centre, University of Manchester. Teaching experience in primary and special schools and ongoing involvement with parents and their interaction with children. She has special interest in parenting, parent-school liaison and early identification of children's difficulties. Her doctoral thesis is entitled 'Mothers' interactive styles: their relationship to programmes of parent-teaching.'

Rosemary Connell Head of Movement Studies Department, Trinity and All Saints College of Education. She has published in the area of motor development impairment and health education and is involved in ongoing school based projects. Her doctoral thesis is entitled 'Cognitive explanations of children's motor development'.

Alan Dobbins Lecturer in special educational needs, Department of Education, University of Swansea. His special interests include motor impairment and more recently difficulties in reading and mathematics. He received a substantial grant from the DES to investigate Specific Learning Difficulties in the South Wales region resulting in a recent text entitled 'Specific Reading Difficulties: Prevalence and Characteristics.'

Ronald Gallimore Professor (Psychology), Department of Psychiatry & Biobehavioral Sciences, and Graduate School of Education, at the University of California, Los Angeles. He is a member of the Sociobehavioral Research Group founded by Robert Edgerton when the Mental Retardation Research Center was created in the late 1960s. He studies the cultural context of competence and performance. He is co-author (with Tharp) of a recent book which summarizes 20 years of teaching and schooling research.

Peter Galvin Educational psychologist with Leeds Education Authority, specialising in children showing emotional and behavioural problems.

Extensive teaching experience in schools for children showing such difficulties and is now involved in producing INSET materials which examine school policy, classroom practices and individual approaches to children showing behaviour problems. He is co-author of 'Behaviour problems: a system of management.'

Robert Rueda Associate Professor in the Department of Curriculum, Teaching and Special Education, University of Southern California. His major research interest is in the social bases of learning and cognition, especially focused on the acquisition and uses of literacy. Much of his work has been with special education students. In addition, he maintains an active research interest in issues concerning language minority students in public school settings.

Jacqueline Rutherford Support teacher with Leeds Education Authority. She has experience in special and mainstream schools with particular skills in language and communication. She has followed the training course for Instrumental Enrichment and taught it in both special and mainstream schools.

Diane Shorrocks Lecturer in educational psychology within the School of Education, University of Leeds. Her special interests are in child language, communication and reading, particularly with young children. She is currently preparing a book on this subject entitled 'Learning through communication'.

Roland Tharp Director of the Center for the Studies of Multicultural Higher Education, and Professor of Psychology at the University of Hawaii. He recently published an integrative review of cultural effects on education in the *American Psychologist*. He is co-author (with Gallimore) 'Rousing Minds to Life: Teaching, Learning and Schooling in Social Context,' 1988 Cambridge University Press.

Peter Tomlinson Lecturer in educational psychology within the School of Education, University of Leeds. Author of numerous publications including 'Understanding Teaching: Interactive educational psychology' and 'Values across the curriculum.' He has received research grants from the Economic and Social Research Council, including one on moral development and a current one on Radio Assisted Practice, examining new methods of helping teachers in training.

Author Index

Subject Index